Sacrifice and Regeneration

Sacrifice and Regeneration

Seventh-day Adventism and

Religious Transformation in

the Andes | YAEL MABAT

University of Nebraska Press | LINCOLN

The University of Nebraska Press is part of a land-grant institution with campuses and programs on the past, present, and future homelands of the Pawnee, Ponca, Otoe-Missouria, Omaha, Dakota, Lakota, Kaw, Cheyenne, and Arapaho Peoples, as well as those of the relocated Ho-Chunk, Sac and Fox, and Iowa Peoples.

Library of Congress Cataloging-in-Publication Data
Names: Mabat, Yael, author.
Title: Sacrifice and regeneration : Seventh-Day Adventism and religious transformation in the Andes / Yael Mabat.
Description: Lincoln : University of Nebraska Press, [2022] | Includes bibliographical references and index.
Identifiers: LCCN 2022017900
ISBN 9781496216700 (hardback)
ISBN 9781496233530 (paperback)
ISBN 9781496233936 (epub)
ISBN 9781496233943 (pdf)
Subjects: LCSH: General Conference of Seventh-Day Adventists—History. | Seventh-Day Adventists—Andes Region. | Andes Region—Church history—20th century. | BISAC: HISTORY / Latin America / South America | SOCIAL SCIENCE / Indigenous Studies
Classification: LCC BX6153.4.S63 M33 2022 | DDC 286.7/8—dc23/eng/20220801
LC record available at https://lccn.loc.gov/2022017900

Set in Questa by Laura Buis.

To my family

Contents

Illustrations

Figures

Table

Illustrations

Acknowledgments

THE JOURNEY TOWARD THIS BOOK HAS BEEN A LONG ONE. It began years ago outside the walls of academia when I was backpacking throughout Latin America and noticed Evangelical churches everywhere. Initially, I thought of focusing my research on Central America, where the mass conversion from Catholicism to Evangelical and Pentecostal Christianity is especially strong. Nevertheless, it seems that the universe had other plans for me, and I found myself traveling up the Andean mountains to Puno, Peru. I would not have made my way up these mountains and to the realization of this book without the guidance, support, and friendship of the many people I met along the way.

First and foremost, to my mentors throughout this journey: Gerardo Leibner at Tel Aviv University and Steven Kaplan at the Hebrew University. Professor Leibner guided me through Andean politics and society, and I am grateful for his critical readings of more drafts than I can remember. Professor Kaplan, a historian of other landscapes, provided me with a comparative perspective on the dynamics of religious conversion, which are essential for a project such as this one.

I also thank Tzvi Medin, my first guide to Latin American history, and Raanan Rein, who is always happy to give advice and encouragement. I have also benefited from the knowledge and support of Rosalie Sitman, Ori Preuss, Nahuel Ribke, Claudia Kedar, and all the other members of the Latin American research seminar at Tel Aviv University during the past years. The Sverdlin Institute of Latin American History and Culture has also provided financial support for this project. The School of History at Tel Aviv University has supported this research along the way, and I am grateful to them.

In Peru, I was lucky to meet Juan Fonseca, Juan Carlos la Serna, the late Jeffrey Klaiber, and Mario Riveros Echeverry, all of whom kindly shared with me their knowledge of the Andean social and religious landscape and opened doors in various places. Monsignor Jorge Pedro Carrion Pavlic granted me entrance to the Archive of the Diocese of Puno and engaged in insightful conversations with me about the contemporary state of Christianity in the Altiplano. This research would never have been possible without the help of the staff in the several archives that I consulted in Lima, Cuzco, and Puno. Specifically, I thank Agustín Gutiérrez, Sonia Sotomayor Vargas, and their team of highly professional archivists at the regional archive of the Department of Puno. Not only did they direct me toward the right collections and specific documents, but they also helped me overcome a few cultural and linguistic barriers and enriched my understanding of Puno and its surroundings.

In the United States, I am indebted to Peter Chiomenti and Benjamin Baker from the General Conference Archive of the Seventh-day Adventist Church for their assistance in the archive and for guiding me through various aspects of their faith and practices. Mark Peters, Dan Serns, and Robert Ford, all related to missionaries who worked in Puno, have been kind enough to share their family histories and personal archives with me. Finally, a special thanks to Erick Langer from Georgetown University. Professor Langer and I met during my trip to research the Adventist archives, and he has become a friend and a mentor ever since. The intellectual and practical advice he offered during the writing of this book was essential, and I can't thank him enough for this. I also extend my thanks to the University of Nebraska Press, especially to Bridget Barry and Emily Wendell, for seeing this book through production and elevating it in many aspects. Cambridge University Press permitted me to reproduce in chapters 2 and 3 portions of "Veterans of Christ: Soldier Reintegration and the Seventh-day Adventist Experience in the Andean Plateau, 1900–1925," which appeared

Acknowledgments

in *The Americas* 77, no. 2 (2020). This book has also benefited greatly from the comments of two anonymous readers whom I thank for their efforts, constructive remarks, and insight. Finally, I thank my family, who supported and encouraged me throughout this project, for believing in me. I dedicate this book to them.

Introduction

AS I WRITE THIS INTRODUCTION, DRAMATIC EVENTS ARE unfolding in Bolivia. After fourteen years in power, Evo Morales has been pushed out of office.[1] The immediate context for these events was that of the disputed results of the October 2019 presidential election. Morales claimed victory, and the opposition accused him of manipulating the results and stealing the election. To what extent these accusations are true, if at all, is unclear at the moment and, like almost every other issue, deeply disputed.[2] What is certain is that a short time later, Morales was on a plane to Mexico and other *masistas* resigned from their positions, including vice president Álvaro García Linera. The country is currently ruled by an interim president, Jeanine Añez, from the department of Beni and a representative of the right-wing Democratic Social Movement.

Shortly after assuming her new role as president, Añez stood on the balcony of the presidential palace and, facing the crowd, brandished a giant Bible and proclaimed that the "Bible has returned to the palace." She was not the only one to use Christian symbols and a Christian rhetoric amid these political events. Another important figure that emerged from the protests against Morales, one Luis Fernando Camacho, also made constant reference to the scriptures both in words and in actions.[3] It was Camacho who knelt before the Bible on the Bolivian flag, which he unfurled on the floor of the presidential palace, and then listened to an anonymous pastor say that "Pachamama will never return to the palace. Bolivia belongs to Christ." These gestures, quite obviously, represent a rejection of Morales's central political project, "the Plurinational State of Bolivia" which established a separation between church and state and granted official recognition to Indigenous religions. In spite of that separation during Morales's first term, religious symbols and rituals played an important part in this political project. To wit, Morales's 2015 preinauguration ceremonies took place at the archaeological site of Tiahuanaco and were conducted by Indigenous priests who made use of perceived Incan and other pre-Columbian religious symbols. The use of these symbols is not coincidental, and they are part of a wider project of indigeneity and decolonization that has deep historical roots in the region.[4]

There is nothing new in framing any political project in religious terms, symbols, and ideologies. In the Andes, as in the rest of Latin America, religion and politics have been closely intertwined, often making it impossible to distinguish between the two. Historically, both the Inca emperor and the Spanish monarchs used religion to legitimize their sovereignty and political authority. The ruling Inca was the "son of the sun," and the cult of the sun was part of the empire's ideological foundations.[5] Columbus brought the cross with him to the "New World," and Christianity served as the ideological justification for conquest, colonization, and the suppression of Indigenous cultures and beliefs. The *inter caetera* bull issued by Pope Alexander VI in 1493 gave the Spanish crown the legal basis to claim political sovereignty. The establishment of the *patronato real* ensured that the relationship between religion and politics would remain indissoluble throughout the colonial period. Even after independence, the Catholic Church was given a privileged status in most of the continent's new nations. Indeed, the first Protestant missionaries who arrived in Latin America earned the support of liberal politicians. These liberals welcomed the Protestants for several reasons, among them the curtailment of the strength of the Catholic Church, which was supported by their conservative political opponents.

The story I am about to tell is about one of these Protestant missions. More importantly, it is about the intersection between religion and politics and the relationship between Indigenous people, the arrival of a new faith, and that faith's foreign emissaries. As such, it sheds historical light on contemporary events, such as the role of the Bible in the recent upheaval in Bolivia. In fact, my story took place not too far from La Paz, although on the opposite side of Lake Titicaca. It occurred in the department of Puno, Peru, and its main protagonists also vehemently waved Bibles at their political contenders. Rather than being the white representatives of a long-time privileged elite, however, they were Indian peasants and a handful of U.S. missionaries from the Seventh-day Adventist Church.

The historical period examined in this book also differs significantly from the recent events in Bolivia. Since the 1980s, there has been rapid growth in the number of Evangelicals in Latin America, and they are now part of the continent's religious landscape. My story occurs at a time when no self-respecting conservative politician would enter the presidential palace with an Evangelical pastor, let alone be baptized by one in the Jordan River as Jair Bolsonaro, the Brazilian president, did in 2016. Instead, it unfolds during a period when men were sent to prison for selling Bibles or preaching Christian doctrines that were not Catholic. During the nineteenth century, the Andean countries prohibited the public practice of any religion other than Roman Catholicism. Religious liberty was granted in Bolivia and Ecuador only after the liberal revolutions of 1896 and 1899.[6] In Peru the Catholic Church was able to preserve its monopoly over the public practice of religion until 1915, at which time the Peruvian congress recognized religious liberty as a constitutional right.

Despite legal prohibitions of public worship of other religions in the Andes, Protestant missionaries worked in the Andes, especially in Peru. Peru was more accessible geographically than Bolivia and more politically friendly to Protestants than Ecuador until the liberal revolution in the latter country and Eloy Alfaro's rise to power.[7] Specifically, Protestant missionaries found allies among Peruvian liberals who believed that Protestantism was much more compatible with modernity than Catholicism.[8]

This general atmosphere made proselytization possible, but not without risks. One well-known case was that of Methodist Francisco Penzotti, who was incarcerated in Peru for illegally distributing Bibles and religious literature as well as inviting people to attend Methodist services.[9] Furthermore, popular hostility continued regardless of the missions' and missionaries' legal status. In 1909 Harry Compton, a Methodist pastor at a congregation in Quito, was viciously attacked by local Indians while visiting a small congregation in the town of Malchinguí. He and his family narrowly escaped alive.[10] A few years earlier, in the city of Cochabamba, Bolivia, the army was sent in to protect Canadian Baptist missionaries from local attacks.[11] Catholicism was an essential part of the region's social, political, and cultural structure, and Protestants were generally looked upon as outsiders and even political agitators.[12]

It was in this conservative region, however, that thousands of Aymara Indians decided to leave the Catholic Church. Instead, they found God in a small Seventh-day Adventist mission station that had been established around 1910, on the Andean Plateau, in the department of Puno, Peru. By the late 1920s, the Seventh-day Adventist Indian mission to Lake Titicaca, as it became known, included twelve churches and about sixty Sabbath schools that served more than seven thousand members, almost all Aymara and Quechua Indians. Hundreds more were waiting for baptism, and many others were "sympathizers" who attended services periodically.[13] According to one report, probably from the mid-1920s, over thirty-five hundred pupils, which represented almost half of Puno's Indigenous school-age population, were studying in Adventist institutions.[14]

The Indians who converted referred to themselves as *adventistas* or *evangélicos* interchangeably, never differentiating between the two. They were also called evangélicos by local state officials and by other Indians, who cared more about the fact that they were no longer Catholics than about the unique features of Seventh-day Adventism. From this perspective, this is the first large-scale conversion of Indigenous peoples from Catholicism to Evangelical Christianity in Hispanic America. The expansion of Evangelicalism, especially Pentecostalism, in Latin America, has been extensively debated in scholarship, particularly since the 1990s. Yet the majority of these studies come out of the disciplines of sociology and anthropology.[15] Historians have been much slower in responding to these changes in Latin America's religious landscape. To be sure, important work has been done on this topic, such as that of Virginia Garrard, who points to deteriorating social and economic conditions as fuel for Evangelical growth.[16] But overall historical research on the emergence of Protestantism in Latin America, especially in the southern part of the continent, is fairly limited.

One reason for this might be that the number of Protestants was negligible until the last quarter of the twentieth century. For example, in 1920 the entire Protestant population in Guatemala was less than two thousand people, and the membership in each of the biggest churches in Guatemala City was under three hundred.[17] Furthermore, scholars divided Protestant history in the continent into phases or "waves."[18] Hence, the Protestant missionary enterprise of the nineteenth and early twentieth centuries is the first wave; the expansion of Pentecostal churches since the 1980s is either the third, fourth, or even fifth wave, depending on who you ask. These recent waves include tens of millions of converts, almost half of the population of Guatemala, a third of Brazilians, and about 20 percent of the population of Peru and Bolivia. In light of these numbers, it is easy to understand why researchers are drawn to the later phases of the Evangelical expansion.

Popular trends in Andean historiography and, specifically, the state of research on Protestantism in the Andes are more reasons for this neglect. During the second half of the twentieth century, Andean historiography was dominated by what is known as Nueva Historia, or the New History school. The New History was an eclectic amalgam of various theories from the humanities and social sciences such as English social history, the French Annales school, and dependency theory.[19] Scholars associated with the New History were influenced by the Cuban Revolution and other insurgencies, and they often chose what to investigate according to the topic's seeming "revolutionary" potential. For the new historians, peasant communities and export economies were themes endowed with this revolutionary aura. Christianity was not.[20] From the 1990s onward, a new generation of scholars emerged and research on religion has been expanding. Although most of this scholarship focuses on the colonial era, important research has been conducted on the period after independence, and even early Protestant endeavors.[21] Nevertheless, the Seventh-day Adventists' success in the highlands, although occasionally mentioned, has not been thoroughly studied.[22]

This book focuses on the social, political, and cultural dynamics between converts, missionaries, and their surroundings that brought about this religious transformation. As such, it is also a part of a broad discussion over the nineteenth- and early twentieth-century Protestant foreign missionary enterprise. Specifically, scholars have been debating missionaries' role in empire building and their contribution to what is known as "cultural imperialism." Some scholars, especially those writing in the 1980s, contended that missionaries were essentially imperialist agents who imposed their own worldview on the natives. More recently scholars have tended to challenge this view, arguing that it deprives converts of agency. This debate has accentuated national identities, cultural gaps, and power relations. The differences in culture and power structures between missionaries and converts are indisputable, and I discuss them in detail in the last part of this book. At the same time, large-scale forces, such as the expansion of capitalism, urbanization, and industrialization, influenced missionaries and converts alike. As we shall see, both converts and missionaries were young men of approximately the same age who were unable to secure their socioeconomic positions within their communities of origin. From this perspective, the nineteenth-century missionary enterprise was a product of global forces that shaped the lives and opportunities of both missionaries and converts.

I have divided this book into three parts. The first part, which includes four chapters, focuses on the Indian converts. It identifies army veterans as a key group in the expansion of Seventh-day Adventism and as the mission's native leadership. Veterans were young men in their twenties who had returned from military service and discovered that the downfall of the haciendas had taken a toll on their properties, leaving them little, if any, resources to rely on. Moreover, the cultural habits they acquired in the barracks put them at odds with hegemonic notions of "Indian-ness" and the local hierarchies that sustained these conventions. Conversion became a means of breaking away from the harsh racial impositions of the Andean social hierarchy and of reconfiguring the meaning of Indian-ness. The second part, composed of three chapters, centers on missionaries and argues that the Seventh-day Adventist foreign missionary enterprise was propelled in part by a specific challenge that a younger generation of Adventists grappled with: Saturday observance conflicted with the demands of middle-class employment. In the secluded Altiplano, however, this challenge did not exist. Adventists missionaries moved closer to mainline Protestantism because their daily experiences were shaped by issues of class, specifically middle-class material culture, and by the fact that they were not Catholic, more than the unique practices of Seventh-day Adventism.

The final section, which includes two chapters, brings together converts and missionaries to explore how all of the above played out within the mission's walls. It also explains how and why the Seventh-day Adventist Church transformed from a liberal, and even radical, institution into a much more conservative one, thus shedding light on long-term trends in Latin American Evangelicalism.

Sources and Methodologies

As part of my proposal for this research project, I had to briefly sketch the different types of documents I was looking for and speculated about where I thought I would find them. My "dream documents," as I often refer to this part of the proposal, included lists of the new converts, information about their backgrounds, local church publications, information about local activities, private correspondences, and perhaps some local gossip written in diaries. These documents, I thought, would be in local church archives, maybe in Lima and probably in Puno. Unfortunately, I was unable to obtain access to the Adventist Church's archive in Lima. In Puno, documents from such early years do not exist, or at least this is what I have been told.

Next, I went to the Prefectura collection in the Archivo

Regional de Puno and the general collection Archivo Arzobispal de Puno. The former was damaged by a major fire in 1994, and the latter had never been systematically cataloged and preserved. I was able to find, in these archives, a few documents that mentioned the Adventists directly and, more important, hundreds of complaints submitted by peasants from the districts of Chucuito and Acora, where the Adventists were most active. The complaints provide a glimpse into the daily life of the Indigenous populations as well as partial information pertaining to peasants' backgrounds. The problem was that I had no way of knowing which, if any, of these Aymara peasants were Adventists. In most cases, documents do not mention religious affiliation. Furthermore, converts had no interest in disclosing that they belonged to the Adventist Church since it was illegal until 1915, and even after that year, members of that church continued to be the target of harassment from authorities and neighbors.

Aside from these documents, I had newspaper articles, letters to the Asociación Pro-Indígena and the Seventh-day Adventist headquarters in Washington, and different Adventist publications in English. Occasionally, these publications mentioned names of specific Indian converts. I therefore created two databases: the first, which included names of all the Indians whom I knew were connected to the mission, eventually consisted of over 280 converts. The second was a comprehensive catalog of just about eight hundred documents categorized according to place, date, subject, and the names of the Indians who appear in each document. Once finished, I juxtaposed the names, eventually discovering which complaints had been submitted by converts.

This methodology has flaws. First, there is the question of identity verification. People related to the same *ayllu* were usually from the same extended family and often bore the same family name. Thus, I found numerous people with the family name Mamani, Chambi, or Arpasi, all from the same place and often with the same first name. It was, therefore, important to verify that the person appearing in the Prefectura documents was the same person as on the Seventh-day Adventists' list. In some cases, usually with the most prominent converts, I was able to identify signatures and therefore quite easily make a positive identification. In other cases, especially with popular names, I looked for additional criteria for verification. Discovering several names of converts in a single document turned out to be an important measurement. Adventist converts often worked together as a group, submitted joint complaints, relied on one another as witnesses, or held power of attorney on each other's behalf. Other important "fingerprints" in a text included declarations on alcohol or coca prohibition, as well as confessions of attempts toward "self-improvement."

The second difficulty concerns the fragmented nature of my databases. Comparing the names yielded information about less than half of the converts, and in most cases, the data was minimal. Indeed, the number of converts for which I have an abundance of information can be reduced to a few individuals who were leading figures. Moreover, with very few exceptions, I do not know when exactly each convert decided to convert, if that person stayed within the Seventh-day Adventist mission, and if not, when they left. As a result, it is hard to know, for example, if certain actions were instigated by conversion or whether it was the other way around. Yet, even so, the contours of the picture are clear and it is possible to make sound deductions about the missing pieces. In other words, scant and partial information can light up the shady corners of history. This is especially true for projects such as this one, which examines the lower classes of society, among whom illiteracy is prevalent and resources for historical conservation, meager.

Locating Missionaries in a Digital World: From Archives to Social Networks

As was the case with converts, my first goal was to gather as much data as possible about missionaries' backgrounds: where they had come from geographically and socially, what other opportunities they had had, and how long they had been associated with the Seventh-day Adventist Church. To that end, I used a variety of sources, such as U.S. censuses, obituaries, appointee files from the Seventh-day Adventist Church, embassy registrations, and in one or two cases even a local newspaper. But the most important sources—which includes to a degree all of the above—were online sites devoted to the research of family genealogy such as ancestry.com, findagrave.com, familysearch.org, and personal blogs.

While the roots of genealogical documentation stretch all the way back to biblical times, modernity has largely created the incentives for this type of ancestral research as well as many of the tools to conduct it.[23] The introduction of the internet and digitalization technologies significantly facilitate genealogy research, turning it into a much more accessible and affordable pastime. As a result, the family histories of a larger segment of the population are now available, representing a variety of experiences.

Technological gaps, access to the internet, amount of leisure time, and other issues created unequal representation within this source. Nevertheless, these sites are a treasure trove for historians, as they provide easy access to millions of personal archives, including official registration, personal photographs, and oral histories. Moreover, forums and discussion threads, where genealogists meet virtually, review new information, and argue over family relations can provide possible "leads" for research. For example, discussions over the location of a grave often involve religious affiliation, which in the context of this study can help establish issues concerning conversion. Constructing horizontal lineages between siblings, death, and remarriage of parents often ties into issues of inheritance, shedding light on the economic opportunities and expectations of future missionaries.

Contacting genealogists is an additional advantage. Of the five genealogists I was able to locate, three were more than happy to help. They answered questions, contacted other family members in search of specific information, and offered insights into family dynamics or specific personalities. Quite obviously, the amount of information a family historian holds about a specific relative depended on the degree of closeness, biological or "spiritual," that the genealogist feels toward that person. Are we speaking about his grandfather or great-uncle? Someone the genealogists knew personally or maybe a distant relative who, for some reason, sparked his imagination? In both cases, the degree of closeness is relatively high and usually translates into abundant information. On the other hand, in cases of distant relatives, information can be scarce, since our subject is just another name on the family tree. Moreover, for genealogists the question of verification, making sure that the person is who we think he is and that his relations to other members of the family are accurate, is crucial. Without it, entire lineages will prove false. At the same time, controversies over extended family history tie into the core issue of popular genealogy and an interesting methodological issue: memory making. Rather than being a means of validating lineage, popular uses of genealogy, as the kind professed in social media sites, are more about heritage.[24] It is an attempt to construct a personal history of the *longue durée* to answer the question "Who am I and how did I get here?" As scholars studying issues of memory and oblivion so often point out, however, the memory of the past is planted in the present.[25] How people, in this case genealogists, present their history has to do with their identity here and now. Thus, while working with genealogies, we must remember to ask what the genealogist would like to remember about his family history and what he would choose to forget. Familial memory, to paraphrase Pierre Nora, is borne by living offspring and constructed out of their own need for "heritage." It remains in permanent evolution (especially while using a dynamic platform such as social media); distant relatives, asleep in their graves, sometimes for decades, are revived to play a part in a present they most likely could not even have imagined.

Sacrifice and Regeneration

PART 1

Converts

1

Wars, Indians, and the Peruvian Nation

AT THE DAWN OF THE TWENTIETH CENTURY, WHILE LIMA'S aristocrats hotly debated the future of a nation filled with "Indians," Manuel Z. Camacho, a thirty-year-old Aymara Indian, set out to redeem his race. Camacho was born in a small Indian community on the shores of Lake Titicaca in the department of Puno but spent most of his early life away from his native home. In the early 1880s, when he was about twelve years old, his father sent him to live with Dr. Higinio Herrera and his wife, a childless couple living in the city of Moquegua.[1] Child circulation, the relocation of a child into a new household through kinship networks, was prevalent in the Andes. The practice stemmed from various motivations such as strengthening relationships between adults and providing the child with new opportunities. Young Camacho lived with the couple for a few years and was fortunate to attend primary school for three years. Then, he left the Herrera couple, worked in various occupations, traveling to Lima and, according to one biography, even to the United States. By 1894 Camacho was back in Moquegua and joined Nicolás de Piérola's rebel army against the incumbent president Andrés Cáceres. When the fighting ended, Camacho left the army camps but remained on the coast, moving from place to place, reaching as far as Santiago de Chile and making a living however he could.[2] Finally, around 1900, after years of wandering, he opted to return to his native Puno.

Camacho's trip to the arid Altiplano was long but not lonely. During the second half of the nineteenth century, many Indians who were either army veterans or deserters were making their way up and down the sierra.[3] In Peru, as in other parts of Latin America, the nineteenth century was one of political instability, intermittent wars, and bloodshed. Between 1821 and 1845, Peru experienced over twenty regime changes, as well as ongoing fighting between *caudillos* and a failed attempt to establish a confederation with Bolivia (1836–39). At least in terms of political stability, things seemed to have taken a turn for the better after 1845. In the middle of the nineteenth century, a small liberal oligarchy whose economic interests were tied to international exports became the most powerful player in the Peruvian political and economic arenas. Specifically, this group exported guano, the accumulated excrement of seabirds, which was collected from the Peruvian coast and nearby islands and sold as fertilizer in European markets. Simply put, they turned manure into money. At first, to secure control over guano mining, the guano oligarchy allied itself with local caudillos, particularly Ramón Castilla. By 1872 this export interest group had diversified economically, and once the political conditions were favorable, they clustered in a new political party—the Civilista party, which was the first organization to achieve power through civil means. But seven short years later, the cannons roared once again, this time against an external enemy: in 1879 Chile invaded Bolivia and Peru, and the War of the Pacific broke out.

The War of the Pacific has its roots in conflicting territorial claims made by Peru, Bolivia, and Chile over the mineral-rich Atacama Desert. The nitrate deposits in the province of Tarapacá, which was then a part of Peru, and those in the province of Antofagasta, then a part of Bolivia, were at the heart of the dispute. In 1875 President Mariano Prado nationalized the Peruvian nitrate industry to create a new source of income, since the prices of guano in the international market had been plummeting. This step agitated European and Chilean nitrate producers, who worked in the region, and they began to lobby for Chilean military intervention. Three years later, Bolivia imposed a tax on all nitrate exported by the Anglo-Chilean Antofagasta company. The imposition of this tax violated previous treaties between Bolivia and Chile and eventually provoked Chile

Wars, Indians, and the Nation

to send warships to the Antofagasta Bay in 1879. Bolivia then responded by declaring war and putting into effect a mutual alliance treaty with Peru, which was now obligated to enter the war as Bolivia's ally. Chile's army was far superior to the Peruvian or the Bolivian military. In the first half of the 1870s, the Peruvian government took direct steps to reduce its military power for reasons both economic and political. The number of soldiers, for example, was reduced from twelve thousand in 1870 to forty-five hundred in 1875.[4] This measure had devastating consequences. First, Chile now occupied significant parts of Peru, including the province of Tarapacá, the sugar plantations on the northern Peruvian coast, and the city of Lima.

Second, Peru's fragile inner stability collapsed with the first gunshots. In December 1879, just a few months after the war broke out, President Prado secretly fled for Europe, under the pretext that he had gone to recruit funds and equipment for the war. He would never return to Peru. The political void was filled by Nicolás de Piérola, who had served as the treasury minister in the 1860s but was hated by the Civilista oligarchy. A native of Arequipa, Piérola was a conservative and, although he established a political party, the Democratic Party, he operated as a caudillo, relying on personal networks in Arequipa and the southern provinces.

Once in power, Piérola established a dictatorship and attempted to defend the city of Lima, which was under Chilean threat. Because of conflicting political loyalties, he was either unable or unwilling to trust some of the experienced professional military officers. Instead, the Arequipeño caudillo mobilized his base in the south. Working through traditional Andean patronage networks, he recruited battalions of Aymara and Quechua Indians who were called to protect a city they had never visited and people whose language they did not understand. Moreover, ill-equipped and with no real training, these Indian soldiers were no match for the Chilean army, and in January 1881 the Chilean military occupied Lima. It is striking that important parts of the Limeño elite were more relieved than frightened by the occupation. The racial mixture that suddenly flooded the streets of the "pearl of the pacific" terrified

Lima's elite more than the white soldiers from Chile did. Reports from the central highlands and the northern sugar plantations about Indian and Chinese coolie uprisings fueled racial anxieties even further, as it appeared that the racial hierarchies that structured Andean society were dissolving rapidly.[5]

After the city had fallen, Piérola escaped to the central sierra to continue the resistance from there. The situation deteriorated, however, and revolts were unleashed across the country, even in regions such as Puno that were not directly under Chilean occupation. Faced with this failure, Piérola left for Europe at the end of 1881, and Andrés Cáceres, a former general in Piérola's army and one of his major rivals, took charge. Cáceres, a Quechua-speaking mestizo, skillfully organized local Indian peasants into a guerilla army that inflicted a major defeat on the Chileans in 1882. These peasants also attacked and occupied large haciendas and in certain regions were able to hold on to this "war booty" well after the war had ended. They also articulated their actions within a wider vision of nationhood and citizenship, which refuted some scholarly assumptions that the Indians did not understand who they were fighting for.[6]

At the same time, in other regions of the country, other figures were taking matters into their own hands. Miguel Iglesias, Piérola's former minister of war, for instance, commanded the resistance in the northern region but ended up allying himself with the Chileans, who recognized him as president. In 1884 Iglesias signed the Treaty of Ancón, which ended the Chilean occupation but also ceded the province of Tarapacá to that country.[7] The cannonballs, however, continued to fly. Cáceres, now hungry for the presidency, mobilized the Indigenous and rural guerilla battalions into Lima and forced Iglesias to resign in 1885.[8] Only then did the fighting cease, and Cáceres established Partido Constitucional, won the 1886 elections, and turned to reconstruction efforts.

While Cáceres dealt with a war-torn country and an empty treasury, Peruvian intellectuals contemplated the reasons for Peru's defeat. Javier Prado and Mariano Cornejo, for example, viewed Peru's defeat through a Comtian lens and pointed a finger at the country's Hispanic past, the Catholic Church, and traditional values that, in their eyes, hindered progress. The writer and intellectual Manuel González Prada was much more radical. Prada also attributed Peru's defeat to its colonial past but pointed a finger at the state officials in the highlands, specifically the district-level judges, priests, and governors. These three groups, he asserted, were the "trinity of brutality" and heartlessly exploited the Indians for personal profit. By leaving the Indians in a state of ignorance, bondage, and servitude, they also hampered Peru's national progress.

These accusations were rooted in long-standing tensions and conflicts between liberals and conservatives that erupted after independence across the continent. In the Andes, conflicts over issues of church and state centered more on controlling the Catholic Church and its social, economic, and political capital than on separating church and state. In Bolivia these efforts were successful, and the Catholic Church was subordinated almost entirely to the state.[9] In Peru the Catholic Church had a strong base of power in Arequipa and the southern provinces and therefore was able to preserve part of its independence. Moreover, after the wars of independence, both liberals and conservatives viewed Catholicism as a unifying force in a linguistically, ethnically, and racially divided nation. Prada's poignant attack on the Catholic Church was therefore significant in sharpening the lines between liberals and conservatives in Peru.[10] Simultaneously, Prada's focus on Peru's Indigenous population also invigorated indigenismo. Indigenismo was an eclectic intellectual movement that encompassed numerous fields and disciplines and became particularly important in the 1910s and 1920s. The indigenistas were mestizos and creoles who lived in cities, took great interest in the country's Indigenous past, and believed that its future depended upon finding effective answers to the "Indian question," or how to integrate the Indian into the nation.

After eight years of political stability, Peru slid into another civil war. In 1894 Cáceres ran for an unconstitutional reelection that provoked harsh reactions, especially from the former Civilista export-based oligarchy. To get rid of Cáceres, they turned to Nicolas de Piérola and called on him to return from exile. Piérola's base of power was, and had remained, in the city of Arequipa and the southern departments, and he used his long-standing networks to consolidate an army. In fact, his strategy was quite similar to the one he used during the War of the Pacific: first, he equipped and aided several groups of Indian battalions that were fighting in the interior; then, he unified them under his banner and recruited others, such as the above-mentioned Manuel Z. Camacho, into his rebel army.[11] Indians from the highlands, therefore, were the ones who cleared the way for this aging general to ride into the presidential palace and unseat Cáceres. Moreover, a new wave of soldiers from the highlands camped on Lima's outskirts, reminding the elite, yet again, that their nation was made of Indians.

The Aristocratic Republic, Conscription, and Indians

In 1895, when the cannonballs were finally silenced, a period known in historiography as the "Aristocratic Republic" began. Coined by the Peruvian historian Jorge Basadre, the term is an oxymoron pointing to a political system that combined republican institutions and aristocratic values, habits, and lineage. Indeed, for twenty-five years Peru was governed by an exclusive elite whose members were often related by kinship and marriage. But this period was one of political stability and relative internal and external peace. During Piérola's four-year administration (1895–99), the country underwent extensive modernization that included establishing the ministry of development, reorganizing taxation, and expanding and improving the nation's financial institutions. Piérola also had a specific interest in reforming the Peruvian armed forces and establishing a modern, professional, and centralized military. To that end, in 1896, Piérola invited a delegation of French military officers and advisers. Two years later, the Escuela Militar de Aplicación de Chorrillos was established under French direction. Furthermore, in 1898, a modern military code modeled after the French one was enacted and laws and regulations concerning conscription were also put into effect. Hence, at least in theory, all Peruvian men between twenty-one and twenty-four were to be drafted for three or four years and subjected

to the same treatment.[12] The law also included the establishment of new institutions and methods for drafting men into
the armed forces.[13] The idea was to bureaucratize the draft and
thus eliminate the personal ties and individual negotiations
that had characterized recruitment in the past. Furthermore,
as a result of these steps, regional elites would lose a large part
of their power to the central government in Lima.[14] Put differently, the military reform was part of the government's centralization efforts.

In practice, not all young men were drafted and most of
the burden fell on the shoulders of the Aymara and Quechua
Indians, who could not buy their way out of service. In the
1910s, prominent indigenistas, such as Dora Mayer and Pedro
Zulen, argued that Indian conscription was just another form
of exploitation. But others, including all the twentieth-century
presidents, beginning with Eduardo López de Romaña, who
succeeded Piérola in 1899, championed the military as a vehicle for Indian education and integration.[15] The army, these men
believed, had an important "civilizing mission," and out of the
cantonments emerged a new, well-trained Indian who could be
a beacon of progress and nationalism in his community. Nevertheless, research has not been conducted on what had actually
happened with these veterans. More broadly, Latin American
historiography, which offers a plethora of studies regarding the
various intersections of military, state, and society, has given
little attention to issues of former soldiers' reintegration into
civil society, particularly into rural society. It is likely that when
soldiers left the barracks, on account of discharge or desertion,
some probably returned immediately to their native communities in the highlands. Others made the outskirts of the cities
their new homes. And yet others, like Manuel Camacho, chose
to ramble about, sojourning in various places and working in
different occupations before they decided where to settle down
permanently.

It is extremely difficult to estimate how many men like Camacho, who eventually decided to return to their communities in
the highlands, there were. One of the main reasons for this difficulty is the lack of exact data on the number of enlisted sol-

diers.[16] Obviously, ongoing wars and the lack of a consistent central government are not conducive to historical preservation in general. But attempts to assess the number of soldiers during the nineteenth century, and even the early decades of the twentieth century, are met with additional methodological problems, since "recruitment was an ongoing endeavor, as was desertion."[17] In other words, the number of soldiers constantly changed as men deserted their posts. Despite the new conscription law of 1898, peasants were still recruited through patronage networks and as part of reciprocal relationships rather than being drafted through bureaucratic mechanisms as faceless citizens. Centralization, in this regard, was not particularly successful, and, similar to the situation in Bolivia, Lima continued to rely on regional elites to implement its orders and fill quotas.[18] In fact, this personalistic style was entirely eradicated only in the 1950s.[19] Therefore, recruitment continued to involve oral understandings, and while, from the mid-1900s on, one can find documents on recruitment, the evidence is still partial and the names of people who appear in them do not necessarily correspond to those who ended up in the barracks. Moreover, there is no documentation of who returned to Puno and when.

That said, contemporaries noticed veterans. Luis Valcárcel, the Cuzqueño indigenista, for example, casually said that "of the millions of Indians who have completed their military service, there are roughly a few thousand who have not returned to their place of origin; all the others returned, not only in body but in soul, to their traditional place."[20] Valcárcel's estimations are exaggerated, as the entire Peruvian military force never amounted to millions, but his comment does indicate that a significant portion of discharged Indian soldiers had returned home.[21] The reunion with their families was a happy occasion for some of them, who quickly found their way back to the field and the pastures. Others, like Manuel Camacho, encountered a very different reality. A soldier who returned home was one more person who wanted a share of the family's and the community's resources. When land and water were abundant, veterans' demands would not pose a major problem. But when

Indians were losing lands to the large haciendas, and natural resources were scarce and expensive, veterans' demands were an additional source of pressure. Additionally, away from home, on the coast, or in the outskirts of cities or growing towns, veterans had adopted new tastes, habits, and practices. A few, like Camacho, even adopted new faiths.

Manuel Camacho and Seventh-day Adventism

There are a few contradictory accounts about Camacho's conversion to Seventh-day Adventism. Although it appears that he was first exposed to Adventist teachings in the late 1890s, it is unclear where exactly Camacho learned about this church. The first Adventist missionary in Latin America arrived in Argentina in 1894. A year later, the Seventh-day Adventist General Conference sent G. H. Barber to labor in Valparaíso, Chile. Generally, the Adventist early work in Chile was unsuccessful and the mission attracted only a handful of converts. Nevertheless, at least according to one account, it was in that country that Camacho was exposed to Seventh-day Adventism. According to another version, Camacho learned about Protestantism, Seventh-day Adventism, and the Bible in Arequipa in the late 1890s. While dwelling in that city, he befriended Eduardo Forga, an Arequipeño from a well-off family with ties to the Seventh-day Adventists.[22] At that time, there was no official Adventist Church in Peru, but Chilean literary evangelists distributed literature throughout the region and some of it found devoted readers. Around 1902, Eduardo Thomann, an Adventist convert from Chile, arrived in Lima to help organize a small congregation. But not until 1906 would the General Conference send an official missionary, Franklin L. Perry, to establish a church in Lima. Other Adventist churches, in Arequipa and the town of Lanca, in the central Andes, would open doors in the late 1910s. In Puno a church was officially established in 1911, when Ferdinand Stahl, then stationed in Bolivia, was authorized to relocate with his family to Puno.

Camacho, however, did not wait for Thomann, Perry, Stahl, or any other outsider to bring this new religious message to his native community and work to save their souls. Around 1900,

Camacho decided to return home, and in his bags, he carried Adventist books, pamphlets, and the Bible, and began teaching these new doctrines, together with reading and writing, in an improvised classroom. His first students were young men like himself, veterans who had also returned home after spending years away from their community. These were men who discovered the difficulties of demobilization and reintegration into rural communities, especially in a region where the penetration of capitalism caused extensive social, economic, and political pressures.

2

Army Veterans Return to the Highlands

KNOWN FOR ITS VAST GRASSLANDS, THE ANDEAN ALTI-
plano was particularly suitable for herding animals. Historically, Andean shepherds herded llamas, alpacas, and vicuñas,
and after the Spanish conquest, sheep were added to the pack.
For centuries, animals were sheared and their wool was used
locally or distributed regionally. But just as in other secluded
regions across the globe, technological innovations and improvements in infrastructure ended the Altiplano's relative seclu-
sion. By the middle of the nineteenth century, southern Peru in
general, and Puno specifically, became a significant exporter of
wool to the world market. The region's role as a wool producer
and exporter expanded through the first decades of the twentieth century, reaching a peak during World War I. The soaring price of wool in the world market also led foreign houses
of commerce, which used to conduct business from Arequipa,
to establish direct representatives in Puno. As a result of this
move, local trade circuits, fairs, and middlemen lost their importance and small producers no longer had the same leverage to
negotiate a price for their merchandise. In a never-ending race
to purchase more land, hacienda owners became increasingly
dependent on credit lines, which weakened their bargaining
position, decreased their revenue, and ended up increasing
their appetite for resources.[1] Endless conflicts over land and
water, which were necessary to sustain large herds, broke out,
destroying the region's "moral economy" and tearing apart its
social and political cohesion.

This situation was particularly acute in the districts close to Lake Titicaca, such as Acora and Chucuito, which would become the heart of Adventist activity. These two districts were (a) suited for both agriculture and grazing and (b) among the most populous in the department of Puno.[2] They were home to one hundred haciendas and thirty-five independent Indian communities.[3] According to the 1876 census, these districts had 15,070 people and a population density of about 9.72 per square kilometer.[4] Thus, while in absolute terms the advance of the haciendas might have been greater in other districts, population density made the competition for land especially fierce in the areas close to the lake.

The Indian peasants were the main victims of this vicious competition. Thousands were dispossessed of their lands between the mid-1850s and 1920, among them Manuel Camacho's family.[5] In endless and ongoing quarrels, mestizos and Indians implemented various tactics to preserve or increase their landholdings and access to natural resources. Military service was one such method. During the War of the Pacific, Puno never came under Chilean occupation, nor was it torn by the civil wars of the late nineteenth century as were other parts of Peru. On the one hand, the region's economy and social structure were not directly affected by war during this period. On the other hand, unlike peasants in the central sierra who fought near home and at times took over the neighboring hacienda, Indian soldiers from Puno were dispatched to faraway places with little or no ability to communicate with their families. This tactic made military service an effective way to dispose of older sons and young fathers who were their families' social and economic backbone. This action also weakened the family socially and politically, since communal politics played out along gendered lines, and men were the ones who assumed the central positions in the local hierarchy. By contrast, women depended on men for access to local sources of power and to promote their interests and agendas. Thus, due to the absence of their close family members, women were pushed toward the social fringes of the community.

Despite President Piérola's efforts to bureaucratize recruitment in 1898, during the first decades of the twentieth century, army recruitment remained highly personal.[6] Like most transactions in the Andes, recruiters and prospective soldiers were usually acquainted with each other and had some degree of shared history.[7] Because recruitment was carried out through personal networks, it was also used to solve personal conflicts and make the balance of power tip in these situations. Local strongmen, also known as "gamonales," often targeted Indians who stubbornly refused their demands for land, labor, or agricultural goods and forced them into the barracks.[8] Furthermore, since power in the Andes was delegated along vertical lines, Indian communal authorities were usually the ones who rounded up recruits. Therefore, they had a degree of influence over who would be drafted, a power that could be used for personal benefit.[9] In fact, any Indian could attempt to use his social outreach and whatever bargaining power he had to "remove obstacles" and send them to the barracks.

Yet the personalistic style of recruitment also gave Indians some leverage, since recruiting peasants as soldiers involved negotiations over their terms of service and, more important, the compensation for that service.[10] Persuading Indians to join a battalion involved offering the prospective recruit "carrots" as well as using "sticks." Exemption from taxes, for example, was one of the privileges that an Indian soldier could earn in exchange for his service.[11] Other incentives included appointing *alcaldes* or other Indian community leaders to positions of power within a district or even creating new districts, which then required funds from the state's treasury.[12] Similarly, recruitment was not always the result of an individual's wish to forcefully remove a rival for the sake of economic or political gain. Indian soldiers were not always the passive victims of stronger men. In some cases, joining the army might have been the best option. Fierce competition over resources left many Indians landless or with landholdings so small that they were hardly sufficient for their livelihood. For some, joining the military provided some sort of opportunity. According to Olinda Celestino, such was the case of the community of Lampián, in the valley of Chancay, district of Lima. In the region, the shortage of natural resources, especially land, and the collapse of traditional mechanisms of reciprocity resulted in bitter conflicts between the younger and older generations. Unable to gain access to economic and political resources, which were mostly in control of the older generation, young men were forced to emigrate from their villages in pursuit of work. Rather than moving to Lima or one of the large estates on the coast, as most of the men did, a few chose to join the military.[13]

A military base, in this context, was a destination for immigration, one that provided a solution for men whom circumstances had "pushed" out of their homes. Moreover, perceiving the military as a destination for rural migrants allows us to grasp the complex role that the military played in civil society: at once both a vicious embodiment of state violence and a refuge from other forms of daily oppression, providing individuals, particularly young men, with an established or semi-established way out of traditional power relations. Therefore, soldiers were recruited under various conditions and arrangements. They were also discharged to disparate realities. Some veterans returned home with more promise and better social and political outreach than others. Nevertheless, even those who came back to the community in a relatively favorable position had to cope with a new reality that took shape while they were away and sometimes at their expense.

Veterans' Struggles over Natural Resources

For veterans who wished to resettle in the district of Chucuito or Acora, as Camacho did, "coping with a new reality" often meant dealing with the Pinazo family, headed by Jorge Pinazo. Pinazo had begun accumulating land at the turn of the century, as a result of the rise in international demand for wool. By 1910 he owned several haciendas in the district of Chucuito and was involved in endless disputes and violent incidents with Indians from that district.[14] In one case a small stream that belonged to former soldiers stood at the center of Pinazo's interests.

In 1912 Miguel Santos Chajo, an army veteran and Adventist convert, submitted a complaint, together with other Indians from his district, against Jorge Pinazo. According to these Indians, Pinazo, assisted by his Indian dependents, had dispossessed them of a small stream that their families had owned for over three hundred years. To settle the dispute, acting governor Pablo del Carpio was sent to the area. Del Carpio questioned the community's authorities, who apparently were the "eldest and most prestigious men" and was told that "the entire community uses the water and while it comes out of the property of the mentioned community members, no resident has the right to interfere (with its flow) nor does it belong to the municipality to be publicly sold."[15] In other words, the distinguished elders differentiated between land rights and water rights, acknowledging Santos Chajo as the legitimate proprietor of the land while rejecting his claims over the ownership of water. The water, in their stance, was no one's private property, and therefore neither Santos Chajo nor anyone else had the right to alter its natural current or divert it to their advantage. It was, in essence, a common resource to be shared by the community members.

Joint management and ownership over water had a long history in the highlands and were embedded in religious views, institutions, and practices. Andean cultures had developed a hydrological cosmology, which had at its center Lake Titicaca, their mythical source of origin, thus bolstering the connection between religion, ideology, and hydrological regimes. Over the centuries, norms and regulations concerning water and its distribution were altered, but a strong connection between religion and water regimes persisted.[16] In fact, in some cases the economic value of irrigation practices was negligible; their importance lay in their ceremonial aspects.[17] The community's high-ranking authorities, its "most prestigious men," as del Carpio called them, were precisely those in charge of water management. These were men who had invested time, sometimes a lifetime, and significant resources in the prestige system.

The prestige system, also known as the politico-religious hierarchy, required community members to perform various tasks, from delivering mail to sponsoring religious feasts, to benefit the community. Usually, although not always, one began by performing the most tedious tasks and then slowly ascended the hierarchy, gaining respect and establishing his authority. Those who had reached the highest ranks controlled many aspects of communal social, economic, and religious life, water being one of them. They oversaw the way water was allocated to the various members and conducted the religious rituals that accompanied and legitimized its distribution. Managing the water supplies was an important source of power, even in the district of Chucuito, where irrigation was practiced on a smaller scale.[18] In other words, it was not a privilege to be given up easily, especially considering the investment made to obtain it. The authorities' agenda, therefore, conflicted with the claims that Miguel Santos Chajo presented. Acknowledging an individual's private ownership of the stream meant losing a vital resource that they controlled through communal mechanisms.[19]

While the Indian authorities were undoubtedly an interested party, the accusations were directed against Pinazo, whose response is not recorded in the files. It is possible that pages are missing from the file and that in them Pinazo claims to be the legal owner, stating that he purchased the stream from a deceased family member. This would not be the first time Pinazo used such arguments to advance his interests.[20] Another possibility is that he was never seriously questioned by the district authorities about the case. Instead, del Carpio, who was closely related to Pinazo, could have declared that the stream was state property, since it belonged to no one.[21] Consequently, Pinazo could take possession of it in a two-step process: first, the owner would be charged with invading state property, and then Pinazo could buy the stream from the state.[22]

The prevalence of such methods would explain why the elders made a point of telling Pablo del Carpio not only that the stream did not belong to Indians but also that it did not belong to the municipality. It also explains why del Carpio never mentioned Jorge Pinazo during his investigations. Del Carpio uses the elders' stance concerning the water to undermine the Indians' claim that the stream had been part of their property for generations. The accusations against Pinazo, however, were never thoroughly examined and the legitimacy of his demands or actions was never questioned. Hence, although the Indians were the ones accusing Pinazo, they were eventually also the ones who were investigated by authorities.

Finally, there was a fourth party involved in this dispute: Pinazo's Indian dependents. Although they are anonymous and silent, the brief reference to them sheds light on the dynamics of Andean social alliances. It may be that Pinazo recruited "his" Indians to help protect his interests regarding the stream. It is equally possible that these Indians had turned to their patron to request his help in a quarrel that they were having with other Indians or that intracommunal tensions over the stream generated an opportunity for this hacienda owner to increase his holdings. In any one of these scenarios, though, the importance of patron-client and reciprocity relationships cannot be overemphasized. "Getting things done" in the Andes, from electing authorities to settling disputes, depended on one's social outreach and ability to construct a strong social web, which included vertical and horizontal commitments. This was a gradual process that took place through continuous daily interactions that included performing various duties and chores, lending favors, coaxing, and persuading functionaries and strongmen from within and outside the community.

Generally speaking, war efforts could provide additional opportunities to strengthen and expand these networks. This situation was precisely what happened in the southern sierra during the War of the Pacific. Because the main contribution of the southern sierra to the war effort was supplying provisions, the war ended up strengthening traditional social structures and forms of domination.[23] Indeed, being part of a patron-client network was especially crucial in this region. Veterans, however, because they had been absent from the community, did not have the opportunity to cultivate strong relationships with communal and district authority figures. They were therefore left without strong allies who could promote their interests and, in Santos Chajo's case, be a counterforce to the Pinazo family.

Besides lacking social outreach, veterans also depended heavily on their families for successful reintegration. Nevertheless, the same forces that had been pitting communities against each other and turning hacienda owners into aggressive land grabbers, were also tearing apart families and extended families. In 1852 President Ramón Castilla, then allied with the Civilistas, enacted a new civil code that canceled the *mayorazgo*, a traditional system of inheritance based on primogeniture and whose main function was to safeguard the wholeness of the estate. Instead, Castilla enacted a system of partible inheritance that divided the estate between living spouses and legitimate children.[24] As a result, estates were smaller and mutual commitments for the economic well-being of family members weakened significantly. Conflict erupted easily when no will existed or in cases of contradicting claims over the property. Moreover, since a variety of notions of tenure existed in the Andes, disputes could break out over the nature of tenure even when a title to a specific land parcel was not contested. For instance, extended family may have recognized an individual's right to cultivate the land without recognizing his right to sell it.[25]

Because recruitment served as a way to "resolve" these conflicts in the first place, it is not surprising that veterans who returned home had to fight for resources they had previously owned or at least had access to. Juan Huanca and Pedro Pauro were probably recruited to the military in the early 1900s. Both men, who would eventually convert to Seventh-day Adventism, struggled for years to regain rights over the land and the yield they had lost while serving. In a series of complaints submitted around 1912, they accused their neighbors and family members of having taken advantage of their long absence to encroach upon both common lands probably used for pasture and private land that had formed part of their estates.[26]

Similar to Santos Chajo, these veterans were in a particularly vulnerable position. The Peruvian state offered next to nothing with regard to programs and funds to support veterans in their demobilization and reintegration.[27] Therefore, aside from their own ability to negotiate terms of recruitment and secure future benefits, soldiers depended on kin to protect their interests while away and then help them reintegrate into the community. For example, Francisco Pilco, a soldier from the district of Ilave, owned a pregnant mare that had been stolen by a local gamonal around 1915. Yet Pilco was relatively lucky, since his father had the time and the means to wage a legal battle on his behalf.[28] Manuel Camacho also relied

Veterans Return to the Highlands

on his extended family after returning to Chucuito at the turn of the century. After discovering that his father had died and the family estancia no longer existed, he turned to the search for his mother, whom he found living with her second husband and children in Chucuito. Camacho's stepfather took him in as part of the extended family, and he reciprocated by working and participating in the household economic activities, both agricultural and commercial.[29] Thus, kinship provided a way "back into" the community and a degree of economic security. Those who did not have anyone to advocate on their behalf and safeguard their possessions, or whose families were deeply torn apart by inner conflict, had little to count on in terms of support and social outreach. In fact, in all likelihood, veterans' return aggravated conflicts even more, now that there were additional demands and needs to consider.

Veterans' Place in the Community's Traditional Political Administration

Veterans were embroiled in a complex and circular dynamic that confined them to the social and political margins of the community: On the one hand, on account of their absence, they did not have the social connections that could help them secure their rights over natural resources. On the other hand, conflicts over natural resources hampered veterans' ability to fulfill some of the tasks required for upward mobility in the politico-religious hierarchy. Owning land was often a prerequisite for holding honorary positions in the prestige system, which required the ability, in terms of both capital and social standing, to sponsor religious festivities. In the best of cases, losing land or dedicating resources to ongoing legal battles only debilitated veterans' economic outreach. In the worst of cases, it left them completely dependent on family and their own labor. Thus, dedicating the funds to sponsoring a fiesta had become difficult or impossible.

Limited resources also made it difficult to conduct important religious ceremonies and sacraments that were crucial to making one's way up the politico-religious hierarchy. Throughout the nineteenth century, the cost of these ceremonies had been increasing as communities became unable to provide a continuous and stable income for rural priests. To wit, the Catholic Church in rural areas was divided into parishes, which included a central town and a few satellite villages, whose boundaries were based on the population's ability to support a priest. As the earning capacity of the local Indigenous population diminished, so did the priests' livelihood. One of the strategies by which the local clergy compensated for this loss was to charge more for sacraments.[30] For young men, as veterans were, marriage was particularly relevant, and high costs often led a couple to choose cohabitation over a formal Catholic ceremony. Different practices of cohabitation were widespread in the Andes, and it was not uncommon for a couple to refrain from formal wedlock.[31] Upward mobility in the communal hierarchy, however, was preconditioned on formal marriage, hindering yet again veterans who aspired to local positions of leadership.[32] Authority positions were, therefore, out of the reach of those veterans who lacked the economic resources to obtain them. But at the same time, veterans' limited social ties impinged on their ability to protect their property or promote their interests within the Andean social web. Because veterans were recruited under various conditions, they also had a differing range of options and opportunities upon their return. Some men might have been able to secure enough guarantees, either for themselves or for their families, to make their reintegration easier. Nevertheless, many did have to struggle for their economic and political viability and actively fight to regain their rights. Puno's incorporation into the global market, together with its population growth, increased the pressure on natural resources and eventually instigated countless and constant quarrels and conflicts over them. Tensions tore apart communities and families, unexpected alliances were made between Indians and mestizos, and brutal rivalries broke out between them. Veterans' return home often burdened the situation even more, because their demands disrupted fragile agreements and status quos that had emerged while these men were away. Neighbors, family members, communal authorities, and hacienda owners often had a common interest in hampering their reintegration, "pushing" them to the community's margins or completely out of it. Moreover, the struggle over economic and political resources was not all veterans had to deal with. Other barriers stood in the way of successful reintegration: cultural ones.

Race and Racism in the Andes

In 1990 Mariano Larico Yurja, an Aymara Indian and political activist in Puno during the 1920s, told his life story to the Peruvian scholar and writer José Luis Ayala. He recalled that "army veterans who return to the estancia changed a lot. . . . They leave the army with a blanket, shoes, uniform, and a cap, they have become accustomed to underwear, they keep their uniforms so they can wear them while dancing in the fiesta."[33] By pointing to the manners and material culture that were associated with the mestizo world, Larico implies that these practices have become part of these men's *habitus* and that they were in no hurry to give it up simply because they had returned home. Yet, in the Andean world, these were not minor details: habitus, or the cultural capital that oriented one's social behavior, was the essence of one's racial identity.

The idea that cultural traits such as clothing, language, and food determine one's racial identity has been a topic of extensive discussion and debate. Scholars, mostly during the 1960s–80s, questioned whether social relations in the Andes had anything to do with race, since phenotype was practically a nonissue. They viewed race as essentially biological and therefore found little use for it, preferring instead to use terms such as *ethnicity, marginality*, and *social inferiority* to characterize social relations in the region.[34] Nevertheless, race and racism continued to haunt Peru and the Andes. "Racism," argued Alberto Flores Galindo in 1987, "exists even if racial terms do not officially circulate in public."[35]

During the second half of the 1990s, however, academic currents changed, the winds blowing mostly from the north. Scholars such as Marisol de la Cadena and Mary Weismantel strongly advocated for the use of the term *racism* in the Andean context.[36] According to them, race, and as a result racism, had been silenced in the Andes because of the "biological essentialism" of race as an ontological category.[37] According to these scholars, race is a constructed category, regardless of whether its parameters are biological or cultural. Just as Flores Galindo did, Weismantel, de la Cadena, and others have contended that what made racism was not its biological aspects but the intense, domineering, and subordinating power structure between humans it manifested.[38] Although terms such as "ethnicity" recognized differences, they did not elucidate power structures well enough and thus obscured reality. The fact that race in the Andes was culturally, rather than biologically, constructed was not meaningless, of course. One of the most salient results was the fluidity between racial categories since, by adopting new habits and manners, or by receiving some education, one could transgress, transform, or emerge as a member of another racial category, or what is often referred to as *mestizaje*.[39]

Veterans' clothes, in this regard, were a salient indicator of the profound change that veterans were supposedly going through. With a racial discourse that focuses on culture rather than biology, it is easy to understand why clothing attracted Larico's attention. With the lack of a clear phenotypical profile that divided racial groups, what a person wore was the most visible marker of his or her racial identity. To wit, in Cuzco during the first half of the twentieth century, people often referred to dress codes as a way to distinguish mestizas from "the Indian women." An apron and a hat, for example, were tokens of mestizo-ness.[40] By contrast, a shawl or a *pollera*, a certain kind of skirt, were perceived as "traditional" Indian clothing, worn since time immemorial, even if historically these styles had originated among whites or mestizos.[41] Specifically, some veterans returned with boots that manifest the "boundary between the higher status people who wear shoes or boots and the others who go barefoot or wear rubber sandals called *ojotas*."[42]

In this regard, clothing also manifests two socioeconomic conditions that were inherent to Indian-ness: being poor and being a peasant in rural areas, as Indians were generally viewed as poor and shoes were expensive.[43] By the same token, wearing ojotas was typically associated with a peasant's chores. The Alti-

Veterans Return to the Highlands

plano pasturelands were wet and muddy, and wet shoes left the feet cold, blistered, and sore. Ojotas, however, allowed the feet to dry quickly, and the layer of mud that formed around them provided better insulation than wet shoes or socks.[44] Changing shoes, in this regard, correlated to changing one's vocation, and once one stopped cultivating the land, he stopped, in the eyes of some, being an Indian.

Another important cultural asset that veterans had acquired away from their community was Spanish. Strongly associated with education, learning Spanish was perhaps the most important watershed dividing Indians from mestizos. How much Spanish soldiers actually learned in the army seems to vary greatly and in many cases was quite limited.[45] Manuel Camacho, in this regard, was not representative, as he entered the army with an elementary education that he had received as a boy in Moquegua. Much more representative of the level of fluency in Spanish of these veterans were the fourteen army veterans who had written to Puno's department prefect in 1926, among whom only six could sign their names.[46] Gregorio Mamani, who had spent a few years in the military camps during the 1930s, was able to sign his name but not much else: "They taught me the alphabet, there in the army. I was able to sign my own name, and—a, o, i, p—I could recognize some letters of the alphabet on paper. . . . Soon after leaving the army, I forgot how to read the letters I'd learned or how to spell my name."[47] With scanty knowledge of the alphabet and no access to adult educational programs, Mamani had little chance of maintaining, not to mention improving on, what he had learned. Such may not have been the case for all soldiers, but it was for many of them, particularly those who were recruited before Piérola's military reform and the construction of military schools.[48]

In terms of comprehension of Spanish and oral communication, the picture seems to be more complex and ambiguous. Mamani vividly explains, "You'd be unable to speak [Spanish] when you entered and unable to speak when you left, Spanish barely dribbling from your tongue. There in the army, those lieutenants and captains did not want us speaking the *runa* tongue. They would say: 'Dammit Indians! Spanish!' So the noncommissioned officers would beat Spanish into us."[49] On the one hand, he declares that Indians did not learn a thing. On the other, Spanish had become a part of them in the most physical sense of the word; it had been violently imprinted into the soldiers through the daily brutality of training. Where the classroom failed, ruthlessness prevailed. Cultural oppression was therefore profoundly interwoven with the acquisition of Spanish in the barracks, sharpening the fine line between those Indians who were able to meet the terms presented to them and go through a process of acculturation, and the many who could not. Although at a cost, the former group had a chance for promotion, both in the military and in society, while other men, such as Gregorio, remained in the lowest army ranks and were the most "Indian" among the soldiers.

Yet even men who were not inclined to learning new languages could not avoid Spanish completely. Accompanying the soldiers from wake-up to lights out, escorting them on their strolls down to the market and the city streets on days off, following them like a shadow into their bunks, *castellano* was all around and some of it had to rub off. Although many soldiers did not receive formal education in the language, could not read, write, or speak fluently, through daily experiences they acquired, at the very least, basic knowledge of the language. As unimpressive as it may have seemed in the city, back in the community, meager knowledge of Spanish turned into an important asset. In comparison with peasants who had never left their district, "a little" became "a lot." Race is therefore a dynamic social construction that changes according to the locale and the participants. "Indians and mestizos emerge from interaction, not from evolution."[50] Consequently, what mattered was not so much the objective quality of that Spanish the veterans spoke, as it was their position in comparison to other interlocutors, who on average knew less than they did. Veterans did not "evolve" into mestizos. They had become mestizos in comparison with their neighbors who had never left the community, did not speak any Spanish, and had never tried on a pair of boots.

Veterans Return to the Highlands

Tense Encounters: Army Veterans, Indians, and Mestizos

Whether one was considered an Indian or a mestizo had direct social and political ramifications. Colonial Peru was a hierarchical caste-based society in which different groups had different rights and obligations. The new Peruvian republic, however, was founded on the ideas of the Enlightenment and the French Revolution. Popular sovereignty, equality, and private property were written and rewritten into the nation's various constitutions. On paper, everyone was now "a Peruvian," and all Peruvians were equal before the law. In practice, however, Peru remained a highly stratified castelike society in which Indians were at the bottom of the social hierarchy and mestizos at the top.[51] Mestizaje, in this regard, also meant upward social mobility, and Indian veterans, who now wore uniforms, had supposedly moved up a notch. The anthropologist Olinda Celestino, for example, quotes one of her informants who liked "the uniform a lot," because the way he looked in it impressed people from his community who visited him in the city.[52]

That, however, was what happened in the city. In the countryside, things were different. Gregorio Mamani, for example, would not return to his community wearing a uniform because he was afraid that the other Indians would mock and insult him: "Your fellow villagers see army clothes and say: 'He'll be a *little misti* only as long as those state clothes last him,'" he testified.[53] By contrast, Severo Qorimaywa had served in the National Guard and decided to return to his family's estancia after he was discharged. Once at home, he hung up his uniform and put on a poncho and a pair of handwoven pants, thus turning back into an Indian. As such, Qorimaywa's reintegration was easier, and he eventually became the community's president.[54] Mamani and Qorimaywa made opposite choices, but their actions stem from the same conventions: returning to the community meant self-re-Indianization.

Veterans who refused to re-Indianize were often treated with suspicion and ridiculed. In the eyes of others, as Mamani testifies, they were "little mistis," outsiders, people who may have reached a higher social status but at the cost of their social belonging and identity. In this regard, the term "little misti" conveys a sense of betrayal and condescension: betrayal, because it appeared that veterans were willing to trade their families and heritage for upward mobility, and condescension, because they insisted on identifying with higher-status mestizos than with their fellow Indians. Mariano Larico thought that veterans saw themselves as superior to other Indians because they believed that their military service entitled them to "another class of women . . . and at times they want[ed] to have more than two women."[55] Former soldiers believed they deserved a "different class of women," or that they could control more women than the average (i.e., more than two). This is revealing of the way these men saw themselves not only vis-à-vis women but also compared with other men.[56] They had made rank, not only in the military.[57]

Yet, at the same time, veterans' mestizo-ness was a disguise, or at the very least it was temporary. To recall Gregorio Mamani's words, one could be "a little misti only as long as those state clothes last him." In other words, veterans were like pretentious actors who would last only as long as their costumes enabled them to play the part. No matter the garments, the person underneath was an Indian, and he would remain an Indian; his real character would slowly reemerge as the shiny fabric unraveled. Laura Gotkowitz describes a similar situation in which an attempt to transgress racial or ethnic categories is called out as a bluff. During an exchange of insults between Ramona Gutiérrez and Gregorio Mendoza, the first said of the second's wife: "There are individuals who wear polleras to please their husbands, but the monkey, no matter how much satin she wears, is always a monkey."[58] As it appears, Mendoza's wife attempted to deceive others and present herself as belonging to a higher racial and social category. Yet the woman's fraudulent efforts were transparent and her real "monkeyish" nature exposed. Scholarly ideas concerning hybridity or the fluidity of racial and ethnic identities tend to overlook the difficulties that can arise from adopting new habits or changing traditional ways of conduct. Although mestizaje undoubtedly existed as a powerful force, it did have limits.

Veterans Return to the Highlands

Scornful reactions toward veterans, in this respect, functioned as disciplinary tools aimed at regulating one another's behavior and punishing deviation. Gregorio Mamani did not want to return to his community in uniform, because he knew that people would make fun of him. Wearing the nice clothes he had bought in the city would turn out to be a barrier to his reintegration.[59] Implicitly Mamani was presented with a choice: assimilate, that is, submit to the community's hegemonic notions of Indian-ness, or self-deport. He opted for the latter.

Moreover, the temporalities and inner dynamics of mestizaje are crucial. Mariano Larico, for instance, believed that the loss of one's Indian-ness happens over generations as sons and grandsons of Indians who had emigrated from the community integrated into mestizo society and denied their cultural genealogy: "The sons of the peasants residing in the town are now mistis, they do not want to know anything about the peasants who stayed in the estancia, neither do the grandchildren of peasants who had left."[60] The first generation, though, was still considered to be Indians, even if they had mestizo characteristics. It seems that in the eyes of other Indians, veterans who had been considered Indians their entire life could not have miraculously transformed into something else. Racial metamorphosis, in this regard, was almost as inconceivable as changing one's skin color, even if phenotype had nothing to do with it.

Local strongmen, including hacienda owners and state authorities, were discontented with veterans' mestizo-ness. These men had a clear interest in sustaining the social and racial order of Andean society. They did not look lightly upon what they perceived to be attempts to overstep racial boundaries, and things could easily escalate into violence, as happened one Sunday morning in 1913. That day Santos Valdéz, Mariano Chuhuaris, and Manuel Camacho visited the town of Chucuito. While there, the three were ridiculed and carried off to prison, spending days and even weeks in custody because they had been wearing mestizo clothes.[61]

Using Mary Douglas's concepts of dirt and purity, Mary Weismantel analyzes the position of the *chola* in the marketplace, pointing out that "an unsettled racial identity is one source of the chola's offensiveness: Indians, when visible in the city, whites among Indians."[62] Correspondingly, because veterans were perceived by others as neither mestizos nor Indians, they were considered a threat to social "hygiene," and as capable of polluting racial categories and geographical spaces. The fact that these racial in-betweens were considered to be dirty or dangerous, rather than humorous or ridiculous, is in itself evidence of the instability of racial boundaries in Andean society. One could pose the question, Why not treat a mesti-fied Indian as a jester clad as a king? The ability to transgress between racial categories, to actually "pass" as a mestizo by adopting certain cultural traits, made the surveillance of racial boundaries necessary and presumably transformed in-betweens into a potential threat. Hence, identifying "frauds" became a crucial and difficult task. Moreover, veterans' familiarity with sophisticated weapons not only raised the fear of armed rebellion but also indicated that Indians had the capacity to handle them and that they were not as ignorant as one may have wished. Similarly, performing military drills, as was done in Adventist schools, demonstrated a capacity for order and organization, undermining notions about Indian idleness.

For some Limeño intellectuals and politicians, this "new" Indian was proof of what they had been arguing since the end of the War of the Pacific: that Peru's defeat was largely to do with the lack of assimilation of Indians and their conditions of servitude that prevented them from integrating into the nation. The qualities that veterans possessed therefore turned them into walking proof that the Indians could be integrated into the nation and that the Limeños' vision for a modern and "enlightened" nation was attainable.[63] Yet, for men such as Jorge Pinazo, the problem was that there was no room for the landed oligarchy in this vision. They were part of Manuel Gonzáles Prada's trinity of brutality and an obstacle that had to be removed for the nation to move forward. Landowners were not simply frightened of the armed threat that veterans posed, nor were they only concerned about losing Indian working hands. Veterans symbolized a national project that had no room for them.

Veterans Return to the Highlands

In this sense, refusing to accept veterans and requiring that they conform to hegemonic racial notions was a way of resisting a liberal national project envisioned by Limeños who had never lived in the highlands.

Veterans' new appearance and military experience, therefore, only exacerbated existing phobias among regional elites, now that the "bloodthirsty" Indian was armed and trained.[64] Hence, military service ended up creating problems as much as solving them: while both state and communal authorities had used recruitment to "get rid" of young Indian men, some had returned and were unwilling to act like Indians. Both state and communal authorities, as well as other Indians, were quick to react. Using methods ranging from diatribes to violence, they sought to regulate veterans' behavior and force them to act according to the hegemonic notion of Indian-ness. In this regard, the process of hybridity, or that of incorporating new elements into one's identity, was hardly a peaceful process or a matter of friendly negotiations over the acceptable cultural norms and practices. Instead, it came at a personal cost and involved oppression, resistance, loss, and sometimes victory. Notwithstanding veterans' central place in the Adventist Church, they were not the only ones who knocked on the mission's door. Hence, before concluding, we will turn to briefly discuss the other Adventist converts and their relationship with veterans.

Mapping an Alternative Community: Veterans and Other Converts

Information concerning the socioeconomic background of the first Seventh-day Adventist converts, especially those who joined the mission between 1911 and 1925, is quite difficult to obtain. Nevertheless, a letter written in 1912 by Marcos Miranda, an active Seventh-day Adventist, sheds some light on the issue. Representing a group of Indians, among them other converts, Miranda complains of tax extortion.[65] The background to Miranda's complaint is that of national fiscal policies, put into effect under Cáceres, and their implementation since the last decade of the nineteenth century. An 1893 legislative resolution resolved that all property units producing an income under 100 soles (meaning an amount of five soles collected as tax) would be exempt from property tax. Nevertheless, many peasants with incomes that fell well below 100 soles were enrolled into the tax registers and paid sums lower than the minimum five soles. In 1908 new attempts to enforce the law were made by the Peruvian government.[66] But instead of being exempt from taxes, Miranda and his companions ended up paying more than they earned because the overassessment of Indian properties was a common practice.[67]

In the province of Azángaro, only 8 percent to 10 percent of the peasants had wealth equivalent to twenty soles or more a year, and only 2 percent made over 100 soles annually. In the areas near the shore, where our story unfolds, the fierce competition over natural resources was a weighty burden on the accumulation of such wealth. In other words, while Miranda may not have been representing the richest of the rich, as tax collectors had proclaimed by including him in their lists, he and his cosigners were likely among the top 10 percent.[68] After all, overassessment was effective only if Indians could pay. Notwithstanding their relative economic security, the wealthier stratum of the community, specifically those who did not have sufficient political ties, found themselves subjected to onerous fines, particularly those they had to pay to buy their way out of labor services.[69] Furthermore, assuming positions within the communal hierarchy, with the aim of gaining religious and political power, bore heavy costs. As discussed earlier, to advance in the politico-religious hierarchy, it was necessary to sponsor costly religious festivals, which only the top 10 percent of the community were able to do and were expected to do. Initially, one of the important functions of the fiestas was the redistribution of wealth, putting a degree of checks and balances on economic gaps within the community. One had to exhibit generosity toward the community to legitimize one's own prosperity.[70] In the turbulent years of the turn of the century, however, it had become difficult to recuperate economically after such an expensive investment.[71] In this regard, Miranda seems to have been like other Protestant converts, in other places in Latin America, who found that conversion had minimized certain socio-religious economic obligations.[72]

Sectors within the upper 10 percent shared sentiments of exploitation and disdain toward the traditional system with veterans who found it hard to squeeze their way into the system in the first place. It seems that rather than being a class-based phenomenon, Seventh-day Adventist converts were a community of peasants who no longer enjoyed the advantages of the traditional system and shared a desire to find an alternative. In a way, their case combines the conclusions that Emilio Willems and Christian Lalive d'Epinay have each reached in their research. Willems and d'Epinay, using Weber's paradigm, identified Protestant converts to be among populations that were transitioning into the capitalistic market. Willems focused on small and medium landowners, while d'Epinay examined new and marginalized immigrants in the cities. Seventh-day Adventists in Puno were more similar to the latter, after they came home, and met the former group.[73]

Because the Andean prestige system was religious, as administrative roles combined with religious tasks and worldview, conversion offered a way out of this system while making it possible to preserve the basic connection between political and religious leadership. Moreover, traditional notions of reciprocity, or new interpretations of them, may have evolved between veterans in weak economic positions and converts from more prosperous families. The latter offered "cultural capital," that is, literacy and acquaintance with certain cultural codes, in exchange for subsistence and respect from the locals.

It was not unheard of for teachers to mobilize in this manner. Luis Felipe Luna Tamayo, for example, was a landless teacher from Urubamba brought to Azángaro by a local hacienda owner to educate the hacienda owner's children. He ended up marrying into the family.[74] Thus, with few financial assets but a relatively high level of education, Manuel Camacho, like many other veterans, found that teaching provided him with an income, status, and a path for social mobilization.[75] But it was precisely the education, habits, and new ideas former soldiers brought from the barracks and the coast that became additional impediments to their readjustment, stymieing reintegration even further. To a degree, veterans found themselves alienated culturally, unable or unwilling, or both, to accept hegemonic notions of "Indian-ness" and act accordingly. Seeking alternatives, some found their way to Manuel Z. Camacho's improvised class-room and then within the newly erected walls of the Seventh-day Adventist mission.

Army veterans were fundamental to the mission's expan-sion and made up its native leadership. They worked as trans-lators, sold Adventist literature, and even began training as missionaries. But above all, veterans served as teachers in the Adventist rural schools. In 1920, Erasmo Roca, at the time head of the labor department in Augusto Leguía's administration, observed that "most of the [Adventist] teachers that we have met are army veterans."[76] As the native leadership of the Adventist Church, veterans generated new cultural spaces that enabled fresh interpretations of Indian-ness, the emergence of new leadership, and the redefinition of Indians' national obliga-tions and responsibilities.

Veterans Return to the Highlands

3

Religious Conversion and Racial Regeneration in an Indian Community

MANUEL CAMACHO'S CLASSROOM OPENED ITS DOORS IN 1901 in a small *estancia* named Utawilaya, in the district of Chucuito in Puno. From the very beginning, local authorities were hostile toward this man's educational endeavors, and he and his students were subjected to constant violence and imprisonment. Despite these obstacles, from 1902 to 1905, Camacho taught at least twenty-five men, many of them veterans, to read and write in Spanish using the Bible and Seventh-day Adventist literature.[1] For almost a decade, Camacho wrote to Adventist representatives in Chile and Lima, requesting that a missionary be sent to Puno and an official mission be built. In 1910, Ferdinand Stahl, an Adventist missionary stationed in La Paz, began to visit Camacho and his students regularly. After spending a year crossing the border back and forth, the General Conference finally permitted Stahl and his family to leave La Paz and move to Chucuito permanently.

When Stahl arrived in 1911, there were probably three or four dozen Sabbath-keepers in Chucuito and a few in the town of Puno. Five years later, six churches served over five hundred members in two or three districts. From across the mountains and the Altiplano, Indian representatives walked for miles to the central mission to submit a petition for an Adventist teacher and missionary. Adventism was growing rapidly. By the end of the 1920s, the church had grown to over seven thousand baptized members and there were hundreds more unbaptized affiliates and sympathizers. The 1940 census shows that about twenty-eight thousand Puñenos described themselves as Protestants,

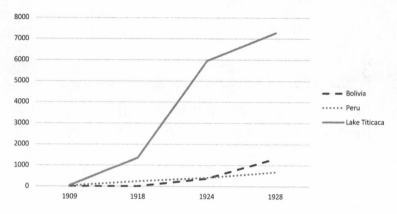

FIG. 1. Seventh-day Adventist membership in Bolivia, Peru, and the Lake Titicaca Mission to 1930. Created by the author from *Seventh-day Adventist Conferences, Missions, and Institutions, Annual Statistical Report, for Years 1909, 1918, 1924, 1928* (Takoma Park, Washington DC: General Conference of the Seventh-day Adventists, 1909–28).

almost all of whom practiced Adventism, even though only a small portion were official members of the Adventist Church.[2]

Hence, the Adventist influence went well beyond the boundaries of the official church establishment. Most of the Adventist activity in the first decades was conducted among the Aymaraspeaking Indians, but in 1920 Pedro Kalbermatter pioneered into Quechua-speaking regions. There were now twelve churches, a medical clinic, and dozens of rural schools, in which army veterans served as teachers, around Lake Titicaca.[3] In terms of Indians' access to education, this development was revolutionary.

Until 1905, elementary schools in the Altiplano were under the supervision of the municipal council and accessible almost entirely to regional elites. In places where rural schools existed, they were usually used as another method to recruit labor or to forge reciprocal relationships. In 1903 the government launched a new educational reform to centralize the educational system under the auspices of the ministry of education. Centralization was supposed to prevent further exploitation of Indians, enable a more balanced allocation of resources, and eventually provide education to larger sectors of the population. Nevertheless, its success was extremely limited, and Peru's educational system remained highly unequal and inaccessible to Indians. In effect,

Conversion and Regeneration

TABLE 1. Seventh-day Adventist converts,
staff, and institutions, 1915–28

Year	Mission	Churches	Membership	Baptized this year	Ordained ministers	Total laborers	Sabbath schools
1915	Bolivia	2	10	3	1	4	1
	Peru	6	514	190	4	18	20
1917	Bolivia	1	10	2	1	4	2
	Titicaca*	4	359	353	2	9	5
1921	Peru	8	340	72	2	15	17
	Bolivia	3	174	155	1	12	3
	Titicaca	10	3,120	917	2	106	18
1924	Peru	8	411	65	3	16	29
	Bolivia	4	373	147	3	9	7
	Titicaca	11	5,963	1,420	4	28	11
1928	Peru	12	678	68	2	18	48
	Bolivia	8	1,325	258	5	87	25
	Titicaca	12	7,267	867	8	145	72

*In 1917 the Lake Titicaca Mission was separated from the Peruvian Mission. Its jurisdiction covered both sides of Lake Titicaca. In 1921 the mission was reorganized, with the Bolivian side returning to the jurisdiction of the Bolivian Mission.

Source: Created by the author from *The General Conference Department of Education Statistics, 1853–1987*, Seventh-day Adventist Church, Office of Archives, Statistics, and Research, under "Statistics"/"Education," accessed January 6, 2022, https://documents. adventistarchives.org/Statistics/Forms/AllItems.aspx?RootFolder=%2fStatistics%2fEducation&FolderCTID=0x01200095DE8DF0FA49904B9D652113284DE0C800ED657F-7DABA3CF4D893EA744F14DA97B.

Adventist schools were among the very few options, if not the only option, through which Indians could obtain some degree of Spanish literacy until the 1930s. They were also among the few institutions that were not tied to local gamonales or part of the traditional Andean power structures such as the Catholic Church. Seventh-day Adventism was the only non-Catholic Christian denomination in the rural Altiplano until other Protestant denominations began to work in the region in the mid-1920s. For anyone seeking a spiritual alternative and willing to take the risk that came along with confronting the Catholic Church, the Adventist Church was the only option available.

Scholarship has often associated conversion to Protestantism

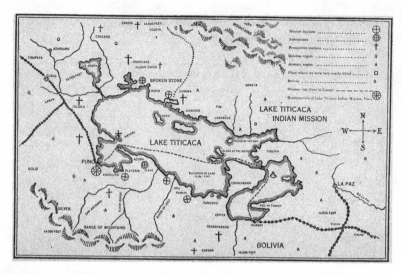

FIG. 2. The Lake Titicaca Mission, circa 1920. From Stahl, *In the Land of the Incas*, 16.

in general, and Seventh-day Adventism in particular, with racial mestizaje. Conversion, in this regard, helped people adopt new practices and habits, lose some of their "Indian" traits, become more mestizo, and achieve a degree of social mobility. While this generalization may be true in some cases, racial transformation, or becoming a mestizo, does not seem to have been the objective of the Adventist army veterans and other Indian converts to Adventism. Quite the contrary. In daily interactions and correspondence, they openly and repeatedly identified as Indians.[4] Indeed, an important part of racial transformation occurred between the lines of bureaucratic paperwork. It was not uncommon for Indians to present themselves as something other than Indians when approaching authorities, and uncontested claims served to validate their mestizo or "whitened" identity. Some people went even farther, creating their own bureaucratic tools to affirm a specific racial identity. For example, in 1876 Indians accounted for about a third of the population in Atun Huaylas, in the central highlands. In 1940 the huaylinos, many of whom came from the families considered Indians in 1876, conducted a census in which they all declared themselves to be mestizos.[5] Furthermore, veterans had eventually found a spiritual home

Conversion and Regeneration

FIG. 3. Adventist presence in Peru, circa 1920. Created by Erin Greb from *The Seventh-day Adventist Yearbook* (Takoma Park, Washington DC: Review and Herald Publishing Assn., 1906–20).

in an institution that proudly declared itself to be "Indian": "The *Indian* Mission to Lake Titicaca" (my emphasis). In the Andean context, no self-respecting mestizo would join such an institution. Thus, through baptism and active participation in the Adventist Church, members reasserted their Indian identity. To an extent, this is not surprising, since "the cult of mestizaje" was never as strong in the Andes as it was in Mexico. In fact, throughout the colonial period and into the twentieth century, being of pure blood, Indian or white, was often considered superior to racial hybridity. In practice, however, mestizos existed and mestizaje occurred, especially among those who no longer enjoyed the legal guarantees of being "Indian," primarily protection of their land and their access to other natural resources. For these men, mestizaje was a way out of onerous taxes and communal obligations as well as a way to open new venues.[6] Subsequently, veterans' insistence that they were Indians is unexpected.

Nevertheless, in a region where race was constructed more on a cultural basis than on a biological one, there is tension between the racial identity veterans professed to have and the clearly mestizo cultural traits they had adopted. In other words, how could they be Indians if they were acting like mestizos? Examining racial constructions in Cuzco, Marisol de la Cadena concludes that a mestizo identity could include practices and traditions generally associated with Indians.[7] Seventh-day Adventist converts engaged in a similar racial adaptation but from the opposite direction—trying to incorporate mestizo traits into an Indian identity. Conversion was an essential part of this reverse adaptation and strongly contributed to converts' emergence as new or, more precisely, renewed Indians. It provided veterans with a space where they could foster a new racial identity and, more important, with an interpretative paradigm that contextualized cultural traits, such as language, food, and dress, in a way that played down their racial implications. Yet, because race, religion, and politics were intertwined in the Andes, conversion also caused communal tension and conflict. Converts no longer accepted the political and religious authority of the community's traditional leaders; they no longer believed that they were subjected to the same kind of obligations as the "old" Catholic Indian who had not converted and, in their words, had not gone through a process of regeneration.

The Shifting Relation between Church and State

After the War of the Pacific, the strife between liberals and conservatives deepened, in part because of the war itself and the debate over the causes of Peru's defeat. This increasing conflict was also linked to the country's economic reconstruction, especially the rehabilitation of its export economy, which was legitimized by positivist ideologies. According to this view, modernization and progress also entailed secularization, separation of church and state, and freedom of religion. Nevertheless, the distribution of power between both sides was relatively balanced, and the lines between being "liberal" and being "conservative" were relatively fluid. In 1888, for example, the Peruvian Congress passed a law establishing civil cemeteries for foreign citizens. This was a victory for liberals, but one they achieved just barely, with forty-two votes in favor and forty-one against.[8]

Issues of church and state continued to spur disagreement after Piérola's rise to power. Yet in compliance with the political arrangements that enabled the existence of the Aristocratic Republic, between 1895 and 1919, disagreements were to be settled among the various components that constituted the ruling oligarchy. Thus these years were characterized by efforts to settle the contradicting visions for the nation circulating among the elite that now formed the country's new government. In this context, issues of church and state were often pivotal points of disagreement. On the one hand, Piérola was the son of a devout Catholic mother and had studied in the San Toribio Seminary. Politically and culturally, he represented values of Hispanism and Catholicism, perpetuated since colonial times, in the southern city of Arequipa. For him, Catholicism and authoritarian political conduct were essential in a country as diverse as Peru.[9] Accordingly, the family, as the nation's basic social unit, had to be under the aegis of one central moral authority, in this case, the Catholic Church. Freedom of religion, which also meant decentralizing one's personal and familial affairs, introduced chaos, and strong and stable nations were not born out of chaos.[10]

Shortly after taking power, Piérola ordered the exclusion of Protestant weddings from the civil registry. According to Peru's civil legal code (1851), marriage could be performed only by the Catholic Church. Nevertheless, it had become customary to inscribe the marriages of non-Catholic foreigners in the civil registry. Piérola broke this fragile but long-standing status quo, thereupon leaving non-Catholics without an official validation of their marital status.[11] This action provoked an angry backlash from Protestant foreigners living in Peru as well as from liberal intellectuals and some Civilista politicians who did not share Piérola's Catholic vision for the nation. Instead, they put forward "modernization" as a national project. This meant following in the footsteps of North America and northern Europe, which prescribed freedom of religion, alongside other measures. In Peru, as in other places, many intellectuals who subscribed to this line of thought believed that Protestants were agents of progress and that Protestantism was more compatible with modernity than Catholicism. In their eyes, it was not a coincidence that the "modern" countries happened to be those that had been divorced from Catholicism for centuries. By the same token, immigrants from northern Europe were particularly welcome, and securing freedom of religion was a way to encourage them to come. Finally, many liberals saw the general idea that church and state were not separated in Peru as a remnant of a colonial mentality and as being stuck in the past. Separating the church from the state was simply something that modern states did.[12]

The triumph of the younger generation of Civilistas, represented by José Pardo, in 1904 tipped the scales in favor of the modernization paradigm. As a result, Protestants in general, and missionaries in particular, had allies in the government and among liberal elites. President Leguía, who was the incumbent in 1911, the year Ferdinand Stahl crossed into the country from La Paz to Puno, had extensive business ties in England and North America. As part of his attempts to modernize Peru, Leguía appointed numerous U.S. citizens to political, cultural, and educational posts.[13] The Seventh-day Adventists, in this sense, were no exception, even though de jure their initiatives were illegal.

Fundamental change in the relationship between church and state would occur only in 1915. That year, the Peruvian Congress amended article four of the 1860 constitution, which had banned the public practice of any religion other than Catholicism, so that it recognized freedom of religion as a constitutional right.[14] Oddly, the events in the small Adventist mission station in Puno, over five hundred miles from Lima, played a pivotal role in securing this change. On March 3, 1913, a group of local hacienda owners and Indians headed by the bishop of Puno, Monsignor Valentín Ampuero, set out from the village

Conversion and Regeneration

of Chucuito to the Seventh-day Adventist mission in Platería. When they arrived at the mission, they broke into the main house, stole property, and took five Indian converts, including Camacho, as prisoners.[15] The story reverberated loudly across the nation. Newspapers reported on the state of the detained Indians; liberals screamed in outrage against the local gamonales and Puno's bishop, denouncing them as petty men who were looking out for their own interests and were dedicated to suppressing the Indians and, with them, the future of the entire nation.[16] In this atmosphere, liberals obtained the necessary political support in Congress to amend article four and significantly change the legal relationship between the state and the Catholic Church.

Back in Puno, however, Manuel Camacho was simply trying to get justice for himself and the four other Indian converts who had been arrested as a result of this incident. In what required great courage and an equal amount of self-confidence, Camacho filed an official complaint against the bishop of the diocese and other district authorities, providing a glimpse into the tense relationship between the parties involved and into the self-perception of the Seventh-day Adventist neophyte. Camacho explains:

> The acts of hate and vengeance committed against us . . . in all their naked truth, absolutely, do not have any other reason than the fact that we have become Evangelicals or Protestant; that is, abjuring the celebrations of Catholic festivals, which have been reduced among the Indians to the payment of large sums to priests and to the worship of an invented God. That is, beginning our personal regeneration, practicing our religion out there, in the countryside, within the walls of the house that Mr. Stahl had built; praising (word missing in original) Jesus, our savior. Studying and putting into practice the teaching of the Gospel that brings harmony and wellbeing into our homes, keeping us away from vices, especially from alcohol and coca. We have begun to see the advantages of hygiene and the early treatment of diseases, through the caring and free medical treatment given by Mr. Stahl to anyone who asks for it.[17]

Sitting in the interrogation room, after having been called for questioning, Camacho draws a portrait of the converted Indians: they abjure Catholic festivals and worship a true God, they study the Gospel and refrain from coca and alcohol, adopting new medical and hygienic practices, and going through personal regeneration. In other words, becoming a Seventh-day Adventist had as much, and maybe more, to do with what one no longer did as with what one had begun to practice. In this regard, abstention from coca, alcoholic beverages, and participation in local fiestas are particularly revealing and merit in-depth discussion.

Abjuring Fiestas and Abstaining from Coca and Alcohol

Celebrating fiestas and consuming coca and alcohol have been part of the Andean religious and cultural landscape practically since time immemorial. These practices carried complex and multilayered symbolisms that linked participants to each other, to the divine, to the supernatural, and to the past and future of their communities.[18] They also fulfilled important social functions, as they were essential to the prestige system and for the creation of social networks and reciprocal relationships within and outside the community.[19] The sponsorship of events during the fiesta, as I have already discussed, was a critical step in one's promotion in the community's politico-religious hierarchy; the way coca and alcohol were consumed manifested norms of reciprocity and hierarchy. But even more crucially, these were central cultural practices and, as such, represented an "Indian" way of life.[20] "*Hallpay* (coca chewing) . . . carries a way of life with it. To do *hallpay* properly . . . is to be *Runa*. . . . To chew coca leaves is to affirm the attitudes and values . . . that are characteristic of indigenous Andean culture."[21]

Hence, by refraining from coca and alcohol, by refusing to participate in local fiestas, Seventh-day Adventists chose to exclude themselves from a significant part of Indigenous culture. They had decided to forswear traditional pathways to the sacred and to reject customs and habits that were considered a fundamental part of what defined an "Indian" in the eyes of both Indians and outsiders. From a sociological perspective, converts ceased to take part in traditional reciprocity rites, cutting themselves out of important social networks. They may have had good reasons to do so. Nevertheless, considering that these rites and customs were central to hegemonic notions of racial identity, one can ask: If chewing coca and dancing drunk in a fiesta were among the parameters that defined an Indian as such, how could one avoid these practices and continue to be an Indian?

It is for this reason that Camacho is not satisfied with simply proclaiming that Seventh-day Adventists "abjure fiestas" but adds that fiestas "have been reduced among Indians to the payment of large sums to the priests and to the worship of an invented God." From his perspective, fiestas have been drained of their deep cultural meaning, severed from their extensive social functions, thus becoming an empty mechanism implemented by greedy priests only to exploit Indians. Rejecting them, therefore, did not amount to a rejection of Indigenous culture, as would be implied in an evolutionary notion of mestizaje; it was, rather, a way of resisting exploitation.

By the same token, the characterization of the Catholic God as "invented" emphasized a deceptive character of a system that, in Camacho's mind, was run by men willing to teach lies in order to profit. Surely, Indians had plenty of reasons to loathe local priests, many of whom had allied themselves with hacienda owners. In fact, Benigno Pinazo, a priest stationed in the nearby province of Chucuito, was related to Jorge Pinazo and owned a hacienda himself.[22] Yet most of the expenses associated with the fiesta were reinvested into the community, providing food, drink, and entertainment for a large number of participants.[23] The converts' focus on fiestas as the emblems of priestly exploitation rather than, say, the soaring prices of religious sacraments, stemmed more from their relationships with Indian communal authorities than from those with mestizo priests.[24]

All of this, to be clear, does not mean that the converts' actions did not have a specific meaning within the framework of the Seventh-day Adventist Church or that they were detached from the doctrine the missionaries were preaching. Seventh-day Adventism was influenced by the nineteenth-century health reform movement in the United States.[25] Adventists spoke in favor of abstinence from coffee, tea, and alcohol; church leaders called upon followers to keep a simple diet, refraining from spicy foods and even meat. The Adventist Church took an active role in the temperance movement and ministered against the harmful effects of certain kinds of drugs.[26] Abstaining from coca, alcohol, or any event that would include the consumption of either, therefore, was a tenet of the Seventh-day Adventist worldview and can be seen as part of its religious doctrine. Nevertheless, what made these theological ideas relevant to the lives of the Indians, what gave them actual transformative power and turned them "true" in the eyes of the new believers, was their ability to respond to local problems and dilemmas, providing a new way of thinking about them. To better illustrate this point, let us turn to two other traits converts had adopted: new hygienic practices and the Spanish language.

The Advantages of Hygiene and Spanish

Hygiene and the prevention of diseases constituted an important pillar of the Seventh-day Adventist health reform and theology. Tying the ideas of health reform to Adventist-specific theology, the Adventist Church taught that the human body was a holy sanctuary and one that needed to remain pure. Missionaries, believing that Indians knew little about personal hygiene, taught them how to wash their faces with soap during the school's first session.[27] Endless comments were made about the state of filth in which Indians lived. Even converts had pointed to cleanliness as one of the qualities that separated them from their surroundings.[28] Yet hygiene turned out to be more than a distinguishing trait between converts and their neighbors; it had become an alternative discourse that emphasized qualities such as cleanliness over the style of dress. Rather than having a clear dress code for services, missionaries emphasized that clothes, of any kind, had to be clean. In 1911 one missionary reported: "When they came to meeting on the Sabbath, many were dressed in clean or new clothes, while others were careful to tell us that they, too, would soon have new clothes, but they had not finished making them."[29] The Seventh-day Adventists' attitude should not be taken for granted or seen as an obvious method to attract converts. Missions across the world often established a policy toward Indigenous clothing. In an attempt to "civilize" the natives or construct clear racial boundaries, they either encouraged neophytes to adopt a Western style of dress or completely forbade them to wear European clothing.[30] The Seventh-day Adventists, however, played down differences in wardrobe, demoting their importance as a racial marker. Photographs of the mission's everyday life indicate that neophytes dressed in both Western and traditional Aymara clothing; both styles filled its rows, blurring the visible boundary between "Indian" and "mestizo" clothing.

Yet the hierarchy established through the association between fashion and racial identity did not cease to exist in the mission. It was still present in many ways. For example, one can roughly distinguish between two types of photos: photos from special occasions and portraits, and "snapshot" images of everyday missionary life. In the second group, one finds more men dressed in native clothing than in the first. Thus, when Adventists wanted to be "presentable," they chose a Western appearance. Secondly, when describing converts' traditional Indian attire, missionaries were inclined to emphasize that the clothes were spotless, a quality that was not mentioned with regard to Western clothing.[31] In other words, Western clothes imbued the quality of cleanliness while Indigenous forms of dress, and the Indians who wore them, needed to be purified. Yet, once "purification" took place and clothes were found to meet the required standard, they were considered appropriate and dignifying. Notwithstanding the palpable Western superiority, hygienist discourse had become a way of discussing and judging appearances without the strict racial implications usually associated to dress in the Andes. Thus, the mission had created a space in which Indians could dress as they pleased, alternating styles, without being subjected to abuse, yet still be considered Indians.

Language was another arena in which cultural discrepancies, which were crucial for racial construction, were systematically minimized: Adventist Church services were generally conducted

FIG. 4. Manuel Camacho (*left*) and Juan Huanca (*right*). From Stahl, *In the Land of the Incas*, 207.

in Spanish. A translation to Aymara or Quechua, however, was provided, making Indigenous languages an integral part of the mission's formal life: "The teacher begins standing on a high podium with an Indian translator to his side, in front of more than 200 students, men and women, all standing reciting a prayer and singing the national anthem and then a few school

FIG. 5. Indian teachers at the Lake Titicaca Mission, Puno, Peru. From Stahl, *In the Land of the Incas*, 269.

songs."[32] One report describes as follows the dynamic of language in the Platería school: "The teacher then gives a lecture on morals, which is translated by the interpreter. Three or four Indian teachers, divided into two rooms among the children, make them read their books, explaining them in their [the student's] own language."[33]

As Spanish was preached from the central podium, it preserved its position as the dominant language. But within the mission's compound, Aymara and Quechua were given the official recognition that they hadn't attained anywhere else. Missionaries made an effort to translate their message. Moreover, formally, converts had to be able to read the Bible, at least at a basic level, to be officially baptized. Thus, in this case, the knowledge of Spanish was not a feature that distinguished mestizos from Indians; rather, it was used to differentiate between Catholics and Seventh-day Adventists. One learned Spanish to be able to convert, not to become a mestizo.

Finally, conversion created bilingual Indians. Clearly, actual proficiency in Spanish varied among converts, and it is likely, as a few missionaries complained years later, that some Indians had little or no proficiency in the language.[34] Nevertheless, in the Andes, where bilingualism, and with it the ability to move between worlds, was the prerogative of mestizos, the mere idea that Indians could be bilingual was radical. In this regard, learning Spanish was about challenging racial hierarchies and distinctions. As Carlos Condorena, the leader of the 1923 Huancané rebellion, who was affiliated with the Adventist Church, said: "The day will come when they [the Indians] will have to learn [Spanish], just as the *mistis* know how to speak Aymara and Quechua."[35]

Conversion provided a space where, and a method through which, Indians could reconstruct their racial identity. By leaving the Catholic Church, they forswore customs such as drinking alcohol and chewing coca, which had connotations that were both religious and social. As a result, converts broke out of the mutual obligations and reciprocity that characterized Andean communal life, exacerbating intracommunal tensions and frictions. Conversion also caused a kind of identity crisis. After all, drinking alcohol, dancing in fiestas, and chewing coca were considered an integral part of Indian-ness. On the other hand, by joining the Seventh-day Adventist Church, converts were able to downplay some of the Andean racial barriers. They were able to dress as they pleased, as long as it met the missionaries' standard of cleanliness, and to speak in both Aymara and Spanish. Within the compound of the mission, they did not have to choose between being Indians and displaying the new, presumably mestizo habits they acquired while away. They were, in a sense, redefining the meaning of being an Indian.

Conversion as Regeneration: The Meaning of Religious Transformation

Describing conversion in their own terms, converts claimed to have "adopted the path of redemption."[36] They also said they were working toward "regeneration."[37] Some had even gone to "far out places across the Plateau" to promote the "rehabilitation of their brothers."[38] Redemption and regeneration are saturated with religious meaning, as these are cornerstone concepts in Christian salvation theologies, commonly found in both Catholic and Protestant doctrines. Broadly, redemption pertains to atonement and Jesus's sacrifice to absolve humanity of its sins, while regeneration points to the believer's own process of spiritual and moral purification from sin.[39] Additionally, a biological meaning was embedded within the concept of regeneration, attesting to man's physical recovery and to the process of regaining the strength lost due to disease or other physical injuries. Finally, rehabilitation carries both medical and social connotations of restoration for those who, for example, are recovering from drug and alcohol abuse.

Converts, therefore, describe conversion as a quest for restoration, rather than a path toward something completely new. They turned their gaze backward toward a presumably ideal time, set in the faraway past, a period prior to their fall, as individuals and as a race, into the decay of the present. In this regard, their perspective stands in contrast to the progressive progress from a low racial and social rank to a higher one, as the evolutionary conception of miscegenation implies. After all, for many Latin American intellectuals and nation builders, mestizaje was an essential part of progress that would eventually pave the way to modernity.[40] Mestizaje, therefore, represents a linear and modernist conception of time, in which just as time progresses, so does humanity, and the future is always more promising than the past. Restoration, on the contrary, extolls the past and paradoxically posits the return to this past as the path toward a new future.

This discourse of redemption and restoration was far from being a unique feature of the mission and corresponded to deep-seated millenarian and utopian currents that were common in the Andes. Specifically, the idea of the "Andean Utopia" contrasts with European notions of utopia, since the European Utopia is located in an unspecified time in the future while the Andean Utopia is understood as the Inca past.[41] Yet converts' description of conversion as a process of restoration rather than a metamorphosis or a complete break with the past also offered them a specific advantage: it allowed them to introduce new elements into notions of Indian-ness while claiming to be embedded within a traditional framework. It was, in effect, a way to legitimize the reconstruction of this racial category by claiming continuity. From the perspective of the Seventh-day Adventists, it was the Catholic Indians who had broken ties with the past by following the degenerate Catholic customs.[42] Moreover, in this context, restoration also is a significant mode of resistance, in particular to notions of evolutionary mestizaje, which were expressed through derogatory remarks such as "little mistis" and put converts at odds with their own culture. Finally, viewing conversion as a form of restoration provided neophytes with a clear idea as to who was responsible for their dire situation: the Catholic Church and its conniving and greedy priests—men interested in making a fortune by teaching Indians to worship a false god. In other words, the priests preached lies, preventing the Indians from becoming good Christians and putting into practice God's true teachings. Conversion, therefore, also entailed the purification of Christianity.[43]

The idea that Christianity needed to be purified was not new. It had been voiced in the past by the rebels during the Túpac Amaru II Rebellion (1780) as a way to justify their actions. For example, at Azángaro, Diego Cristóbal Túpac Amaru, one of the rebellion's leaders and a cousin of Túpac Amaru II, asserted that the Spaniards were all criminals who "caused the Indians to become heretics, and who were apostates in contrast to the true Christians."[44] Furthermore, the idea that one could adopt Spanish habits and practices but remain an Indian also has historical precedence. The kurakas, a native elite during the mid-colonial period, held a dual Hispanic and Neo-Incaic identity. In the 1570s, as part of the Toledo Reforms, the Spanish Crown implemented a settlement policy that created the "Republic of Indians" and the "Republic of Spaniards," each with specific legal obligations and privileges. The Republic of Indians was governed by Spanish bureaucrats and by the kurakas, a native elite that either was, or claimed to be, successors of the Inca. The kurakas adopted Spanish material culture, such as some articles of clothing, and were instructed in Spanish, mathematics, and forms of European art. They were still, however, considered Indians, albeit Indian royalty, and remained within the domain of the Republic of Indians as leaders of their communities.[45] Significantly, a major site for shaping the kurakas' dual Hispanic and Incaic identity was the Colegio de San Borja

Cuzco, a school established in 1621 by Jesuit missionaries. Jesuits also established a school and mission for Aymara Indians in the town of Juli, where they successfully instructed the Aymara in European ways.[46] Here, as in Cuzco, the Aymara neophytes were generally recognized as Indians, despite Hispanic acculturation. In the 1910s, the Adventists would establish a mission station in Juli.

There is no direct historical connection between the kurakas and Jesuits, on the one hand, and the Adventist missionaries and the Aymara veterans, on the other. Major events, including the expulsion of the Jesuits from Peru in 1767, the Túpac Amaru II Rebellion, the suppression of the kurakas, independence, and endless wars, profoundly altered the region's political, social, and cultural structures. Notwithstanding these important transformations, the long-standing notion of an elite that adopted Spanish traits but was considered of the Indian race indicates that the Adventist converts were not operating in a vacuum. Their ideas about the "regenerated Indian" had roots in the region. Intriguingly, the idea that one could be a "Hispanicized Indian" flourished among those who were particularly interested in Inca history and culture, such as missionaries sent to evangelize Indians in the sixteenth and seventeenth centuries. Broadly, these trends would disappear after the expulsion of the Jesuits and with the emergence of Enlightenment ideas and modernity among elites in the eighteenth and nineteenth centuries. The Indian and the Inca would be revived again only in the late nineteenth century with the emergence of indigenismo.

The Seventh-day Adventist Converts and Visions of the Nation

At the twilight of the nineteenth century, after looking toward Europe for decades, elites in Lima discovered that their country was actually filled with Indians. The first signs of the renewed urban interest in the "Indian" appeared in literature, novels, and stories whose main protagonists were rural Indians. The novel *Aves sin nido* (1859), which tells the story of a fictional rural Indigenous village named Kíllac and the abuses its people are subjected to by local elites, is considered a landmark in the development of literary indigenismo. After the War of the Pacific, the indigenista currents became stronger and a growing number of intellectuals and artists, who looked inquisitively into the history, anthropology, geography, and economy of the rural Andes, became critical of certain social and economic mechanisms they believed left Indians in a state of ignorance and servitude. In 1909 Pedro Zulen, then a student at San Marcos University, established the Asociación Pro Indígena, which aimed to raise public awareness about the conditions under which the Indians live and to stimulate social and political reform. This organization was inspired by antislavery organizations and was a successful attempt to move indigenismo from the confines of intellectual and artistic discourse to political advocacy.[47] To that end, the association published newspapers and pamphlets, met with legislators, and assisted Indians from rural areas on various issues. After World War I and into the 1920s and Augusto Leguía's regime, other centers of indigenismo emerged, such as the indigenistas of Cuzco and the group that clustered around the Marxist intellectual José Carlos Mariátegui and the journal Amauta. Indigenistas differed from each other significantly.[48] But they shared a common gaze of white and urban mestizos and criollos, and a general agreement that Peruvian progress and modernization depended on "uplifting" the Indian.[49]

As cities turned their gaze to the mountains, however, so did the mountains stare back. Perhaps veterans had been exposed to discussions of indigenismo during the years they spent in the barracks, as occurred to some extent in Bolivia.[50] Maybe they learned of these debates through local and regional newspapers, now that some had learned to read. Maybe the missionaries served as intermediates, disseminating their own take on local politics. Whatever the source, the fact was that the various aspects of converts' religious renewal and regeneration corresponded with indigenista concerns over the Indians' "degenerated" state. If elites were in search of a "new Indian" who would push the nation forward, then Seventh-day Adventists seemed to be creating the prototype. In this regard, Indians participated in the discussion about the future of their race, and their role was not limited to being subjects in the conversations of others. In fact, they had proposed their own solution: conversion. Proposing religious change as a remedy for the Indian's poor state, or more precisely choosing to transform a belief system and the local sociopolitical institutions embedded in it, was a uniquely Indian solution. Indigenistas, it is true, looked favorably toward Protestantism and even lent support to missionary initiatives.[51] Yet they tended to distinguish between the missionaries' social and religious messages, embracing the first and ignoring the second.[52] They recognized the biosocial meaning of regeneration but considered its religious content to be irrelevant. Luis Valcárcel, for example, bluntly declared that he was ignorant of Seventh-day Adventist creed and uninterested in knowing it.[53] What was important for this Cusqueño indigenista were the social changes and self-confidence he recognized in converts.

Conveniently, indigenistas overlooked the facts that Indians were reading the Bible and that hygiene carried significant religious meanings within Seventh-day Adventist theology. Some of them even went so far as to project their own constructed division between the social and the religious on the Indians, believing that they had little interest in, or understanding of, religious creed: "Also, one should not be scared of the religious labor that they [the Seventh-day Adventist missionaries] do, because, for the Indian, religious beliefs are a materialistic question. . . . The philosophic and moral principles on which each religion is based can only be understood by educated people."[54]

Nevertheless, for converts, forswearing fiestas was as much a religious act as an act of social protest. It was not only about avoiding the onerous expenses incurred in preparing fiestas, as some indigenistas would have liked to believe; it was also a quest for an alternative, "authentic" divinity. Moreover, contrary to the condescending remark quoted above, Indians both understood and took interest in the "philosophical and moral principles of religion." From the time of the Reformation, the Catholic cult of saints had been treated by Protestants as idolatry.[55] Already in 1910, before Stahl had permanently settled in Puno, the local priest of the Santo Domingo parish in Chucuito denounced the religious blasphemies that Seventh-day Adventists had been teaching the Indians:

"A foreigner and an Indian named Manuel Camacho are going from estancia to estancia, corrupting and converting the incautious and the weak of spirit, like our Indians. Like heathens, these two men are telling them blasphemies and denying the existence of supreme beings like devils, even having them agree that there is no God, or purgatory, or hell or glory and that when a person dies everything is over, that there is no worse hell than the material sufferings of this life, that a rational being concludes his life with death like an irrational animal."[56]

The priest's testimony does resonate with some of the theological and pastoral points emphasized by Adventists. For one, missionaries often commented that they preached godly love rather than fear.[57] The idea of purgatory had already been fiercely criticized and then cast out of doctrine by prominent Protestant theologians.[58] Adventists had gone a step farther, persistently arguing against the concept of an "intermediate state" or the notion of the soul's immortality. For Seventh-day Adventists, as this priest perceptively points out, life was believed to end with death, the soul lying dormant with the body until reawakened by Christ. Conclusions reached about irrationality, or the inexistence of a soul, however, are related to Catholic ideas about death and resurrection. While the priest's understanding of Seventh-day Adventist doctrine may have been partial and heavily clouded by Catholicism, his testimony indicates that Indians were in fact interested in the doctrine. The fact was that indigenistas were unable or unwilling, or both, to recognize the role that religion and conversion played in Indians' lives. Catholic Indians and district authorities, on the other hand, understood all too well what the ramifications of conversion might be. In the Andes, where religion was a communal activity, any claim that it was a "private matter" was simply a misreading of reality.[59] Without religious cohesion, and a broad consensus over one's religious commitments, maintaining any kind of social and political coherence became extremely difficult.

4

Religious Conversion and
Communal Cohesion

IN THE ANDES, AS IN OTHER PARTS OF LATIN AMERICA, religion, politics, and sovereignty have long been intertwined. Before the Spanish conquest, political relationships between Cuzco and various Andean villages included exchanging political leaders, gods, and priests. Alongside weapons and germs, the Christian cross was brought by Spaniards to the Americas, and Catholicism served as the ideological framework for the continent's conquest and colonization. Specifically, the legal foundation of the Spanish claim over the New World's territories was the 1493 papal bull issued by Pope Alexander VI. Among the Indigenous population, the relationship between Catholicism and political authority was cemented during the Toledan reform of the late sixteenth century. The Indian *reducciones*, or resettlements, had two major functions: to convert the Indians to Christianity, so they could live like "civil" people, and to make tribute collection more feasible. Although these new settlements did not necessarily become the permanent dwellings of Indians, they did emerge as significant "administrative and ceremonial centers, theaters of political and religious ritual,"[1] thus tying together religion and sovereignty, a bond that was recognized and legitimized through the payment of tribute. Over time, and especially after the idolatry campaigns of the seventeenth century, the authority of local Indian leaders, the kurakas and alcaldes, would "increasingly lie in the public demonstration of their Christianity."[2] Patron saint festivals linked tribute collection, communal identity, and the kurakas' prestige.

By the end of the eighteenth century, the hereditary kurakas were replaced with the *alcaldes de indios* in a move that laid the base for the modern prestige system. The reasons for this shift are diverse and have much to do with dynamics within the Indian communities. The reasons are also linked, however, to Bolivarian republicanism in its rejection of monarchism, especially the Spanish monarchy, and in its view of the Indian aristocracy as part of that old, degenerate, and exploitative form of government. From this perspective, supplanting the "old" colonial kurakas with a new kind of communal leadership would better fit a "republic" and could make citizens, rather than tributers, out of the Indians.

Nevertheless, religion did not vanish with the kurakas, as perhaps some liberals wished, and it continued to play a vital role in the consolidation of political authority, sovereignty, and ideas about citizenship. Communal activities such as taking on a political position, forging alliances, even cleaning out water channels and demarcating plots of land, all carried religious meanings and were legitimized through religious beliefs and symbolism. By the same token, how rituals were conducted, who participated in them, and which religious images and symbols were honored was of utter political importance, often pointing to social and political loyalties as well as to the boundaries of the community. It is in part for this reason that widespread veneration of Catholic saints or local *cofradías* frightened both state and ecclesiastical authorities.[3] Indeed, popular religion was a "crucial site of 'everyday state formation'" in the Andes throughout the nineteenth century and beyond.[4]

The importance of popular religion in Peruvian state formation both resulted from liberal reforms and was asserted in spite of them. On the one hand, despite liberal reforms and general hostility toward the Catholic Church, the state relied on Catholic missions, especially in the frontier region, to civilize the Indian and turn him into a productive citizen.[5] On the other hand, liberal reforms, namely the appropriation of church property and the abolishment of tithes, severely reduced the Catholic Church's revenue. The result was apparent across the Andes, but it was particularly noticeable in rural and Indigenous areas where Catholic edifices were becoming dilapidated and ecclesiastical posts were vacant for years. Even in places such as Chucuito, where religious services were relatively accessible, months could go by before people saw a priest. The absence of official ecclesiastical authorities had two significant consequences: first, it buttressed the authority of the Indian communal authorities, who supervised religious rites and were responsible for meeting the community's spiritual needs. Furthermore, by the late nineteenth century, sacraments had become so expensive that some peasants looked for alternatives regardless of whether a priest visited them regularly or not. As a result, communal authorities also conducted "unofficial" sacraments such as burials and baptisms, expanding their religious authority even further.[6] Second, free from the gaze of the church and without ecclesiastical authorities who could regulate everyday religious practices, popular forms of Catholicism flourished. The veneration of saints became widespread and decentralized, thus enabling the public enactment of a variety of identities and political loyalties. Attempts to subdue Indian fiestas and processions in honor of local saints accentuated the importance of the religious sphere as a site for envisioning the nation and its prospective citizens even further. In 1880, during the War of the Pacific, the council of Huancayo, in the central sierra, worked excessively to subdue popular religious festivals. The regional elite feared that the image of these religious celebrations would reflect badly on the province and present it as an uncivilized, and even barbaric, province.[7] Moreover, because religion and local politics were intertwined, by honoring specific saints and disengaging from other saints, Indians were also professing political loyalties that did not always match the loyalties and political preferences of local elites. Similarly, during the Atusparia uprising (1885), fiestas and Catholic rituals became an arena of contested power. On the one hand, mestizo priests used their religious authority to achieve political gains and "pacify" the rebels. On the other hand, Indian communal authorities were not passive bystanders and conducted their own popular Catholic rituals to accumulate authority and consolidate alliances.[8] Peru was not unique in this regard. Discussing the Mexican War of Independence, Eric Van Young pointed out a similar connection between popular religion, sovereignty, and local politics, writing that "communalist thinking and politics depended in large measure on sources of religious legitimation."[9]

Within a broader framework, Catholic saints played an important role in the construction of Peruvian nationalism and were incorporated into the state apparatus. In 1823, when the nascent republic was still at war with Spain, the Virgin of Las Mercedes, for example, was named the patron of the Peruvian armed forces, tying Catholicism to the institution that was emblematic of national sovereignty.[10] Around the same time, the Bolivian government was busy establishing a civic celebration in honor of national events such as the Battle of Ayacucho, on the one hand, and reducing the number of Catholic popular fiestas on the other. The result, however, was the convergence by the mid-nineteenth century of the "civic" with the religious, evident in celebrations commemorating national events that included prayers, churches decorated with flags, and portraits of national heroes presented on the alter. Thus, the intertwining of religion and politics on the communal level was framed in a larger national context that wove together Catholicism, national identity, and national sovereignty. Engaging in politics, therefore, inevitably meant engaging in religion, and vice versa; saints formed a nucleus through which communal politics were integrated into the larger framework of the nation and thus became a site for contesting notions of Indians' citizenship.

Subsequently, attempts at discerning between the two misrepresent Andean social and political reality in which political spaces, values, practices, and even people's imaginations were deeply rooted in a religious worldview. José Antonio Encinas, for instance, the Puneño educator and indigenista, noted the centrality of religion in the Indigenous worldview, writing that "the regeneration of the Indian race cannot be resolved but within the religious framework since the Indian's conscience does not have the strength to get by without this control."[11] Encinas's words are patronizing, implying that Indians, like children, lack reason and need to be subjected to external control. Yet, even so, his observation concerning the importance of religion in any attempt at generating significant social change should not be easily discarded. Encinas, in this regard, saw exactly what eluded the gaze of other indigenistas, who constantly imposed their own desired separation between religion and politics on Indigenous populations.

This framework accounts for accusations made in 1913 by Catholic community members against converts according to which "the rains are not falling as they did before, causing a bad yield."[12] In other words, two years of official Adventist activity in the area and the emergence of an alternative religious community of two hundred converts had caused a drought. What might at first seem to be a baseless accusation or a cynical attempt to create outrage toward the growing Seventh-day Adventist community reveals how religion was embedded in local politics. It also attests to the very real anxieties that conversion to Seventh-day Adventism provoked among the Catholic members of the community. Andean hydraulic cosmology has long included local professions of faith such as drinking alcohol and pouring it on the earth. Such rites were understood as part of man's reciprocal relationship with nature and were popularly believed to secure the ongoing cycle of the rains.[13] Based on that belief, if the community was not reciprocating to the earth properly, then the rain would stop falling. Hence, as the converts' regeneration led them to abstain from alcohol, this stance could have serious repercussions for the entire community. Moreover, the cosmological anxieties over a supernaturally inflicted drought reflect very earthly concerns over the future of crops and subsistence in a community that was not cohesive.

Historically, in the rural Andes, communal authorities were responsible for the administration of common natural resources. Their duties ranged from supervising access to shores or pastureland to managing agricultural lands and husbandry practices. Communal lands, for example, were divided among members at the beginning of the season, each peasant being assigned to cultivate a strip of a larger field.[14] The land was then cultivated through a fixed rotation system, which demanded a high level of coordination, cooperation, and enforcement.[15] Additionally, peasants were not free from rotation obligations even on the lands they privately owned, and harvest success often depended on cooperation.[16] Sectorial fallowing, in which part of the land was cultivated while the rest lay fallow, was widely practiced across the Andes. In places close to the lakeshore, such as Chucuito and Acora, for instance, a rotation of three or four crops took place, as this soil was richer.[17] After the last yield, the plots were left fallow, at which time all members of the community had access to the land for the purpose of herds' grazing. This system offered some major advantages for peasants, as it reduced the workload, regenerated soil fertility, and even contributed to pest control.[18] Its success, however, depended on peasants' adherence to a specific set of rules that governed planting, harvesting, and grazing, and had to be strictly observed.[19]

The agricultural cycle was deeply integrated into a religious worldview, and its different stages were celebrated with religious rituals. For example, festivities held during the sowing period focused on seed fertility, and prayer was devoted to a prolific harvest. During the period of growth, rituals were performed to secure and improve the development of crops. Then, when crops ripened, the community gave thanks to God for his generosity, through ritual and prayer.[20] These rituals were conducted, as mentioned, by the men who held office in the communal hierarchy and were endowed with the religious and political authority to distribute communal resources. Thus, rituals and festivities enhanced the community's commitment toward the land tenure regime and those in charge of it. By rejecting the religious framework, converts (a) challenged the legitimacy of the system and those who oversaw it and (b) weakened a system that depended on cooperation, therefore posing a threat to the community's ability to sustain its livelihood.

Returning to the rains that refused to fall in 1913, we see how anxieties over the political and economic future of the community were expressed through the religious paradigm. The community had to work together to ensure a fruitful yield, whether by cooperating in rituals intended to secure enough rain or by working together to observe a set of rules. Once a part of the community refused to cooperate, the stability of the entire system was shaken. Conversion, therefore, created real fears for the future, as a religious change would inevitably have a major impact on the communities' political and social structure. Furthermore, converts aroused additional suspicion by refusing to take part in what were considered to be traditional Indian obligations, emphasizing instead how their religious regeneration contributed to the uplifting of the "Indian race."

The Regenerated Indians and Education

Education, which meant above all literacy in Spanish, was one of the main components of regeneration. From the Adventist Church's perspective, baptism depended on one's ability to read the Bible at least at a basic level of proficiency. More broadly, the question of Indian education was a central part of indigenista discourse and was often brought up as an answer to the "Indian question." Prominent names such as Hildebrando Castro Pozo, Julián Palacios, and Moisés Sáenz argued over whether education would uplift Indians, what kind of education Indians should receive, and who should teach them. The renowned educator and director of the primary school "Centro Escolar 881" in Puno, José Antonio Encinas, argued that Indians were suspicious of the outside world because of their longtime exploitation and gamonales' land grabbing. Education, he thought, was the only way to overcome these suspicions and integrate the Indians into the nation.[21]

From the grassroots, however, sectors among the Puneño Indians had been demanding greater access to education and schools since the beginning of the twentieth century. Access to education was one of the primary goals that the first group of Indian messengers from Santa Rosa, Puno, presented in Lima in 1901. The Indians who had participated in the delegation claimed to have fulfilled their duty as taxpayers and hence argued that, as citizens, they were entitled to an education.[22] "Good citizenship" or "good republicanism" had long been associated in the Andes with paying taxes, particularly the *contribución personal*, and providing free labor services.[23] The seeds of this notion of citizenship were planted during the colonial era with the reciprocal relationship based on "land for tribute": Indians were expected to pay a head tax and provide labor power for a range of public initiatives, and in return, the government would protect their lands and guarantee their access to natural resources. Throughout the nineteenth century, a series of legal, social, and political developments had compromised and altered the "land for tribute" pact, dissolving it completely in certain parts of the northern and central sierra. In the southern sierra, however, it remained relatively strong.[24] The building of schools, in this regard, was considered to be another "favor" that Indians should receive in return for their taxes and labor.

In 1908 a group of Seventh-day Adventist novices had decided to present a petition to the president as well. Like their predecessors, they too requested better access to education. But taxes were not mentioned: "In our fervent desire to obtain an education for our sons and turn them into conscientious citizens, useful for society and the fatherland, and stimulated by the noble purposes of the supreme government that strives to disseminate basic education in all parts of the republic, we also wanted to contribute to such a beneficial enterprise by founding two rural schools on our own and sustaining them with our own funds."[25] Indians had joined the broader discussion on issues of citizenship, adopting a long-held stance, which had major supporters among indigenistas, by which education would turn Indians into citizens. Hence, converts viewed their endeavors in the educational field, establishing schools and using the Indians' resources to maintain them, as a contribution to the nation, which the government should endorse, praise, and protect. Education, from this perspective, had ceased to be a favor to be earned through taxes or free labor; rather, it was proof of good citizenship and a national contribution in its own right.[26]

The shift between these two paradigms is best illustrated in a letter Camacho wrote in 1911, three years after the Adventists' initial petition. In it, he once again requested that national authorities protect his school:

Complying to the purest sentiments of humanity and love for thy neighbor I maintain, without charge . . . a primary school for Indian children . . . without ever receiving in any form encouragement or protection from the local authorities. . . . Under the pretext of Public works . . . the actual governor, Don Pablo del Carpio . . . employs them [the Indians], for his own benefit to work on the reconstruction of his house . . . and cultivate his lands . . . giving them no compensation for their forced labor.[27]

Thus, while Camacho was busy working for the Indians, providing them with access to free education, del Carpio was taking advantage of them, using Indian labor for personal profit. Del Carpio, though, answered Camacho's accusations, stating that the exact opposite was true: "The municipal agent gave an order to repair the roads that were in a bad state. . . . Camacho is using the pretense of the school to spread propaganda for the evangelist sect."[28] Thus, according to del Carpio, the work to which he had assigned the Indians was for the benefit of the community and district. From his perspective, Camacho was the one exploiting the Indians, using his school to proselytize his religious ideas. Therefore, this quarrel ensuing from the petition for schools points to two different notions of good citizenship: education versus free labor. These two ideas quickly came to be at odds, as each side postulated that the total good depended on his contribution, while the other side was alleged to be looking out for selfish interests.

Besides the academic curriculum, students participated regularly in military drills and exercises. Being veterans, for the most part, teachers took pride in their past service and in their present efforts to create loyal citizens prepared to answer any call to the flag. They also believed that military service was another acceptable substitute for taxes or free labor. For example, during the heated legal battle over land ownership that Juan Huanca and Pedro Pauro were embroiled in during 1912, Huanca declared that of the four plaintiffs, "three of us [referring to himself and two additional converts, Pedro Pauro and Ciborcio Cupita] have been serving the state in battalion n. 3 while the fourth one [Hicarcio Calisaya] paid tribute for the estate."[29]

Hence, military service and property taxes were used to legitimize Huanca's claims over the disputed land. All four plaintiffs had fulfilled an obligation to the state, and in return, their property rights should be respected. Significantly, among the Bolivian Aymara, paying tribute was also invoked as grounds for exemption from military service. In Bolivia, after the civil war of 1898–99, Liberals instituted obligatory military service and annulled Indian tribute, thus directly substituting one for the other. Considering the geographical closeness and the social and cultural relationships between Aymara peasants around the lake, it is likely that the changes in notions of citizenship in Bolivia influenced those of veterans in Puno.[30]

From the authorities' vantage point, however, replacing taxes or free labor with military service diminished their ability to fill quotas and burdened other community members. In other words, to fulfill their commitments to district authorities, communal authorities depended on the cooperation of the entire community. Thus, it is not surprising that the authorities from a community in Juli denounced the recruitment of Juan de Dios Villca, a reliable taxpayer, who had been forcefully conscripted by the Nacionales.[31] From their perspective, not only had Villca fulfilled his duties and rightfully earned protection, but they stood to lose a docile taxpayer.

Similar to water regimes and the management of agricultural lands, tax administration and labor recruitment were embedded in an Andean religious worldview that tied together the community, the state, God, and faith. Until the 1850s, when the *contribución personal* was abolished, Indians referred to themselves as "religious contributors," which specifically addressed their status as taxpayers.[32] In the Bolivian highlands, well into the twentieth century, annual tribute was split in half and collected in December and June, on Christmas and Saint John's Day. The religious ceremony was conducted by the tax collector, and a kind of symbolic reciprocal relationship was forged between himself, the taxpayer, and the taxpayers' dependents.[33] The ceremony underlined communal unity, while also legitimizing the authority of the tax collector through religious ritual. The act of paying taxes was as symbolic as it was economic.

Conversion and Cohesion

Consequently, attempts to change the way tax was collected, institute new taxes, or transfer the responsibility of tax collection to different agencies or officials were considered an attack on a sacred order. In 1884 the Bolivian government enacted a new stamp tax that Indians had to pay to receive an official title to their lands. The Indians were outraged, arguing that they had already paid tribute and in effect already paid for the land. A year later, when the tax commissioners arrived in the highlands to implement this new tax, the Indians threatened to sacrifice them in an attempt to appease the deities and preserve the sacred order.[34] For the tax commissioners, who barely made it out of the community alive, the Indians were challenging their authority and, as a result, the authority of the state. Thus, we once again witness how popular religion was a crucial arena for state formation and served as a setting in which Indians fulfilled their obligations as citizens. This framework also helps explain why conversion was understood as a form of treason.

Conversion and Local Authority: Are the Regenerated Indians Citizens of the United States?

"An accusation against the Indians Manuel Camacho, Estaban Miranda, Jacinto Tarqui, Mariano Chambi, Simón Nuca and Malcheor Ignacio for treason; because they declared, on distinct occasions, that they themselves, and their colleagues in the Seventh-day Adventist sect, had converted to this sect, and have also become US citizens; and for this reason, they have nothing to do with the political constitution of Peru, nor with the ecclesiastical authority of this department."[35]

Did the Indian converts really claim that they were U.S. citizens? Or was this simply a false allegation aiming to defame converts? I contend that within the Indians' perceptions of citizenship and considering that sovereignty was intertwined with religion, it made sense for converts to see themselves in some way as "U.S. citizens." The meaning of citizenship, however, had nothing to do with a putative naturalization process held in the United States and everything to do with being entangled in reciprocal commitments involving a U.S. authority figure.

Historically, Indian peasants had no direct dealings with the central colonial, and after independence, national, administration; rather, communal authorities paid taxes or filled recruitment quotas on behalf of the entire community. In the late colonial period, tax collection was the responsibility of the local *caciques*, but after 1812, it moved into the hands of the Indian communal authorities.[36] In 1900 the *contribución personal*, which had been abolished by President Castilla and later reenacted, was permanently repealed. Instead, Piérola's government implemented a property tax and established a new and independent national tax collection agency.[37] The idea was to centralize and bureaucratize tax collection and consequently curtail the power of regional elites. Moreover, for some liberals the contribución personal was a national embarrassment, a vehicle through which gamonales exploited the Indians, preventing them from becoming productive citizens. Yet this change was slow and limited, and district and communal authorities still acted as an important link between the state apparatus and Indians living in communities. In some cases, there was no national representative, which gave Indians little choice but to depend on local brokers. In other cases, it was the Indians themselves, who preferred to pay taxes to local and familiar authorities to whom they were bound by ritualistic and reciprocal relationships.[38] Simply because in many communities collecting taxes was part of a larger reciprocal relationship that was legitimized by religions and through religious rituals, unfamiliar secular agents of the state were not trusted.

Seventh-day Adventist missionaries helped fill the vacuum left by the rejection of local power structures and the absence of the central state. The fulfillment of one's civic duties largely remained a matter to be settled vis-à-vis the communal authorities and continued to be inscribed within the boundaries of local communal political culture. As a result, "subalterns struggled to create their own national-democratic vision. They used the notions of reciprocity, communal responsibility and accountability and solidarity present in communal political culture to reinforce the universal promise of national democratic discourse."[39] Simply, Indians' notions of "big" concepts such as nationalism and citizenship were understood through the prism of local political manners, values, and conduct.

Yet what would be the case if these civic duties were performed with the help of a group of foreign missionaries rather than local authorities? What if reciprocal relationships and communal obligations were maintained via authority figures from North America? Converts created alternative networks of reciprocal relations within the framework of the Seventh-day Adventist Church. For example, in exchange for a Seventh-day Adventist teacher, Indians pleading for education had to provide a building for the school and a home for the teacher.[40] When a community had grown, making it necessary to expand the infrastructure in a specific mission station, the Indians were the ones who supplied the labor power as well as some of the materials.[41]

Entangled in such relationships with missionaries, how did converts understand citizenship? Considering that local political commitments and reciprocal relationships shaped the way converts understood national politics, it made sense for Indians to believe that conversion influenced their citizenship. Conversion effectively meant breaking away from "old" political commitments, hierarchies, and social networks. Instead, converts forged new ones, with foreign missionaries. From that vantage point, they had, indeed, become U.S. citizens. It was not that they intended to demand voting rights in the United States; rather, they justified their right to citizenship in Peru through their relationship with the missionaries and obligations to the Seventh-day Adventist community. Thus, paradoxically, for them, true patriotism meant leaving one's native religion and adhering to a foreign prophet.

Additionally, because sovereignty was inseparable from religion, certain Seventh-day Adventist teachings were translated into the political realm and understood by locals, mestizos, and Indians as undermining the social hierarchy in the Andes. For instance, the idea that all human beings were equal before God or that the Bible was the only true source of religious authority was interpreted as a call to disregard authority. In March 1913, mestizos from the town of Acora wrote a letter to the department's prefect in which they expressed their fears that missionaries and converted veterans teach Indians that "social hierarchy does not exist, and the superiority with which the blind Romans treat the priests, governors, judges, and *vecinos* is a deception characteristic of a Christian era that today is dead. Secondly, that the idea of serving and obeying the authorities is an old invention brought by the Spaniards, but a man only has to subject himself to the Bible that they have provided, sanctifying the Sabbath and subjecting themselves only to their [the missionaries'] command and to the Gods that had come from North America."[42]

Missionaries dismissed the Catholic ecclesiastical hierarchy and saw it as illegitimate. Their attitude toward state authorities, however, was much more complex. Missionaries were highly critical of district authorities, denouncing their abuses and commenting on the feudal characteristics of the Andean social structure.[43] On the other hand, they did not wholly discredit these authorities as they had done to the priests. In their eyes, rebuking priests had nothing to do with obeying state officials, as they viewed religion and state as two separate spheres. In contrast to this separation, the residents of Acora linked "priests, governors, judges, and vecinos." For them, they were all one body of authority, a view that resulted from the deep connection between sovereignty and religion in the Andes. In this regard, district authorities and local townsmen understood converts much better than the missionaries did. When converts proclaimed that "all were brothers, including Bolivians, Chileans, and that the headquarters of their religion was in the U.S. and [that] therefore they did not recognize any authority by the virtue of their humanity," they understood that Seventh-day Adventists were not simply quoting theological teachings.[44] Brotherhood and equality were not strictly a heavenly matter. Through these values, converts challenged authority in the here and now. Nevertheless, passive resistance of this sort was not the only means converts used to achieve their goals. Neophytes had other methods at their disposal, such as litigation and even violence, and they resorted to these, sometimes at high personal risk.

Conversion and Cohesion

Taking Action: Litigation and Violence

The quest for justice had led Indians to the courts since colonial times. Although legal proceedings were costly, time-consuming, and (more often than not) prejudiced, Indians turned to that avenue in an attempt to fight for their rights. Adventist converts often worked as a group, submitting joint petitions and using legal channels to oppose communal authorities and promote intracommunal reform. It is noteworthy that they did so before Ferdinand Stahl's arrival and the official establishment of the "Lake Titicaca Indian Mission." In 1908 the eighteen Adventist converts who were studying with Camacho submitted a petition to the president requesting schools for their communities. By then the school had been functioning for a few years and Camacho was a known activist. This probably was not the first petition the group submitted. Four years later, this time with Stahl's backing, over twenty-five men signed a communal petition addressed to the department's prefect, requesting that "this superior office . . . put into effect all the [word missing] supreme resolutions enacted in favor of the Indian race and among them we refer to the most crucial one which is act n. 1183 concerning the abolition of services and the suppression of local community authorities[;] by prohibiting these abuses, carried out by the political authorities, we will be freed from being victims of these authorities."[45]

The aforementioned act n. 1183 was passed in 1909 and prohibited all government authorities from demanding free service from Indians for either private or public projects.[46] The suggestion that the act stipulates the "suppression of local community authorities," which had risen to their positions through the system of prestige, seems to have resulted from the converts' interpretation of the act, as part of their attempts to delegitimize the traditional politico-religious hierarchy and promote reform within the community. Yet, as Pablo del Carpio, the acting governor of Chucuito, remarked, the positions granted to communal authorities were grounded in history and local consensus.[47] Their role within the existing system was crucial because they executed most orders, ranging from the capture of criminals to filling army quotas. Similarly, del Carpio evoked notions of local tradition and unwritten social agreements to justify Indian labor. Indian labor, he contends, does not fall under act n. 1183, even though it is uncompensated because Indians "among themselves and with the townsmen work out of habit and custom and for that reason, the services are not paid."[48] In other words, these services were not forced labor, but habit or custom; as such, they were legitimized by a long-standing consensus.

The fact was that reaching communal consensus for the coherence of the community involved "constructing communal hegemony," which was "the product of complex articulations of interests, discourses, and perspectives within the village society."[49] But what if consensus was not achieved? What would happen if a group of community members developed a worldview that rejected everything sacred to the rest of the members? How could Seventh-day Adventists and Catholics reach a consensus if they could not even agree on what made an "Indian" an "Indian" and what their obligations should be?

Seventh-day Adventists now followed a different religious authority and had committed themselves to an alternative community. Moreover, conflicting notions of citizenship, which translated into practical obligations and rights, created new internal conflicts and exacerbated old ones. In such a reality, it became extremely difficult to bridge these gaps, since doing so required yielding power and agreeing to compromise over a system in which some had invested their entire lives while others wished to see it perish from the face of the earth. Finally, ideological battles over the possession of heavenly truth and mutual discredit did not help to achieve common ground. Hence, it was particularly laborious and demanding to reach a widespread agreement that would foster solidarity and intracommunal coherence.

In such circumstances, tensions easily escalated into violence. Seventh-day Adventists have been portrayed as victims of religious persecution by narrow-minded hacienda owners and priests who were afraid of losing their grasp over a captive workforce.[50] To a large extent, this perception is correct, yet it does not tell the entire story. Evidence from the 1920s demonstrates that Adventist converts also resorted to violence and attacked Catholic Indians. Documentation is rare, and it is difficult to say how frequent these events were, when they began, or if they were related to specific developments in the 1920s. By that time, Seventh-day Adventism was well established in the region; converts had become a significant force among Aymara-speaking Indians and perhaps even a majority in certain moieties. Therefore, it may be that they were confident enough to directly attack Catholic symbols.

Furthermore, developments in Peruvian politics may have also contributed to these events: in 1919 the period known as the Aristocratic Republic came to an end. The outbreak of World War I accelerated social and economic transformations that resulted in deteriorating conditions for laborers as well as growing insecurity among the urban middle classes. Rebellions, strikes, and protests occurred nationwide and peaked in 1918–19, when Lima's working class and students took to the streets. These events, coupled with the fear of election fraud, set the stage for political change, and in July 1919 Augusto Leguía executed a preemptive coup against President Prado. This was not Leguía's first time in the presidential palace—he had served as president between 1908 and 1912—but this time he entered the presidential palace with a political project that was to replace the Aristocratic Republic: the construction of La Patria Nueva, the new fatherland (1919–30), which included the expansion of the state bureaucracy, foreign investment, and the inclusion of larger sectors of Peruvian society in the political arena. During the first years of his administration, Leguía implemented important indigenista policies such as the legal recognition of Indian communities, the establishment of an office for Indigenous affairs, and recognition of the Comité Central Pro-Derecho Indígena Tahuantinsuyu, an organization that was founded to promote Indian causes and had branches in the highlands. Such an atmosphere may have also contributed to converts' confidence, emboldening them to attack Catholic Indians.

One man accused of violence against Catholic Indians was Juan Huanca, who reached an advanced position in the Lake

Titicaca Mission and during the late 1910s had been stationed in Umachi, Moho Province. He was also an activist in the Comité and would leave the Adventist Church in 1922 due to conflicts with the missionaries over his political activities. In any case, until his departure, Huanca was a successful missionary and was prospering in his efforts to evangelize.[51] Yet, at that time, a small-scale holy war was underway in the community. A group of Catholics had approached the authorities, complaining that Indians who were Seventh-day Adventists had physically abused them, burned their property, stolen their land and animals, and prevented them from baptizing their babies. These actions were rooted in economic factors, and as stated in the report itself, conflicts over land did spur at least some of the tensions between the two sides.[52]

Nevertheless, in many cases, these actions offered no economic advantage. What mattered was their political meaning and their purpose in establishing authority. Violence, in this sense, has important performative aspects and contributes to the consolidation of power.[53] Pablo Huanca, one of the Catholic Indians who was continuously harassed by the Seventh-day Adventists, was walking around the village one day when a group of converts ripped off his scarf and poncho. Why? Clearly, not to sell them in the market. Ripping off items of clothing was a way of asserting control. Huanca's scarf and poncho were pulled off of him in public, in front of spectators, to humiliate him, to present him as powerless in the eyes of others. It is very possible that Huanca had held a position in the traditional hierarchy and was targeted in an attempt to highlight the helplessness of someone in a position of power. Yet, even if he did not hold any official position, he was still identified as a "Catholic Indian" who, in one very symbolic moment, was at the mercy of a Seventh-day Adventist. Spectators, who heard the Seventh-day Adventists calling this Catholic a "degenerate Indian," could have interpreted this assault as a warning sign, letting them know it was time for "regeneration."

Another example of how violence could be used to consolidate or delegitimize power was to be found not in Seventh-day Adventists' attack on authorities but, rather, in their attacks on

Conversion and Cohesion

buildings that represented authority, celestial authority. There is evidence that during the 1920s, on a few occasions, Adventist Indian converts entered Catholic churches and destroyed images of saints, smashed crucifixes, and even dismantled the church's physical structure: "Entering the church on a planned day, insulting and humiliating ... the sacred images, it is insignificant for them to ravage the church in Occopampa, together with the images, and turn their [the images'] heads into toys. ... These are acts of travesty and mockery, to insult our Lady of Carmen and our Lady of Candelaria is a source of satisfaction for those called evangelicals."[54] Aggressions toward religious symbols could be traced to the Spanish Reconquista and the Protestant Reformation. During the Reconquista, mosques were often converted to churches and Muslim religious symbols were destroyed as a part of the proclamation of religious and political sovereignty. Francisco Pizarro, for instance, entered Inca temples, defaming them and then erecting crucifixes and "explaining" to the Indians that they had been deceived and should no longer follow these false gods.[55] Throughout the colonial period, Catholic missionaries also professed violent attitudes toward autochthonous religious symbols as part of their attempt to extirpate idolatry. Missionaries believed that "simple-minded" Indians could not grasp the complexities of religion and that only authoritative and coercive methods would bring them into the arms of the Lord.[56]

Four hundred years later, Catholic Indians from the community of Umachi echoed a similar argument. They claimed that there was no war between them and the Seventh-day Adventists because, they said, "We are not concerned with analyzing which religion is the best one for us because our state of ignorance as well as our hard work in the fields do not allow us time to dedicate ourselves to this sort of specifics."[57] In other words, in an attempt to claim that no one was being persecuted on religious grounds, the Catholic Indians claimed that the entire theological argument was irrelevant for them because they did not understand the differences between faiths.

Did converts resort to coercive methods to make Catholics convert? Perhaps some hoped to do so. Seventh-day Adventists, however, had few practical tools to force conversion in the way that sixteenth- and seventeenth-century Catholic missionaries did. In this context, violence was an extreme measure of theatrical persuasion, close to coercion in its coloring but lacking the necessary tools to force people to act against their will. Violence was used to convey a message of strength and authority. If Indians could not understand the complexities of theology and, as a result, freely choose the "correct" religion, perhaps they would be convinced by seeing holy images smashed on the floor and discovering that the world did not tremble in supernatural fury as a result of this sacrilege.

Moreover, since saints played an important role in local celebrations, the fact that communal officials could not protect them reflected poorly on their authority. If they could not uphold the honor of the holy saints, or if those saints were nothing more than worthless plaster rather than symbols of celestial grace and power, on what grounds did these authorities base their right to rule? Converts, therefore, turned to flamboyant and highly dramatic acts of violence to cast doubt on Catholic beliefs and practices that legitimized the politico-religious system.

These acts of violence were not limited to the destruction of images of saints and the interior of churches. Church buildings were subjected to looting when converts physically tore them down. One church in Occopampa was left in ruins after converts took raw materials for their own use. Another church, in Chucuito, was partly destroyed and its cemetery converted into a potato field. In 1927 Luciano Chambi, head of the Occopampa mission, proudly explained to the delegation from the General Conference why Indians were entitled to destroy or confiscate Catholic Church property: "it was our labor that went into it; it is our material in it; we need some of the material for our own homes, so we will go and help ourselves from the Church."[58]

Churches were built or renovated, and their lands farmed, through an institution called *faena*. The faena was a form of communal labor in which the entire community lent a hand to complete a specific task that was supposedly for the general good.[59] Nevertheless, in communities that were torn regarding the nature of Indians' obligations to the district and the state, as the quarrel between Camacho and del Carpio demonstrates, it became increasingly difficult to determine exactly what the "general good" was. Moreover, the "general good" was often related to religious activities, meaning that converts did not benefit from the fruits of the *faena* in the long run. For example, the produce from the fields adjacent to the church was often used during local fiestas.[60] Since converts did not participate in fiestas, they felt comfortable farming these lands on their own terms and consuming the produce when necessary. Since Seventh-day Adventists no longer received services from the Catholic Church, they felt that it was their right to recuperate the "investment" they had made, and they exercised this right by taking back materials invested in the church's structure. In this regard, Chambi's account of the dilapidating church is a metaphor for the slow crumbling of authority in the Indian community.

The gradual disintegration of communal cohesion was not unique to communities in which Seventh-day Adventists were active. The turmoil of this period prompted others to set out on a similar search: the leader of the Rumi Maqui rebellion in 1915 sought to construct a new form of solidarity around a few estancias that split off from the old, established community, freeing themselves from its authority.[61] Platería itself was an example of such a schism. So was Wancho Lima, the new urban center built by the commoners of the Wancho community in the province of Huancané as part of their rebellion in 1923. In other cases, changes made within the community enabled new forces, often representatives of the central state, to take part in the communal social hierarchy. These processes varied greatly from place to place. This variance explains why the communal authorities were left intact in many areas, more or less until the 1960s, while others went through major shifts.[62]

In any case, the Adventists did not cause these deep underground currents, but they contributed to them. The fissures facilitated the missionaries' entrance into communities that were searching for their own way. Seventh-day Adventism, in this sense, provided a marginalized group with an identity and legitimacy, as well as a certain degree of protection by the foreign missionaries. Conversion, in this regard, provided a way out of the traditional system. Yet, at the same time, it exemplified and enhanced the relationship between Christianity and authority. Indians chose an alternative form of Christianity rather than espouse secular ideas or attempt to "return" to a "pure" Andean religion. They did so with the religious support and practical assistance they received from a group of U.S. missionaries, whose way to the Andes was paved by the pressures, challenges, and opportunities they had faced in their home society, the United States.

PART 2

Missionaries

5

Seventh-day Adventism and the Foreign Missionary Enterprise, 1850–1920

HARRY WILCOX'S JOURNEY TO THE ARID ANDEAN HIGH-
lands began on a farm on the Oklahoma prairie in the 1890s.
Orphaned at a young age, he and his brother John were reared
by their aunt Tris and uncle Bent Etchison. The Etchisons were
devout Adventists, and on Friday evenings, just before Sabbath,
the family would pray, sing hymns, and give thanks to the Lord.
Thirty years later, these moments of family intimacy and religious piety would take on a special meaning for young Wilcox:
they were moments of revelation. In them, he understood that
"Jesus would come soon" and that he should dedicate his life "to
help[ing] others know about this glorious event and the preparation needed to be saved."[1] Wilcox eventually left his aunt and
uncle's home to study at Keene academy, an Adventist educational institution in Texas. After graduation, around 1910, he
became a literate evangelist and a teacher in one of the denomination's schools. Finally, in 1918 Wilcox and his wife, Belle,
decided to pack their bags and join the missionaries laboring
abroad. Their destination was the department of Puno, Peru.
While working among the Indians, Wilcox discovered that his
childhood on the farm had not only inspired him to become a
missionary but had also prepared him for this mission. As a boy,
he was taught "to work, not only at tilling the soil and caring
for the farm animals but also at household tasks such as cooking and washing dishes."[2] This, Wilcox would tell the readers
of his memoirs, proved to be "valuable training" because missionaries in a remote corner of the world "must be able to do
many practical things."

Wilcox's description of his routine chores on the farm as "training" contributes to his greater narrative according to which he was destined to become a missionary. In this regard, his memoirs follow the conventions of the missionary writing genre. Wilcox's book was published by the Adventist Church to promote its religious cause and socialize others into it.[3] Thus, the narratives of these publications follow a specific structure that leaves little room for early life experiences, and whatever information the author does reveal is usually presented as inherent to the eventual decision of becoming a missionary or to life in the mission field. Yet, even within these limitations, Wilcox's story provides a glimpse into his life trajectory: he was born around 1888, grew up on a farm, obtained a tertiary education, filled various roles in the Adventist Church, and sailed for the foreign field, reaching Peru in 1918. This was the road that almost all the missionaries had taken before reaching Puno.

In fact, this was the professional trajectory of many young men and women who became missionaries, regardless of their religious affiliation. The years 1880 to 1930 were the heyday of the Protestant foreign missionary enterprise. During those years, more than fourteen thousand men and women left the ports of the United States holding a Bible in their hand. Churches formed mission boards and established ecumenical organizations aimed at increasing the number of North American Protestant missionaries and supporting their endeavors in foreign countries.[4] The most salient example, in this regard, is the Student Volunteer Movement for Foreign Missions (SVM). Established in 1886, this organization sought to invigorate what it believed to be a sagging of Americans' missionary zeal and expand the number of American missionaries sent to foreign countries. To this end, the SVM conducted recruitment tours to colleges nationwide and signed students up for missionary work. Their success was phenomenal. Between 1886 and 1920, the organization recruited a nearly nine thousand new missionaries who were sent through denominational channels to places as far away as China and Oceania.[5]

There was, of course, nothing new in Protestant missionary efforts, and missions to "nonbelievers" were almost as old

Adventism and the Missionary Enterprise

as the colonies themselves. Already in the middle of the seventeenth century, missionaries had set out to convert North American Indigenous peoples.[6] Nevertheless, the size and vigor of the nineteenth-century missionary enterprise were unprecedented. In fact, the thousands of men and women who left for the foreign field were only the tip of the iceberg. From the comforts of their homes, millions of others read about missionaries' adventures, admired their courage, and supported their efforts spiritually, politically, and economically. Scholars have offered several explanations for the upsurge of missionary zeal during this particular time. One such explanation is that the foreign missionary enterprise served to bridge gaps in other areas. Specifically, it has been argued that although the fundamentalist-modernist controversy would fully take shape only after World War I, tensions between liberals and conservatives began to surface. In this atmosphere, the foreign missionary enterprise became a common ground on which parties who disagreed about evolution or higher biblical criticism could cooperate.[7]

More broadly, foreign missions were fueled by U.S. territorial, political, and economic expansion. To put it simply, it was an inherent part of U.S. imperialism. "Manifest Destiny," or the notion that the United States is destined, by God or enlightened reason, to spread its religious and political ideologies, legitimized its territorial and economic expansion. As recent scholarship demonstrates, the relationship between the missionary enterprise and American imperialism does not necessarily reflect on the specific roles of individual missionaries in their host societies.[8] Missionaries did not, by default, share the economic and political agendas of their country, let alone feel obligated to promote imperial political or economic policies. In fact, missionaries could be, and were, critical of U.S. foreign policies. Nevertheless, at the same time, we should not ignore the power structures at work. Missionaries were sent from the global north to the global south, and they were white men and women who were bringing their idea of salvation to darker-skinned people.[9]

Wilcox's journey to Peru is therefore embedded in the social and religious landscape of the time. In this regard, he is far from unique. Yet, his decision should not be taken for granted, and not just because no decision to go and save the souls of strangers in faraway lands should be taken for granted. The fact was that the Seventh-day Adventist Church was historically opposed to missionary work. Wilcox's journey to Peru, like the journeys of other young Adventists made across the globe, was the result of a transformation within the Seventh-day Adventist Church itself as much as it was part of the spirit of the time.

The Seventh-day Adventist Church's Shut-Door Policy, 1844–1880

Seventh-day Adventism was born out of grave disappointment. On October 22, 1844, thousands of people gathered on hilltops, meadows, and lakeshores in deep expectation for Jesus to return. It was the time of the Second Great Awakening, and tens of thousands of people participated in religious revivals from Kentucky to New York. New ideas were preached from the pulpits, and new religious movements emerged. Twenty years earlier, for example, Joseph Smith claimed that an angel named Moroni directed him toward gold plates, which were buried in a hill not far from Smith's home and contained the Gospel as preached to the ancient inhabitants of America. Smith attracted hundreds of followers, and in 1830 he established the Church of Jesus Christ of Latter-day Saints.

The men and women who awaited Jesus's Advent on that day in October 1844 were followers of one William Miller, an autodidact preacher from upstate New York. Miller was reared a Baptist and read his way to Deism and then back to the Christian scriptures. For two years he meticulously studied the Bible, reaching a series of conclusions, among them that Jesus would return to the earth before the millennium and that this event would occur around the year 1843.[10] Later, his followers set the exact date for the Advent: October 22, 1844.[11] When the Lord did not return as predicted, the thousands of believers who expected him went into despair, and the event became known as "the Great Disappointment."[12]

After the Great Disappointment, many left the movement. But others continued to believe in Miller's predictions and tried to make sense of this failure. Among them were Joseph Bates, Ellen and James White, and a few others.[13] From biblical interpretations and a series of visions Ellen White claimed to have received from the Lord, they argued that the Millerites had been right about the date but wrong about the event. Drawing on various sources from the New Testament, this group developed what would become known as "the sanctuary doctrine." Miller predicted the Advent from a prophecy in Daniel 8:14, according to which after twenty-three hundred days Jesus would return to the sanctuary, which Miller understood as earth. After the Great Disappointment, it became clear to the early Seventh-day Adventists that the sanctuary could not be earth. Instead, they came to believe that the biblical source was referring to a sanctuary in heaven where Christ ministered to believers as the high priest had done in the holy temple in Jerusalem. For twenty-three hundred days, Christ's ministry was one of forgiveness and redemption. On October 22, 1844, however, Christ moved from one location in the sanctuary to another and, with this physical move, so did a new phase in his ministry begin. Christ took on a new role as an investigator who examined peoples' lives and assessed their sins in preparation for his return to the earth and the final judgment.[14] The purpose of these investigations is to reveal the Lord's true believers, those who abide by all his commandments, which included the fourth: "Remember the Sabbath day and keep it holy."[15]

This interpretation was vehemently rejected by the Millerite leadership; the group clustered around the Whites, and Bates was alienated from the rest of the Millerite movement. Nevertheless, from their marginalized position, and perhaps because of it, the founding fathers and mother of what would be Seventh-day Adventism developed ideas and a self-perception of a remnant church of Saturday-keepers. In this context, Adventists found the prophecies of Revelation 14:6–12 and those of Revelation 13:1–10 especially important. Revelation 14 tells of three angels, each carrying a message to the people. According to the Adventist interpretation of these passages, the first two angels brought messages about the second Advent as voiced by Miller. The third angel communicated that those who did not observe all God's laws, including the one about the seventh-day Sabbath, were essentially worshiping the beast and would therefore receive "the mark of the beast."

Revelation 13 provides the identity of the beast. In these verses, the author records his visions of two beasts: one rose from the sea and had multiple heads and horns, and the other looked like a lamb but spoke in the voice of a dragon. The first beast was commonly recognized by Protestants as the Catholic Church. The identity of the second beast was contested, and Adventists uniquely recognized it as the American republic. The United States, they believed, had betrayed its principles of civil and religious liberty, and therefore, although it looks like a lamb, it is really a dragon. Moreover, Adventists believed that U.S. Protestant churches were still very much "in the image" of the Catholic Church, since they kept Sunday, a false institution promoted by the papacy, instead of the biblical Saturday.[16]

In this context, early Adventists also fostered an antimissionary stance that claimed that the door to salvation has been "shut" to all those who closed their ears to the angel's messages.[17] This was not a new idea, and they shared it with other Millerites.[18] But Seventh-day Adventists were especially fastidious about it and particularly suspicious of their surroundings. The fact was that Adventists had suffered from double rejection. First, they were ridiculed as Millerites and then dismissed by other Millerites for their particular theological ideas. Consequently, Seventh-day Adventists opted to stay isolated and have as little contact as possible with their social, religious, and political surroundings. In their eyes, nothing could be done to save the souls of the men and women who did not listen to Miller and insisted on filling the pews of the Sunday services. Consequently, missionary work made little sense.

Spreading the Third Angel's Message to the World, 1880–1920

These attitudes remained intact for about two and a half decades. By the 1870s, however, it became clear that a theological and eschatological change within the Adventist Church was slowly taking place. First, like other Protestant denominations of the time, the Civil War and the end of slavery profoundly impacted Seventh-day Adventist theologies and religious imagery. For Adventists, slavery was part of what made the U.S. a beast, and although many Adventists were involved in the abolitionist movement, they believed that slavery would end only by divine intervention. The fact that the end of slavery was brought about not only by humans but by the Union raised questions about the beastly nature of the United States.[19] Second, in practical terms, Seventh-day Adventists found it harder and harder to keep their distance from federal and state authorities. For example, issues concerning the Adventist Church's legal status and the conscription or exemption of Adventists from the Union Army obligated the church to cooperate with state authorities. From a theological perspective, this cooperation meant complying with the "beast's" laws and regulations and therefore caused internal tensions and arguments among members.[20] But eventually these tensions contributed to the reassessment of the U.S. eschatological role. As time passed, Adventist leaders began to refer to the United States more as a lamb and less as a dragon. Adventist visual culture illustrates this shift clearly: in the 1850s Adventist publications depicted the U.S. as an atrocious monster. By the early twentieth century, the most frequent choice for portraying the U.S. in Adventist apocalyptic art was the buffalo.[21]

As the U.S. eschatological role softened, so did the Seventh-day Adventist antimissionary policy loosen.[22] For instance, in 1874 Ellen White remarked that she never had a vision about the shut-door policy.[23] It was, therefore, a human notion rather than an infallible divine message. Jonathan Butler argues convincingly that the eschatological change was influenced in part by Adventists' new and positive attitude toward missions: if Adventists wanted to spread the third angel's message, then they had to present their ideas in ways that would appeal to the widest audience possible.[24] By the same token, a more positive outlook on the United States also made the nation appear much more redeemable, which in turn made mission work logical. Furthermore, by the late 1870s, it was clear to Adventists that the Lord's return, while near, would not occur in the very immediate future. The Lord, Adventists now believed, had left them some time to spread the message of the Sabbath, and as faithful followers, it was their responsibility to take advantage of this time frame and save souls. Furthermore, in 1888, the Seventh-day Adventists convened in Minneapolis for what would become a landmark session of the General Conference. This meeting was a turning point for the Adventist Church, which moved toward mainstream Protestantism on certain doctrinal issues. Among other things, the third angel's message was expanded to include justification by faith alongside the observance of the Ten Commandments.[25] Adventists now had answers for those who blamed them for "dry" legalism and the marginalization of faith. They also had more to offer prospective converts, especially those in Protestant nations— where Adventists began their efforts—for whom *sola fide* (forgiveness on the basis of faith alone) was central.

The Seventh-day Adventist missionary enterprise remained limited throughout the 1880s and focused on North America and other Protestant nations. In 1889, when missionary Harry Wilcox was about one year old, the Seventh-day Adventist foreign mission board was established.[26] Around that time the Adventist Church had a handful of missionaries working in very few countries, namely Australia, South Africa, and Scandinavia. Seventeen years later, in 1906, the Adventist Church had about 280 missionaries working in forty-five countries. By 1916 the number of missionaries tripled and stood at 880 men and women who worked in ninety-two countries.[27] In absolute terms, in 1916 the Methodist Episcopal Church was the largest exporter of missionaries, and it sent out 1,428 people to thirty-four countries. In terms of missionary growth, however, the Methodist Episcopal Church grew much more slowly than the Seventh-day Adventists; from 1906 to 1916, it grew by only 70 percent.[28] In fact, it appears that the only church whose missionary outreach was growing faster than that of the Seventh-day Adventists was the Pentecostal Church of Nazarene, which grew by 600 percent, going from eight to fifty-one missionaries.[29]

Adventism and the Missionary Enterprise

The number of Seventh-day Adventist missionaries is even more staggering when compared with the number of Adventist Church members in the United States, which was just about seventy-nine thousand in 1916. That year, there were 110 foreign missionaries for every ten thousand Adventist Church members. No other church came close to this ratio. The Church of Jesus Christ of Latter-day Saints and the Pentecostal Church of Nazarene, who tailed the Adventists, sent out thirty and fifteen missionaries for every ten thousand members, respectively. Far behind were the mainline churches, such as the Methodist Episcopal Church and the Northern Baptist Convention, which sent four or five missionaries for every ten thousand members.[30] Thus, the churches that sent out the most missionaries in comparison with their membership were all native forms of American Christianity and products of the long nineteenth century. These denominations were often ridiculed by the members of mainstream churches, which is perhaps why they chose to proliferate their message abroad. Even within this group, however, the relative number of Seventh-day Adventist missionaries is exceptionally high. Additionally, the Adventist Church was the only church in which the rate at which missionaries left for the foreign field exceeded the rate of growth in foreign membership. To illustrate, between 1906 and 1916, the Adventist overseas membership grew by 240 percent, increasing from around twenty-seven thousand members to sixty-five thousand members, yet the number of U.S. missionaries grew by 310 percent.[31]

Furthermore, Adventists sent more college-educated midwesterners overseas than the svm, which recruited most of its volunteers from midwestern Christian colleges. Specifically, between 1892 and 1904, students from the Moody Bible Institute and Ohio Wesleyan College were the most responsive to the svm's recruitment initiatives.[32] Notwithstanding the svm's success, in relative terms, it was dwarfed by the Adventists' success. About 13 percent of students who graduated from the Adventist Union College between 1895 and 1906 left for the foreign field. Comparatively, only 2 percent of students and graduates from Ohio Wesleyan College and 6 percent of those from the Moody Bible Institute embarked on boats for foreign lands.[33]

Thus a small church that represented 0.07 percent of the U.S. population in 1916 was responsible for 10 percent of all American foreign missionaries.

As Adventists were gearing up their missionary operations, they were also vocally criticizing U.S. foreign policy. The Spanish-American War had ended in favorable terms for the United States, which gained control over Cuba and ownership of Puerto Rico and the Philippines. Some saw this result as a part of the nation's manifest destiny; others, among them Adventists, charged the nation with imperialism. These accusations were not as intense as the apocalyptic hostility that Adventists had professed toward the U.S. in the 1850s and 1860s. But, at the same time, Adventists did see the suppression of the Philippines' independence movement as additional proof of the beastly nature of the United States and its disregard for liberty. Adventists also accused other Protestant churches of legitimizing this territorial expansion and suppressing other nations' quests for liberty in the name of Christianity.[34] But Adventists did not abstain from missionary work in the Philippines or Cuba, and by 1906 the third angel's message was brought to both these countries. Missionary work, therefore, was not exclusively tied to imperialism and could go hand in hand with anti-imperialist ideologies, discourses, and sentiments.

Malcolm Bull has argued that Adventists' antagonism toward the United States fueled the church's institutional expansion to the point that it had erected an entire array of institutions that supplanted national institutions.[35] Foreign missions, in this context, were no exception. Yet, Adventist internal and external expansion was not only an outcome of the realm of ideas and eschatology. As we shall now see, life in industrialized America posed particular challenges for practicing Seventh-day Adventists, and for some of them, the foreign field was the answer.

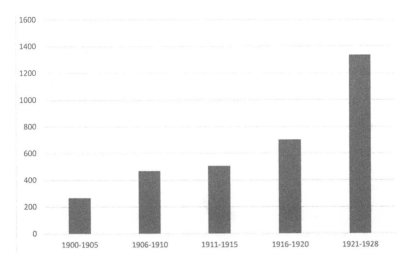

FIG. 6. Number of Seventh-day Adventist missionaries sent to the foreign field, 1900–1928. Created by the author from *The 1928 Yearbook of the Seventh-day Adventist Denomination* (Takoma Park, Washington DC: Review and Herald Publishing Assn., 1911–28), 3.

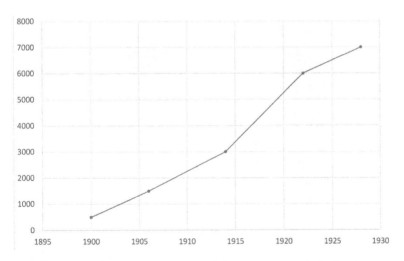

FIG. 7. Number of Seventh-day Adventist laborers stationed in the foreign field, 1900–1928. Created by the author from *The 1928 Yearbook of the Seventh-day Adventist Denomination* (Takoma Park, Washington DC: Review and Herald Publishing Assn., 1911–28), 3.

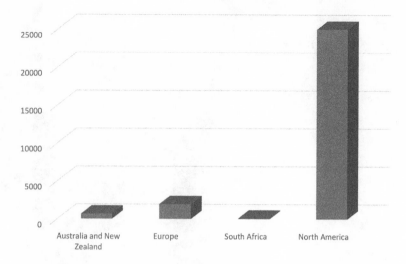

FIG. 8. Seventh-day Adventist global membership, 1890. Created by the author from *Seventh-day Adventist Conferences, Missions, and Institutions, Annual Statistical Report, for Years 1909, 1918, 1924, 1928* (Takoma Park, Washington DC: General Conference of the Seventh-day Adventists, 1909–28).

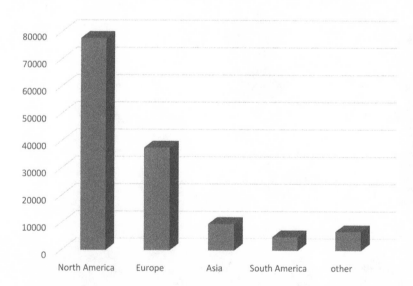

FIG. 9. Seventh-day Adventist global membership, 1915. Created by the author from *Seventh-day Adventist Conferences, Missions, and Institutions, Annual Statistical Report, for Years 1909, 1918, 1924, 1928* (Takoma Park, Washington DC: General Conference of the Seventh-day Adventists, 1909–28).

6

Seventh-day Adventists and the Challenge of Modern Times

IN 1914, AFTER LIVING IN LIMA FOR JUST NINE MONTHS, Edgar Maxwell seemed to have had enough of the view from his window:

> All the houses that we are able to rent . . . front directly on the street, with one or two little windows . . . and without any place for a garden or green or a few chickens or anything to break the dull monotony day after day. It is like living in a dismal prison. Such conditions can only produce homesickness at first, and later nervousness and sickness. . . . There can be no comparison between this side and the East Coast of South America. The wide plains of Argentina and Uruguay are ample to give land to our workers.[1]

For Maxwell, as for many other Protestants, rural life was healthy and close to God, while city life was both physically and spiritually debilitating. His words mirror larger concerns about "perils of the city" and a "paradise lost" that preoccupied ministers and laymen from all denominations at that time.[2] Yet beyond religious symbols of nature as God's creation and theological reflections about the meaning of city life, Maxwell appears to be yearning for home in the most intimate sense of the word. He, like Harry Wilcox, grew up on a farm on the Oklahoma prairie, an area that closely resembled the wide grasslands of the Argentinean pampas. Now, living in the crowded city of Lima, he longed for familiar scenery. In all likelihood, he was not alone in this sentiment. The fact was that the majority of missionaries in Peru, like the majority of Seventh-day Adventists in general, were raised on midwestern farms and were strangers to city life.

Growing Up on a Farm: Seventh-day Adventism and the Rural Middle Class, 1850–1890

As an offspring of the Millerite movement, the Adventist Church began in New York state and New England. Nevertheless, in the early 1850s, Ellen and James White followed the flow of New Yorkers who sailed up the Erie Canal and settled in Calhoun County, Michigan. The Whites moved to the town of Battle Creek in part for the same reason that other northeasterners immigrated westward: the surging costs of living in the East, such as Rochester, New York, where they had lived. Publishing the *Advent Review and Sabbath Herald*, the Adventist Church's mouthpiece, from Rochester had become expensive and burdensome. In Battle Creek, the Whites were able to purchase a printing plant and ensure the continuity of the Adventist publishing enterprise. No less important was the religious landscape of the Midwest. In the "Yankee" Northeast, Adventists were religious outsiders who had followed the eccentric William Miller and refused to acknowledge the failure of his predictions. By contrast, in the Midwest, they were simply another church among many new religions that immigrants brought with them. During the nineteenth century, the Midwest was a budding platform of faiths that included Catholics, Jews, mainline Protestant denominations, holiness churches, and Greek and Russian churches.[3] Native American religions also contributed to the region's religious diversity. At the confluence of the Kalamazoo and Battle Creek Rivers, Adventists were less peculiar and, like other immigrants, had "the freedom not to become American."[4] A comfortable location for a church that believed America was a dragon, indeed.

At least at first, the heterogeneous religious landscape of the Midwest did not affect the internal composition of the Adventist Church. On the contrary, the movement lost some of the heterogeneous aspects that characterized the Millerites, especially in terms of followers' socioeconomic characteristics. The Millerites came from various social backgrounds, had different occupations, and they lived in cities or towns, or on farms at the edges of townships. Farmers were a relatively large group, but not

membership
50   1308

FIG. 10. Seventh-day Adventist presence in the United States, 1867. Created by the author from *Seventh-day Adventist Conferences, Missions, and Institutions* (Takoma Park, Washington DC: General Conference of the Seventh-day Adventists, 1867).

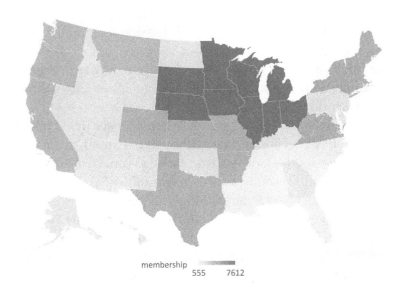

membership
555   7612

FIG. 11. Seventh-day Adventist presence in the United States, 1890. Created by the author from *Seventh-day Adventist Conferences, Missions, and Institutions* (Takoma Park, Washington DC: General Conference of the Seventh-day Adventists, 1890).

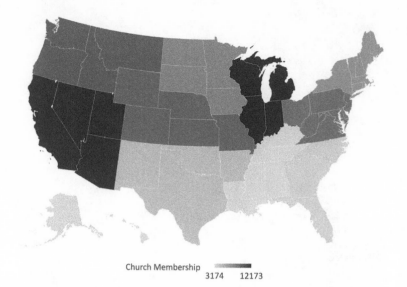

Church Membership

3174   12173

FIG. 12. Seventh-day Adventist presence in the United States, 1916. Created by the author from *Seventh-day Adventist Conferences, Missions, and Institutions.* (Takoma Park, Washington DC: General Conference of the Seventh-day Adventists, 1916).

one that dominated the entire movement. Among Seventh-day Adventists, however, farmers were the overwhelming majority. In 1860 they accounted for about 80 percent of followers, while in Michigan, where most Adventists lived, farmers accounted for only 40 percent. This trend continued well into the twentieth century.[5]

Moreover, Adventism was more homogenous than Millerism was in terms of social class. Although not among the nation's wealthiest families, Adventists tended to come from the higher socioeconomic strata of their communities.[6] A microhistoric examination of the Puno missionaries' backgrounds lends further support to this conclusion. For example, Orley Ford, who was born in 1893, grew up on a farm on Palouse prairie, in Pullman County, Washington. Like most farming enterprises in the area, the Fords were involved in wheat production, one of the main export products of the United States for the world market at the time. They also engaged in dairy farming that was curated regionally. The family had contributed greatly to the establishment of the Walla Walla Seventh-day Adventist College,

Adventists and Modern Times

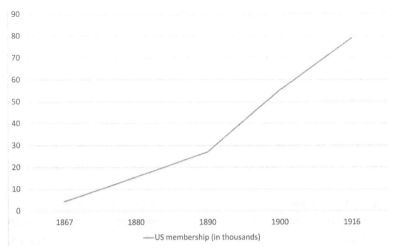

90

80

70

60

50

40

30

20

10

0

1867   1880   1890   1900   1916

——US membership (in thousands)

FIG. 13. Seventh-day Adventist presence in the United States, 1867–1916. Created by the author from "Seventh-day Adventist Statistics," copied from *Review and Herald* 29, no. 24 (1867): 283, https://documents.adventistarchives .org/Statistics/ASR/ASR1867.pdf; "Seventh-day Adventist Statistics," copied from *Seventh-day Adventist Yearbook for 1891*, https://documents .adventistarchives.org/Statistics/ASR/ASR1890.pdf; *Seventh-day Adventist Conferences, Missions, and Institutions, Annual Statistical Report for Year 1916* (Takoma Park, Washington DC: General Conference of the Seventh-day Adventists, 1916).

which also attested to their economic prosperity.[7] Ellis Howard's path to Puno's missionary stations seems to have been a bit more challenging: his father left the family when Howard was a very young boy, sometime around 1890, and he and his sister ended up growing up with their grandmother and aunt. The family operated a small boardinghouse in Tampa, Florida, and then moved to Graceville, Tennessee, where they owned ten acres of "stony ground" for a farm. At Graceville, Howard put himself through school, attending the Southern Missionary College. At the same time, he also had to contribute to the family's income. Howard's family may have not been as well off as the Fords, but the fact that he was able to go to school, rather than work full-time to support his family, and spent his leisure time taking violin lessons, points to the family's secure income and a relatively comfortable living standard.[8]

Interestingly, the Argentinean missionary Pedro Kalbermatter also belonged to the upper middle class of his locality. His family owned a six-hundred-hectare farm in the department of San Cristóbal, Santa Fe Province.[9] The Kalbermatters' property and access to labor were modest in comparison to Argentina's great haciendas that encompassed thousands of hectares, fed hundreds of heads of beef, and had extensive historical patronage networks that provided them with cheap labor. Yet, in comparison with small and medium farms—in particular, those that produced grain and wheat in Santa Fe— they were very prosperous.[10] In other words, without ignoring the important discrepancies between the "middle class" in the U.S. and its Argentinean counterpart, the missionaries in Titicaca had a similar class provenance. They were all sons of farmers "who owned the property with which they worked" and part of "the old middle class."[11]

The "old middle class" is a term coined by Charles Wright Mills and refers to people who had control over their modes of production. By contrast, the "new middle class" comprised salaried employees.[12] Some scholars argue that Mills overemphasizes production modes over other aspects of class formation, such as discourse, identity, values, and habits.[13] My objective here, however, is not to analyze the formation of the middle class in the United States. Rather, I aim to analyze how social and economic changes in the United States affected young Adventists and how these changes influenced their decision to become missionaries. For this specific end, Mills's differentiation between an old and a new middle class based on control over modes of production is most suitable, because such control was crucial if one wanted to observe the seventh-day Sabbath.

Controlling labor was practically a prerequisite for joining the Seventh-day Adventist Church. Ownership over means of production secured the self-management of time, which in turn allowed one to ignore mainstream divisions between sacred (Sunday) and secular (weekdays) time, without paying a high cost.[14] Adventists who controlled their workload could compensate, at least partially, for losses on Saturday by working on Sunday. Laborers did not have the same liberty. They depended on others for work, and their employers decided where, and especially when, their hands were needed. For them, living outside the mainstream weekly time cycle posed a much bigger threat. As one Seventh-day Adventist poor laborer wrote in 1874: "It is extremely hard times here for poor folks—the hardest I have known. And it comes harder on poor Sabbath-Keepers (and we are all poor in this place), than on others because those who are able to hire, choose not to hire those who will not work on the Sabbath."[15]

Furthermore, an alternative time cycle also had drawbacks for industrialists or large employers. Obviously, Adventists did not work on Saturdays, but the Adventist Church's leadership also took an uncompromising position against hiring Sunday-keepers to work on that day. The "Fourth Commandment," they preached, "requires abstinence from labor, not only on the part of the individual himself, but also on the part of those in his employ."[16] Adventist leaders did not want followers to take advantage of a possible loophole and profit on the Sabbath from the work of Sunday-keepers. The result, however, was that the Adventists' workweek was two days short: keeping the Sabbath would have meant unavailability for business on Saturdays and, in turn, operating on Sundays when trade centers, banks, and other financial institutions were closed. In a competitive market, this was not efficient and, in addition to watching over their own profit, large enterprises were also accountable to stockholders. An industrialist might have been self-employed but was not self-reliant and thus would find it difficult to keep the Sabbath in a Sunday-keeping world.

The economic obstacles created by Saturday-keeping also had a significant impact on the ethnic composition of this church. Seventh-day Adventists were racially white, as were the Millerites.[17] In fact, in the 1850s and 1860s, the entire church membership was made up of the whitest people in the United States: Anglo-Saxons. Whereas Adventists would remain predominantly white until deep into the twentieth century, in the 1870s, around the same time the church's shut doors opened, their ethnic composition diversified. By the early 1880s, about 13 percent of Adventists were immigrants, primarily from Germany and Scandinavian countries. The large share of German-speaking immigrants in comparison with other ethnicities, such as Poles and Italians, can be explained at least partially by the patterns of settlement and occupational choices of the former. German-speaking immigrants usually settled on small, independent farms in frontier areas and were thus able to control their time. By contrast, Italian and Polish immigrants, who settled in cities and joined the ranks of paid labor, were underrepresented in the Adventist Church.[18] Hence, paradoxically, those who owned their working time were the ones able to claim that it belongs to someone else—God.[19]

Coming of Age: From Farm Boys to the Religious Professions of the New Middle Class, 1890s–1910s

Between the mid-1890s and about 1910, Ferdinand Stahl, Alvin Allen, and Reid Shepard, all of whom would meet on the cold Altiplano, came of age. It was now time that they left home and took the first steps toward establishing their own households. As these young men prepared to leave their fathers' farms, it became evident that the prospects their generation had were quite different from those that existed a generation earlier.[20] The last decades of the nineteenth century were a period of intense changes as the United States was transformed from a rural, relatively homogeneous society to an industrialized, heterogeneous, and corporate nation. During these years, farm boys from the old middle class discovered that it was increasingly difficult to establish a family farm, as their fathers had done.[21] For one, entry fees to the market had gone up, the real price of land rising throughout the period, even though new areas, particularly in the Great Plains, had been opened for colonization.[22]

For those who were lucky enough to accumulate the necessary funds to purchase land, additional expenses awaited, such as the cost of land improvement or of the agricultural machinery that was imperative for a farmer's survival in a competitive market.[23] Machinery had also altered the relationship between the farmer and his hired hands, further hampering the attempts of a younger generation to reach the high rung of being independent farmers. In the antebellum Midwest, hired help was usually a neighboring farmer's son who was taking his first steps toward economic independence.[24] These personal and stable labor relations provided the hired help with security to earn money toward buying their own farm. After the Civil War, more and more farmers were looking for only seasonal help to fulfill specific tasks, and as competition increased, they also wished to pay as little as possible. As a result, personal and moral aspects of labor relations were deteriorating, leaving farmworkers with little security in the short term and diminishing their chances of making their way up the ladder in the long term.[25]

Finally, the accelerating rate of industrialization, urbanization, and population growth had fomented the demand for agricultural products. With so many mouths to feed, the production of meat, flour, and other types of food became a profitable business.[26] Improvements in transportation and storage infrastructure promised consumers fresh produce and brought the global market even to remote corners of the country, sweeping more and more farmers into international trade currents.[27] Like peasants in the Andean highlands, farmers growing wheat or grazing cattle on the grasslands of the United States were now subjected to fluctuating prices influenced by the fortunes and misfortunes of peasants in Ukraine, ranchers on the Argentinean pampas, and the changing tastes and fashions of anonymous men and women.[28] Commodities prices were now set by large international trade dealers, and additional costs, such as transportation, were cutting into revenue. Consequently, farming became a risky business, making "entry for the next generation of aspiring yeoman farmers . . . that much more difficult."[29]

Within the family framework, sons who had no prospects of inheriting their father's farm were particularly affected by the soaring entrance fees and unstable market conditions. In some cases, it could have been the eldest son who inherited the farm. But in other cases, it was the youngest son, or simply the one who came of age around the time his father was ready to retire.[30] Other children relied on cheap and accessible land outside their birthplace as the first steppingstone toward independent ownership.[31] Most of the missionaries to Puno came from the latter group. Apart from Orley Ford perhaps, none stood to gain from an inheritance that would have significantly facilitated their path toward independent ownership of any sort.

Edgar Maxwell, for instance, was born in McPherson, one of the richest wheat counties in Kansas, in 1878. He lived there until 1890 at which time his family moved to Pottawatomie, Oklahoma, where his parents worked as tenants. Around the same year, John Howell was born, in Rutland, Iowa. His parents also moved around before settling as tenants in Humboldt County, Iowa, in the mid-1890s. Aside from the important factor of land inheritance, local mutual aid networks, which were available to farmers' sons, were not always open to tenants' sons, contributing to their inferiority.[32] Other missionaries were also in precarious positions: Alvin Allen was born in 1880 to an elderly and sick father who passed away when he was six, leaving the family farm to his eldest brother, Arthur, who took upon himself the family responsibilities.[33] When Allen reached eighteen he did not have much choice but to leave home and pursue other opportunities. Finally, Ferdinand Stahl was an orphan whose father had committed suicide after stabbing another man with a pair of scissors during a fight.[34] Stahl's mother remarried and bore more sons, while young Ferdinand and his stepfather, at least according to one report, did not get along particularly well.[35] Somewhere around 1890, Stahl left home in search of other opportunities. In this regard, he shared a common history with his primary aide in the Andes, Manuel Camacho, who also lived with his mother and stepfather and had little chance of inheriting land.

Parallel to the increase in fees and the risks imposed by an expanding capitalist market, other opportunities were emerging, specifically in the Midwest. From 1880, around the time most missionaries were born, to 1910, when they reached adulthood, the number of employees in this region had risen by 150 percent.[36] The expanding industries, commercial enterprises, and bureaucracy were constantly seeking clerks, sale agents, bookkeepers, and numerous other white-collar employees. These new venues often required a costly professional education. But for young men whose families could do without their working hands and perhaps even provide some support during schooling, many career choices with good wages were now available. For example, the average annual net income of a farm in Illinois was about $850 a year, while the average salary of clerks and managers in Chicago was around $1,000 a year.[37] In Michigan, the gap between white-collar earnings and farm profits was much more significant: while the annual salary for male officials and clerks was $900 a year, the average profit from a farm was about $450.[38]

High wages were a significant variable in "pulling" farm boys into other occupations, and the places where young men chose to leave farming in favor of other professions were "the most urban-industrial regions of the United States and the counties with the highest wage levels, manufacturing activity, and urbanization."[39] Residents of these counties were aware of the new opportunities the market had to offer and thus were better informed of prospects outside farming. Furthermore, they did not have to travel far to take advantage of these opportunities and therefore did not have to risk much. This macro conclusion is also valid at the micro level and evident among the missionaries in Puno, 70 percent of whom came from industrialized and urbanized counties. For example, Reid Shepard was born and raised in the township of Otsego, Allegan County, Michigan. This county had about 250 established manufacturers, the growing town of Holland was within its boundaries, and it was near the cities of Grand Rapids and Kalamazoo. Additionally, Berrien Springs, home to the Adventist college of the same name, was only seventy miles away from Otsego and easily accessible by train.[40] In other words, Shepard's commute to school was relatively short and inexpensive. He could come home on weekends, vacations, or whenever help was needed, thus limiting the economic and social investments entailed in acquiring higher education. Missionaries were therefore a part of a generation whose life trajectories were changing in response to industrialism and urbanism. These were men who discovered that the occupational paths their fathers had taken were now full of dents, bumps, and stop signs. Yet, at the same time, they also found out that new roads led to rewarding final destinations. Because missionaries came from a segment of society that was socially, economically, and geographically privileged, they were in a good position to seize new opportunities. They needed, however, to get an education.

The fact was that during the last quarter of the nineteenth century, demand for education, including higher education, was surging across the United States, and Adventists, like members of many other religious denominations of the time, set out to establish schools and colleges of their own. Indeed, Adventist educational institutions mushroomed: In 1890 the Adventist Church had sixteen schools, from primary to tertiary. By 1900 it had established 245 schools, of which six were institutions of higher education. Additionally, the Adventist Church also allocated funds for scholarships and encouraged educational institutions to create schedules that would allow students to work while studying. Making Adventist higher education accessible to the younger generation of followers was a central goal, one not to be taken for granted. Originally the church held strong antieducational views, according to which it made little sense to invest resources in the future since Christ would soon arrive.[41] These attitudes dissolved, hand in hand with the church's anti-missionary attitudes, eventually creating space for professional missionary training.

In sum, coming of age at the dawn of the twentieth century, young Adventists, like other farm boys of their generation, discovered that establishing a farm was difficult and risky. On the other hand, new opportunities in nearby towns and cities that offered high wages and other conveniences were now in close reach. Those who wished to obtain a higher education could now choose from several denominational institutions, three of them situated in the Midwest. But, as luck would have it, white-collar employment and keeping God's fourth commandment did not go together easily.

Coping with Conflict: Seventh-day Adventists and White-Collar Employment

"A brother in Milo has received the following notice from his employer: It has been decided by the management that there can be no discrimination made in the working hours of our men and that, therefore, if your scruples will not allow you to work on Saturday, your services will not be required after one week from this date," reported Pastor E. H Morton of Maine in 1908, and then he added, "Let us all pray for the brethren who are facing the trial of losing their positions because of keeping God's commandments."[42]

This anonymous brother, as it appears, discovered that the Adventist week, that ran Sunday through Friday, conflicted with the traditional Monday-to-Saturday Christian week, which Adventists commonly called the "American week." And that he was to pay the price for this difference. As mentioned, this conflict was not new, and from the church's early years, laborers had to cope with it. During the last quarter of the nineteenth century, however, the problem became more severe, affecting more young men who belonged to the church's backbone: the upper rural middle class. It is hard to know how much more of a problem it was in quantitative terms. Florey and Guest have estimated that about 40 percent of young sons of white farmers left farming in favor of another occupation.[43] But it very well may be that Adventists did not follow this pattern and that they were less inclined to leave the farm because of their religious practices. While numbers are uncertain, church officials recognized that a growing number of young Adventists were leaving the farm in favor of the city, as one lamented: "In many instances it [the city] is taking the brightest of our farmers' sons away from agricultural pursuits, to swell the ranks of professional men, merchants, artisans, factory employees, and city workers of all sorts."[44]

Nevertheless, some of these young Adventists who now swelled the ranks of the new middle class quickly found themselves in conflict with their employers over their working days. During the early decades of the twentieth century, Adventist newspapers reported on many incidents resembling the one that Pastor Morton reported. Clerks and managers wrote about the hardships they experienced in their attempts to keep the Sabbath. In one example, a midlevel manager in a department store agonized over the choice between the Sabbath and his job, eventually notifying his employer that he would not work on Saturdays.[45] In another case, a sister working as a stenographer and bookkeeper in a factory had "made up her mind to suffer" through unemployment for the sake of "the truth."[46]

While most Adventists lived in the Midwest, these incidents were not limited to that region. This problem occurred anywhere and everywhere from New York to Nebraska, inasmuch as the counties in which these young Adventists lived were industrializing and incorporated into the capitalist market. As E. P. Thompson famously argued, the rise of capitalism was closely connected with the commodification of time and the emergence of new time regimens. Time had become a commodity that people could buy and sell in the marketplace, and the more efficient they were, the more their time was worth. Yet this commodification of time came at a cost. On the one hand, time was "confiscated" from people who had to "surrender" their working hours to strangers' clocks.[47] On the other hand, these strangers now depended on others to profit.

Adventists were not the only ones dealing with this problem. Jews faced it as well, and by the late nineteenth century, a small group of reform rabbis was debating the "Sunday option," which essentially meant moving Jewish worship from Saturday to Sunday. The Sunday option remained marginal, even within Reform Judaism. Saturday, contenders thought, was not only an ancient Jewish institution but also too central to Jewish identity to simply be "rescheduled" to another day of the week.[48] Yet, the mere discussion about it demonstrates that the standardization of the workweek caused problems for religious groups whose sacred time conflicted with mainstream secular time.

Adventists were not deaf to the discussions within the Jewish community concerning the Saturday Sabbath. Reporting on the 1902 Conference of American Rabbis in New Orleans, one newspaper editorial speculated that Jews in the United States were on the verge of substituting Sunday for Saturday.[49] Showing little interest in Jewish denominationalism, the writer ignores the fact that the Conference of American Rabbis was part of the nascent reform movement and that the "Sunday option" was highly contested even within that specific movement.[50] Instead, the writer asserts that Jews, in general, were simply unwilling to make the economic sacrifices that living in opposition to the general time cycle demanded. Drained of genuine religious sentiment, he continues, Jews were interested primarily in convenience and financial profit. For Adventists, on the other hand, "no thought of sacrificing the Sabbath for any worldly consideration" would even cross their mind.[51] In this sense, they were God's one true remnant church who were willing to sacrifice whatever necessary to keep his commandments.

Adventists' experiences in the job market—their difficulties in finding employment and facing demands to work on Saturday—were therefore presented as a test to believers' faith and a way to express devotion to God. True believers were expected to make the necessary sacrifices to observe the Sabbath even at the cost of losing one's livelihood. In this sense, Seventh-day Adventist discourse on the Sabbath was set in the larger framework of Christian discourse that accentuated the relationship between truth, salvation, and sacrifice.[52] Nevertheless, what exactly could be considered a sacrifice or what sort of suffering deserved to be divinely rewarded depended on context and changed in accordance with time and place. During the High Middle Ages, for instance, stories about virgin women upholding the faith against excruciating violence and humiliation, attempting to avoid apostasy and rape, were particularly popular.[53] In a time of anxiety over economic security and considering the growing importance of one's profession to their middle-class identity, the pressure to give up a position that provided economic security and social status was a cause of suffering.

As if this were not enough, these problems were fueled by acute political controversy, as local and national lawmakers attempted to reenact the "Sunday Blue Laws," that were imposed to restrict or completely ban activities related to work or leisure on Sundays. Blue law legislation in America dated to the seventeenth-century New England colonies, and its main goal was to ensure a day of religious rest and worship. By the last quarter of the nineteenth century, the idea that Sunday was a social institution devoted to God was constantly threatened. People, especially in cities and towns, had new ideas about how to spend their time. Rather than spending it on the pews of a church, they preferred to pass Sundays in the various commercial and entertainment institutions that were now open for business on that day. Others were less fortunate and were compelled to work on Sundays, either in the factories or by providing services to those who could afford leisure on Sunday.[54] These changes sparked reactions from Christian moralists and progressive activists who formed a coalition and worked to promote legislation that would secure Sunday's status as a day of rest and religious devotion.[55]

The blue laws not only threatened Adventists with further vulnerability in the job market but also deepened Adventist social marginalization, as a result of the public and legal disregard of their Sabbath. Adventists understood Sunday legislation as an attack on religious liberty and particular persecution of their beliefs. "Christians," an editorial in the *Review and Herald* argued, "should oppose religious legislation," especially the blue laws "which in the mind of Satan, their instigator, are always an expression of treason against God, and a rejection of the gospel of Jesus Christ."[56] Thus, the real or imagined predicaments caused by blue laws, especially from 1890 to 1930, were incorporated into the Adventist larger narrative, according to which it had long been tormented by mainline Protestant churches.[57] In this context, suffering through these challenges and remaining committed to the seventh day was of eschatological importance and manifested the victory of God over Satan. Notwithstanding the significance religious praise and the promises of an eternal reward in the next world had for believers, they still had to cope with the practical implications, and pressure on livelihood, that resulted from observing Saturday in a Sunday-keeping world. Adventist authorities were quick to respond to these challenges. Already in 1886, they established a labor bureau aimed at helping Adventists find work with other Adventists.[58] The scope of these efforts was limited, however, and could not provide solutions for the growing number of young Adventists looking for professional employment. Under these circumstances, the church sought out additional solutions, finding them in its own ranks.

For example, Brother Chas Elliot of the Elmira Church in New

York was one of the Adventists who lost his job on account of
the Sabbath. Unable to reach an agreement with his employers
that would allow him to keep his position as a telegraph oper-
ator and remain loyal to his religious beliefs, he found himself
without work. Looking for a way to make a living without com-
promising his beliefs, Elliot decided to "enter the book work";
in other words, he became a door-to-door salesman of Adventist publications, which was referred to as canvassing.[59] Elliot, it
appears, was not alone in his new occupational choice. According to the Adventist press, numerous young men found a solution to their employment problems in the "book work." With
the help of God, the writers of these publications continued, a
dedicated colporteur could secure his family's livelihood and
even more.[60]

Stories about colporteurs' success accentuate God's commitment toward Adventists and are presented as evidence that true
believers are rewarded. At the same time, selling religious literature served Adventists' spiritual aspirations and economic
interests now that the shut door had opened and non-Millerites
were invited to enter this church. In this regard, selling church
publications was considered an effective way of exposing the
general public to the third angel's message.[61] For this purpose,
the church established numerous publishing houses that then
had to become profitable, or at the very least self-sustaining.
To do this, they needed to recruit men who would be willing to
knock on strangers' doors and persuade them to buy both the
product and the message.

Sometimes matters were complicated by conflicts between
the Adventists' religious and spiritual aims and the need to operate in a competitive and capitalist market. Such, for example,
was the case of the church's main publishing house, which was
in Battle Creek. In 1885 this plant was valued at US$150,000
and topped US$61,000 in sales. About a decade later, in the late
1890s, it had become the largest publishing house in Michigan.[62] Success, however, had its costs. To uphold such a siz-
able enterprise, the press provided services to corporations,
factories, and department stores, and by 1899, 60 percent of
its publications were commercial. For the church's leadership,

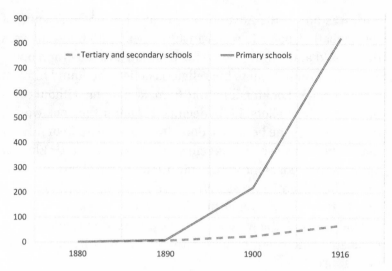

FIG. 14. Number of Seventh-day Adventist schools in the United States, 1880–1916. Created by the author from *The General Conference Department of Education Statistics, 1853–1987*, Seventh-day Adventist Church, Office of Archives, Statistics, and Research, under "Statistics"/"Education," accessed January 6, 2022, https://documents.adventistarchives.org/Statistics/Forms/AllItems.aspx? RootFolder=%2fStatistics%2fEducation&FolderCTID=0x01200095DE8DF0 FA49904B9D652113284DE0C800ED657F7DABA3CF4D893EA744F14DA97B.

who saw the press as a vehicle toward evangelization, this was a cause for dismay and dissatisfaction.[63] But downscaling on commercial publications while remaining profitable required an increase in the sales of religious literature. In other words, the press would have to reach a larger public, and, to that end, it would need more colporteurs. Yet, persuading men to leave their families, often for an extended period, and engage in work that demanded a certain kind of patience and "people skills" was quite difficult. Moreover, this work did not provide secure wages, and one was completely dependent on what one could sell. Henceforth, it was widely considered a precarious occupation for anyone who had to support a family.[64]

Clearly, the fact that Adventist newspapers were part of the publishing enterprise and depended on colporteurs to sell subscriptions pushed editors to report about success stories that helped refute the negative portrayals of the work in the field.[65] Yet, economic interests alone cannot explain why the heroes of

Adventists and Modern Times

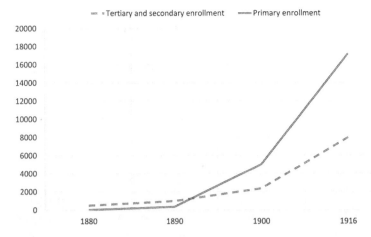

FIG. 15. Student enrollment in Seventh-day Adventist educational institutions in the United States, 1880–1916. Created by the author from *The General Conference Department of Education Statistics, 1853–1987*, Seventh-day Adventist Church, Office of Archives, Statistics, and Research, under "Statistics"/"Education," accessed January 6, 2022, https://documents.adventistarchives.org/Statistics/Forms/AllItems.aspx?RootFolder=%2fStatistics%2fEducation&FOLDERCTID=0X01200095DE8DF0FA49904B9D652113284DE0C800ED657F7DABA3CF4D893EA744F14DA97B.

so many of these stories were white-collar employees who had lost their jobs. To fully understand this phenomenon, we also need to consider the growing pressures on Adventists to work on their day of rest. In this regard, the book field was only one possible solution for this conflict between temporalities, and other attempts to remedy the situation were being made. In one meeting of the New York Conference in 1903, Elder Burrill suggested that the conference establish a health food factory, since "it would provide employment for these individuals (people living in the cities) and grand work could be accomplished."[66] Subsequently, the Adventist Church had become a major employer, and about a quarter of all members served as teachers, ministers, and missionaries within the church.[67] In comparison, only about 10 percent of Latter-day Saints and Methodists were employed by their church.[68] Furthermore, according to one report from 1906, most students who graduated from Union College, Nebraska, which at the time had the largest student enrollment of all Adventist colleges, were eventually employed by the Adventist Church.[69] Of the 208 students who had graduated by that year, 151 men (or 72 percent) were church employees, filling positions that ranged from ministers to doctors.[70]

It is difficult to establish how these numbers compare with other denominations, since statistical reports include graduates' occupations (or disciplines) but do not address the issue of placement. A report from the U.S. Bureau of Education, however, provides statistics about graduates of Wesleyan College, a Methodist institution, thus shedding some light on this issue. According to this report, between the years 1901 and 1905, graduates of Wesleyan College were employed as follows: 14.3 percent, ministry; 10 percent, law; 6 percent, medicine; 27 percent, education (including women, who are not represented in the Seventh-day Adventist figures); 25 percent, business; and 15 percent were unclassified. In other words, assuming that all the teachers, doctors, and nurses, with no exceptions, found positions within the Methodist Church, the proportion amounts to 47 percent versus 72 percent among Adventists. Even if we were then to suppose that some businessmen, lawyers, and unclassified graduates ended up in the denomination's bureaucracy, the gap is still significant.[71] The fact was that the church's bureaucracy and affiliated institutions were expanding rapidly and becoming an alternative job market for many young and educated Adventists who wished to join the white-collar middle class.[72]

As one contemporary observer remarked, Adventist health institutions were not only caring for the sick but also providing "employment for the young people of the Church, who find the keeping of the Sabbath (Saturday) a bar to employment elsewhere."[73] Leaving for the foreign mission field was part of this greater trend. Simply put, local social and economic pressures fueled the Adventist foreign missionary enterprise.

In sum, like other white farm boys who had relatively prosperous fathers, a growing number of Adventists left the farm to acquire an education. Nevertheless, the social and political standardization of the workweek conflicted with the Adventist sacred time cycle, and for a growing number of Adventists, the temporal conditions of white-collar employment conflicted with their religious beliefs. One way out of this conundrum was to find work within the church, the foreign mission field being one option. It is not that missionary work was simply about social mobility or that religious dedication was insignificant when making this career choice. Quite the contrary is true. The conflict described, between the changing modes of employment and the unique Adventist time cycle, is applicable only to those devoted Adventists who were unwilling to compromise the observance of Saturday despite the challenges modern times presented. Hence, religious belief shaped the range of opportunities men like Alvin Allen and Harry Wilcox had to begin with. The decision to leave for the mission field was set within the larger framework of the changing choices, opportunities, and aspirations these young men had at the time. In fact, at times the challenges missionaries had at home followed them into the field.

Off to the "Land of the Inca": The Adventist Mission in Peru

"As soon as we cast anchor," Orley Ford recalled of January 9, 1918, "there was the worst scramble I ever saw." After twenty days of excitement and seasickness, twenty-four-year-old Ford and his wife, Lillie, finally reached the port city of Callao, Peru. Because of its size, their ship had to anchor a few miles offshore and passengers disembarked into small paddleboats that took them to shore. Ford described the commotion as a "swarm" and seemed genuinely relieved when brothers Wilcox and Minner arrived to escort him and his wife to the mission house. There, the couple rested for a few days before journeying to Lake Titicaca, where they joined the other Seventh-day Adventist missionaries laboring among the Aymara Indians.[74]

Notwithstanding the difficulties the Fords experienced in adjusting to their new surroundings, they arrived at a relatively hospitable environment. Or at least one that was much more tolerant of their presence than it had been toward missionaries who had arrived a decade earlier. For one, two and a half years had passed between the time the Peruvian Congress amended article four of the Constitution, now permitting the public practice of religions other than Catholicism, and the Fords' arrival in 1918. Hence, this couple could work without fear that legal actions might be taken against them. Second, there was an established and vibrant, albeit small, Protestant community in South America. Even in the Andes, one of the last destinations missionaries entered, Protestantism had set its roots. To be sure, Latin America became home to numerous Protestant communities during the early colonial period. They usually chose, however, to dwell on the geographical and social periphery, keeping to themselves and rarely engaging in missionary efforts.[75] The nineteenth century, however, brought with it winds of change: the wars of independence that ended the symbiosis between the Spanish Crown and the crucifix; new national policies that intended to encourage white immigration from perceived progressive Protestant countries; and evolving business ties, first with northern Europe and then North American countries. All of these factors contributed to the attractiveness of Latin America as a destination for religious work. Generally, it was the British, who had established commercial ties with South America, especially Argentina, beginning early in the nineteenth century, that ushered Protestantism into the region. North American missionaries joined their British counterparts in the 1830s, and in 1836 the first North American Methodist church was established in Argentina. By the 1860s several Protestant churches were serving both foreigners and locals.[76] In 1891 the Methodist Church would send Thomas Wood from Argentina to Peru, where he became that country's first official Protestant missionary. A few years later the Canadian Baptists gave Bolivia its first official Protestant missionary.[77]

As could be expected, the Seventh-day Adventist shut-door doctrine resulted in this church's late entrance into Latin America. The first ordained Adventist minister, Frank H. Westphal, arrived in Argentina in 1894, sixty years after the Methodists. However, there were Seventh-day Adventist pockets among German-speaking immigrants in northeastern Argentina and southern Brazil already in the 1870s. Some of these immigrants came across Adventist literature while still in Europe and brought it with them across the Atlantic.[78] This was the main reason why so many of the U.S. missionaries in Latin America were first- or second-generation German Americans.[79] The General Conference purposely used transnational connections between immigrants to carry out their religious message, sending German-speaking U.S. citizens to evangelize other German-speaking communities in countries across Latin America.

The Adventist path to the Pacific coast and its way up into the Andean countries was much slower due to geographical inaccessibility, political upheavals, and Adventists' own failure to attract followers. Yet in 1905, after hearing reports about Saturday-keepers in Peru, the General Conference sent Franklin L. Perry to establish a church in Lima. In this regard, the expansion into the Andes was more a response to calls from the field than a meticulously planned endeavor from above. When the Fords arrived in 1918, there were 314 members in the Peruvian mission, which did not include the Titicaca region.[80] Most of these new Adventists worshiped in Lima, but Seventh-day Adventism was also able to gain footholds in Arequipa and the Central Andes, especially the town of Lanca, in the Huarochirí Province.[81] It is hard to say who filled the pews of these churches. In Lima, they appear to have been immigrants from the interior that were swelling the ranks of the lower middle class during the first decades of the twentieth century.[82] As for Lanca, missionaries described adherents as Indians who were native to that specific region, but this description should be taken with caution.[83] The transformation from silver mining to copper mining in the 1890s brought with it the emergence of a mining proletariat, and a growing number of rural migrants arrived in the region seeking employment. It is possible that converts to Seventh-day Adventism in this area resembled converts to Protestant churches in the southern states of Mexico who were also rural migrants.[84] In comparison with other Adventist missions in Latin America, the Peruvian mission, even without the Lake Titicaca mission, was growing fast. By 1925 the Peruvian mission was the seventh-largest among the twenty-one missions and conferences in the South American division of the Seventh-day Adventist Church.[85]

FIG. 16. Seventh-day Adventist presence in Latin America, circa 1916. Created by the author from *Seventh-day Adventist Conferences, Missions, and Institutions, Annual Statistical Report, for Year 1916* (Takoma Park, Washington DC: General Conference of the Seventh-day Adventists, 1913–17).

Nevertheless, in comparison with other Protestant churches in Peru, the Adventist Church was relatively small. In 1918 there were eight other Protestant denominations in Peru besides the Seventh-day Adventists. Among them, the Methodist Episcopal Church, which was the first Protestant church established in the country (1889), had approximately one thousand adherents. The Evangelical Union of South America had about nineteen hundred adherents, and the Holiness Church had about five hundred followers.[86]

Adventists and Modern Times

The reasons why Seventh-day Adventism was relatively small ran the gamut from its late entrance into the field to the fact that the Inca Union, the Seventh-day Adventist administrative unit that included Peru, Bolivia, and Ecuador, spent much of its resources on the work in Lake Titicaca. The Adventist temporality also played an important role in this regard. Generally speaking, conversion to Protestantism, no matter to which denomination, was conditioned by clocks, calendars, and schedules. Conversion is a time-consuming process that requires participating in classes, church gatherings, and other activities. Not everyone can dedicate the hours and days required by this process. Furthermore, the tempo of religious life and the specific timing of religious events within a Methodist or Holiness Church was not necessarily compatible with that of the Catholic calendar, which dominated Peruvian life.[87] Consequently, conflicts over temporalities could occur in any church. But they were especially frequent and acute in the Seventh-day Adventist Church. Study classes could be rescheduled to fit people's needs, but refraining from work on Saturday could not be compromised and only six days separated one Saturday from the next.

The Adventist Church's overseas expansion might have solved the problems for young Saturday-keepers in the industrializing American Midwest, but it did not reconcile the chasm between the Adventist Sabbath and the standardization of time during the late nineteenth and early twentieth centuries. This difference continued to be a challenge in foreign lands. In 1907, Ramon Beltrán, a recent convert to Seventh-day Adventism, was fined by the municipality of Lima. The reason for this fine, according to Franklin Perry, was the fact that he had opened his small textile shop on a certain Sunday in November 1907. At first, Beltrán refused to pay and suffered the consequences: a soldier was placed at the doorstep of his shop and prevented customers from entering. Finally, Beltrán agreed to pay the fine, but only after his lawyer advised him to do so and initiated proceedings against the government.[88] Whether or not the fine was issued on account of municipal Sunday laws is unclear. What is obvious is that Beltrán responded as a true believer should respond and was willing to "suffer" for his new faith. In another case, a convert from Lanca, who was a bricklayer, refused to drink or do any work on Saturdays. In the beginning, this man was ridiculed and persecuted for his actions. Despite these hardships, he continued to observe the Sabbath and preach his new faith and was eventually rewarded: "he won the hearts of the people and even of his enemies. . . . They also call for a pastor to instruct them, so that they may receive baptism."[89] These stories correspond to the wider narrative promoted in the Adventist press in which the conflicting temporalities are presented as a test of faith and true believers; those who observe the Sabbath despite the difficulties are rewarded.

Not everyone, however, was willing to make such sacrifices, and, on occasions, missionaries were frustrated by prospective converts who refused to make the earthly sacrifices that the "truth" demanded. "We have been shocked," Edgar Maxwell lashed out in 1914, "to find the slight hold that the truth has on some of our best members when it comes to choosing between the Sabbath and their 'jobs.'"[90] Maxwell's remark is rather arrogant, as voiced from the relatively comfortable spot of an established missionary, in that it views converts' preoccupation with their livelihood as superficial. Nevertheless, at the same time, he was also well aware that very few, if any, would be able to go without work for an extended period. Thus, if the Adventist Church wanted to make substantial progress, it would have to focus on converting "independent working men, or physicians."[91] In other words, individuals who exercised control over their time might be able to adopt an alternative time cycle without jeopardizing their livelihood.

In 1912 Alvin Allen, at the time stationed in Lima, had established relationships with a Dominican Friar, Father Toalino, who eventually left the convent. This former priest found work in a local newspaper, and although he showed much interest in Seventh-day Adventism and saw the "truth of the Sabbath," he did not observe it. The reason, according to Allen, was that "his circumstances at present necessitate he help himself any way he can."[92] Livelihood came before religious commitment. Try-

Adventists and Modern Times

ing to solve this problem, Allen appealed to the General Conference, asking that Toalino be given a one-year allowance that would allow him to keep the Sabbath and eventually be baptized into the Adventist Church. To be sure, Allen did have particular reasons to help this man that he may not have had in dealing with other converts: Firstly, as Toalino was a former member of the Catholic clergy, his conversion carried particular symbolic capital. Secondly, he was highly educated and proficient in Spanish, while most converts came from the lower social classes, many of them unable to read, write, or even speak the language at a satisfactory level. These abilities, according to Allen, made Toalino "well worth the expenditure," as he could help promote the cause and aid in ways that others could not.

Finally, because of his religious background and education, Toalino also attracted the attention of other Protestant missionaries who tried to lure him into their ranks.[93] This was no minor issue, and denomination competed over converts, especially of this sort. Specifically, the relationship between the Adventist missionaries and other North American missionaries was ambivalent. On the one hand, being in a foreign land did accentuate their commonalities. Franklin Perry, for example, was walking the streets of Lima one morning during August 1906, when the host was carried out of the local church. "The carriage was surrounded by men, bare-headed, carrying candles." He reported and continued to say, "I had no respect for this idolatry. . . . Such a mocking of the Lord made all my *Protestant blood* rise in indignation" (my emphasis). Perry then goes on to tell of a Methodist colporteur who was attacked on the street by two Catholic priests.[94] Whereas, in the United States, Adventists harshly reprimanded mainline Protestants for their Catholic Sunday observance, in Lima the intensity of Catholic visibility overshadowed any disagreements Protestants had over the issue of time. From an Adventist perspective, the Reformation may not have quite ended in the United States, but in Peru, it had never begun. Additionally, all Protestant denominations were now religious minorities in a country that recognized Roman Catholicism as its official religion and the only one that could be publicly practiced until 1915. Thus, while in the U.S., Adventists were blaming mainline Protestants for religious suppression on account of blue laws, in the Andes they joined hands with Methodists, Baptists, and Presbyterians to advocate freedom of religion. The attack on the Adventist school in Platería, which was led by the bishop of Puno in 1913, was central to ecumenical advocacy efforts that eventually brought a change in the Peruvian constitution.

On the other hand, Adventists were never considered part of the "Protestant" camp and were excluded from or refused to take part in many common platforms.[95] Adventists were suspicious of other denominations and fought with them over the credit for various political and spiritual successes. In one such incident, Edgar Maxwell blamed Rev. John Richie, whom he calls "our bitterest enemy," of stealing Adventist glory. According to Maxwell, Richie (who was of the Evangelical Union of South America) credited all Evangelicals for a supreme court decision that abrogated the use of force to compel Indians to serve as *mayordomos* of local fiestas. From the correspondence, the details of the case brought to the supreme court are unclear, but Maxwell makes a point that the plaintiffs were Adventist Indians and that, in his view, this was an Adventist victory rather than a general "Evangelical" one.[96] In this competitive environment, Toalino was a prize. Baptizing a Catholic priest, which other Protestant missionaries had also been wooing, into the Adventist Church was a victory over the Catholic Church and other Protestant denominations. Notwithstanding the advantages of Toalino's conversion, the General Conference declined to support him, stipulating issues of religious commitment and faith. Paradoxically, the tension between temporalities that propelled the Adventist overseas expansion "chased" the missionaries across international borders and posed challenges for missionaries in Lima. This, however, was not the case for the Indian Mission at Lake Titicaca.

7

Everyday Sacrifices and Missionaries' Experiences in the Andean Highlands

WHEN ORLEY AND LILLIE FORD FINALLY REACHED PUNO in January 1918, they found a vibrant Adventist community that amounted to over thirteen hundred members. Among these, 548 were recently baptized. This figure overshadowed all other baptisms per mission or conference in the Adventist Church worldwide.[1] These new Adventist adherents were willing to walk for miles to attend sermons and other religious activities. On Saturdays, they spent the entire day in church, studying the Bible and discussing moral conduct. From missionaries' perspective, these poor and oppressed people did not let "worldly" concerns, such as their "jobs," interfere with their newfound truth. The conflict in temporalities that hindered part of the Adventists' efforts in Lima was not much of an issue in the Andes. The reason is obvious: Andean society was to a large extent a task-oriented society where work was dictated by seasonal agricultural chores. Work on Saturday could be substituted with work on Sunday. Moreover, converts owned their means of production, and although their lands were constantly threatened by large landowners, peasants still had a relatively high degree of freedom over their laboring hours. The Adventist converts were also among those better off in their local communities, thus conforming to the socioeconomic conditions that characterized Adventists elsewhere. In other words, the fact that these temporalities did not conflict in the highlands made Adventism more accessible and missionaries' task easier.

Another challenge that Adventists had to deal with on the coast but disappeared into the highlands' thin air was direct competition from other Protestant denominations. During the 1910s, there was a handful of Protestant missionaries, from a few denominations, working in La Paz, but no church was present in the rural, and Indian, areas that engulfed Lake Titicaca. Attempting to increase Protestant outreach in Peru, English-speaking Protestant missionaries, not including Adventists, met in Panama during the congress on missionary work in Latin America in 1916. A year later, they reached an agreement concerning missionary work in Peru that divided the country between the different denominations: Northern Peru was designated to the Free Church of Scotland, the Church of Nazarene, and the Holiness Church. Central Peru was to be the territory of Methodist Episcopal Church. Southern Peru, including Puno, would go to the Evangelical Union of South America. But that church obtained a permanent toehold in the highlands only in 1925, when the Urco farm was established near Cuzco.[2] All in all, Adventists were the only religious denomination in the region until the mid-1920s. Besides, of course, the Catholic Church.

The importance of the Catholic Church to missionaries' experiences in the Andes was momentous. Within the broad Latin American context, the Andean nations tended to cluster around the conservative pole when it came to issues of church and state. Although there were plenty of liberal intellectuals and politicians who viewed the Catholic Church as a remnant of the colonial past and an impediment to modernization, anti-clericalism never reached the heights it did in Mexico and Central America. Even mild reforms, such as the one enacted in Argentina in 1853, were viewed with suspicion and resistance.[3] In the absence of religious freedom, missionaries calculated their steps with caution. They were often subjected to harassment from neighbors, arrested by local authorities, and vilified by members of the clergy and political allies of the Catholic Church. Marriage and burials were under Catholic jurisdiction, and therefore, in their most intimate moments of happiness and grief, Protestants faced an unsympathetic bureaucracy. For example, it was practically impossible for non-Catholics to inscribe non-Catholic marriages in the country's register and at times needed approval from the president. Without the legal recognition of marriages, couples found themselves in a state of concubinage. In other words, issues of church and state had implications that went well beyond proselytism and impacted the most intimate spheres of missionaries' lives.

Adventists' experiences with the Catholic Church in Puno were no exception. In fact, when it comes to the interactions with the Catholic Church, nothing distinguished the Adventists from other Protestants. As mentioned, Adventist Indian converts described themselves as protestantes, evangélicos, and adventistas interchangeably, never really differentiating between these categories. To a large extent, the Catholic Church acted the same. High ecclesiastical authorities and conservative intellectuals who resided in the cities of Lima and Arequipa were usually well educated. These men were probably knowledgeable about the theological and liturgical differences that separated Protestant denominations. Or at least about some of them. In the social and political arena, however, these discrepancies carried little importance, if any at all. It was not as if the Catholic Church accepted the presence of Anglicans in Peru but rejected that of the Adventists because of their doctrines. Nor did the Catholic Church inscribe Presbyterian marriages in the register but refuse to do the same for Methodists. The fact was that in the public debate about Protestant presence in Peru, theology rarely came up. At stake were not issues of salvation and grace but the social and political implications of freedom of religion. The Catholic Church argued that freedom of religion threatened national unity, since Catholicism was the only unifying force in a nation separated by race, language, and customs.[4] From this vantage point, the non-Catholic presence was dangerous, and there was no difference between Adventists and any other Protestant denomination.

Among rural priests, viewing all foreign missionaries as one monolithic group also had to do with their social and educational backgrounds. By the end of the nineteenth century, the Catholic Church in the rural Andes was in a dire condition. Liberal reforms, particularly those implemented in the mid-nineteenth century, profoundly affected the church's sources of revenue, leaving priests, especially those who served impoverished populations, without a sufficient income. As a result, the racial and socioeconomic composition of the rural clergy changed. Instead of upper-middle-class white men educated in Peru's best schools, a growing number of mestizos from the lower middle class who only had a basic education now entered the priesthood. The Catholic Church's elite, because of its racism regarding the ability of these men to understand theological issues, and due to lack of funds, did not invest much in their training.[5] Consequently, by the end of the nineteenth century, the priests that were stationed in the periphery were impoverished both materially and intellectually. The Adventists in Puno were probably the first non-Catholic Christians that Tomás Bravo, the priest in Chucuito, had ever met. It is highly unlikely that he, or even the bishop of Puno, was aware of the unique history of Adventism or its strained relationships with other Protestant denominations. In Bravo's eyes, the Adventists were Evangelicals, U.S. citizens, and strangers.[6] Other members of the local elite viewed Adventists similarly and spoke of the "Protestant sect" or simply referred to the Adventists as "the Evangelicals." In one letter, missionaries were described as "Adventists sent by the Bible Societies of North America."[7] On the one hand, this quotation shows that the anonymous writer had at least some knowledge about Protestant denominations. On the other, it indicates how limited this knowledge was, since Adventists had no connection to the Bible societies. Henceforth, the important chasm was between those who were Catholics and those who were not, and all the non-Catholic Christians were labeled as Protestants.

The Adventist missionaries in Puno were well aware that the locals, including their own converts, thought that "whoever was not a Catholic must be an Adventist."[8] But this became an issue only in rare cases when other Protestant denominations encroached on their work. On most days, missionaries seemed to be indifferent to this kind of generalization and were even willing to overlook converts' doctrinal inaccuracies. Sources are silent on how missionaries reacted to converts' interpretations of Adventist doctrines. But one short remark made by Juan Huanca in 1911, and reported by Frank Westphal, is somewhat

Sacrifices and Experiences

revealing. That year, Westphal, who was serving as head of the South American Union Conference, visited the nascent Lake Titicaca Indian Mission, where he met Juan Huanca. Huanca had converted to Adventism a few years before and had recently been the victim of a violent attack in which the local priest and twenty-five men stormed into his home and beat him with a club. "It was at this time that he [Huanca] told the priest that he might kill his body, but he could not kill his soul," Westphal reported proudly to the General Conference.[9] This comment is interesting first because Huanca, an Adventist, thought that his soul would live after his body had perished, and second, that Westphal enthusiastically reported this to the General Conference.

A central pillar in Adventist doctrines was that of "Conditional Immortality." Most Christians, Catholic and Protestant, followed Greek philosophy and believed that the soul was immortal. Thus, when one's body died, his soul continued to live in either heaven or hell. Adventists, however, chose to follow Hebrew teachings that denied the immortality of the soul, believing instead that the soul was resurrected with the body upon the coming of the Messiah. Immortality was a gift to the faithful, while those who did not accept God's message would suffer a second death.[10] Paradoxically, while he was beaten by the Catholic priest, Huanca professed beliefs that were much more Catholic than Adventist. And it appears Westphal did not even notice this contradiction, nor did he think that anyone in the General Conference would raise an eyebrow when reading it. What Westphal saw, and what he conveyed to the General Conference, was the story of a martyr: the weak Indian suffering at the hands of Catholic agents and never letting go of his newfound truth, which was Seventh-day Adventism.

The fact was that living in the Altiplano reduced some of the specific challenges Adventists faced elsewhere and brought them closer to the experiences of mainline Protestantism. From their early days in the Millerite movement, Adventists believed that they were part of a persecuted religious minority. Mid-nineteenth-century blue law legislation reinforced this sentiment and created a sense of urgency as the Adventist Church in the United States fought to preserve its central beliefs and practice. Adventist newspaper reports about people having to choose between their livelihood and their religion exacerbated fears of persecution and exemplified the intimate price that people had to pay for their beliefs. Things changed in Lima. "Dissent was a necessary element in the Adventist view of history," and Adventists believed that they had to "remain a suffering minority."[11] Because of this outlook, Adventists in the United States often aligned with other religious minorities, including Catholics, against Protestant hegemony. In essence, this view did not change in the Andes, but now the religious minorities were Presbyterians, Baptists, and Methodists. Adventists were being persecuted along with other Protestants, and as Protestants, by the Catholic Church, which did not differentiate between non-Catholic Christians.

Nevertheless, in the shadow of Lima's Cathedral of Saint John the Apostle, Adventists still had to deal with being religious outsiders among the British and Americans in Peru. Adventists were not part of joint ecumenical organizations and activities; they were often looked upon suspiciously and had to apologetically explain their doctrines to other missionaries. Saturday observance continued to be a problem both for prospective converts who did not want to risk their livelihoods and for Adventist children who had to attend local schools that taught on Saturdays.

By contrast, Puno offered an entirely different experience. In this rural, task-oriented society, Saturday observance did not cause the same problems it caused in Lima. Here the better-off stratum of peasants was relatively free to set their working hours. Additionally, in this secluded area, Adventists were the only active church aside from the Catholic Church. For the locals, including converts, priests, state authorities, and the mestizos in the nearby town, Adventists represented North American Protestantism. At the same time, living in a faraway place brought about new concerns, drawbacks, and difficulties that overshadowed former difficulties. The material conditions in the field were one such concern. No matter where missionaries were stationed, they spoke about the material compromises the field entailed. In remote areas such as Puno, however, this

Sacrifices and Experiences

topic was particularly salient and profoundly shaped the missionaries' experiences. As Franklin Perry, the head of the Peruvian Mission wrote to the General Conference in 1907: "Men who come to Peru should be able to endure hardships in traveling and living among natives. Here in Lima and in other cities, one can do very well, for he has all the conveniences of modern times. But go ten miles or less from town, and all is changed."[12]

Sacrifice, Self-Denial, and the Foreign Mission Field

In 1915 Edgar Maxwell, head of the Inca Union Mission based in Lima, wrote a letter to his superiors. In it, he expressed deep concerns over the discrepancies between the realities of the field and prospective missionaries' fantasies about it. Life in exotic, faraway lands, Maxwell wrote, was "not nearly so interesting nor romantic as appears at a distance." On the contrary, "coming to a foreign country where all the people speak a different language . . . where there are none of the conveniences of the States, or at the best, only a few of them," was a hard, burdensome experience.[13] Only a few, Maxwell thought, were truly willing to pay the price of "a life of discomfort in all things that we are used to in the United States . . . for the privilege of adding their mite to the efforts of those who are laboring to raise up the fallen."[14] Missionary work meant personal sacrifice and withstanding hardships. Not everyone was up to the task.

Maxwell was not alone in his thoughts and the "self-denials" missionaries would have to endure. The complete and utter unselfishness they had to possess was discussed in the Adventist press.[15] In fact, this discussion went well beyond the Adventist Church and was an inherent part of a religious and secular discourse of the late nineteenth- and early twentieth-century United States. Within the religious field, the foreign mission field was the "kingdom of Character," and a space in which Victorian values such as "personal heroism, lofty humanitarianism, self-sacrifice and Christian dedication" were displayed.[16] Stories of self-sacrificing missionary-martyrs, such as Horace Tracy Pitkin, who was murdered in China's Boxer Rebellion in 1900, were produced by the Student Volunteer Movement and then circulated among the men and women preparing for the field.[17] During the same period, tropes of pain, sacrifice, and hardships were also popularized in other fields and made martyrs out of anyone, from geographers to travelers.[18] For instance, descriptions of strong-willed men enduring psychological and physical pain for the sake of making a discovery proliferated within and outside academia to portray scientific breakthroughs in the press.[19] Without a doubt, the adventure, action, and suspense made for a good read, and, for commercial purposes, these features were likely indispensable. After all, who would want to indulge in a story where all goes well and nothing happens? But prolonged descriptions of danger and sacrifice did more than add excitement to what would otherwise be a rather ordinary story. These stories were usually constructed along the following lines: the protagonist embarked on the journey with a purpose, underwent endless calamities and misfortunes, but never gave up. Finally, the mission is fulfilled, and discovery brings light to the darkness. The scientist uncovers a crucial fact about nature, the author is enlightened by a cultural revelation, and the power of the Lord is revealed to the missionary. Within this narrative structure, therefore, getting to "the truth" entailed strenuous efforts, but not everyone could overcome such difficulties. Consequently, hardships and sacrifices functioned as barriers in a process of natural selection of sorts that ensured that only those who are genuinely worthy would reach an epiphany. Simply put, by relating their perils, narrators were constructing their exceptionalism.

Adventists' concerns, therefore, were embroiled in larger discussions that were taking place in living rooms and study halls across America from the 1880s to the 1920s. In this regard, Adventists shared white America's middle-class values and cultural attitudes. Moreover, by the dawn of the twentieth century, Adventists had also developed theological commonalities with mainline Protestantism, specifically regarding justification, righteousness by faith, and salvation. Indeed, it was their position on these topics that were part of an answer to a much larger question: what is Christian about Seventh-day Adventism? From the Great Disappointment up to the mid-1880s,

Sacrifices and Experiences

Seventh-day Adventism was busy articulating its distinctive doctrines. During this period, particular Adventist teachings about the Seventh-day Sabbath, the heavenly sanctuary, the third angel's message, and conditional immortality crystallized. From the mid-1880s to the end of World War I, Adventists' focus shifted to topics such as justification, righteousness by faith, and atonement. Broadly, during those years, Adventists stood at a crossroad: either follow a relatively unique understanding of justification that stressed obedience to God's laws or move toward the wider mainline Protestant understanding of it.[20] With the support of Ellen White, the second option prevailed. One of its main advocates, Elder Waggoner, commented that his view brought Adventism "a step nearer the faith of the great Reformers from the days of Paul to the days of Luther and Wesley."[21] Adventists' "Protestant" views of sacrifice were therefore grounded in cultural norms as well as in certain parts of Adventist theology.

But what did sacrifice entail for missionaries? Or, to put it differently, how were abstract ideas about sacrifice put into practice in the Andean highlands, and what were their social and political implications? Sacrifice could of course mean martyrdom, and some missionaries, or their family members, did meet death in the field. Although this was not uncommon, especially in places where medical aid was limited, it did represent the extreme and most tragic manifestation of sacrifice. On most days missionaries' sacrifices and sufferings were much more mundane and much less heroic. They included the predicaments of travel, the tedious daily encounters with foreign bureaucracy, and, for those who lived in remote areas such as the department of Puno, Peru, settling for basic living conditions.[22] Material comfort was one of the most salient sacrifices made by the missionaries stationed in the highlands. Although Adventists faced special difficulties obtaining white-collar employment, they shared the same material aspirations and consumption patterns that characterized this class. The Adventist week put religious limitations on production much more than it dictated unique forms of consumption, as is the case in Judaism.[23] Intriguingly, in the high Andes, where Saturday did not restrict production and no one had to "sacrifice their jobs," middle-class commodities were put on the altar.

Comforts on the Altar: Middle-Class Material Culture as Sacrifice

The year 1917 introduced a sense of insecurity in Frank Varney's life. Varney, a twenty-four-year-old bachelor and one of the few missionaries who entered the field unmarried, was now awaiting the arrival of his fiancée. Aside from securing her travel arrangements and safety, he seemed to be preoccupied with the kind of living arrangements, particularly material ones, that he would be able to provide for his future bride in the field: "Now comes the question about what furniture you will allow her to bring," he wrote to the General Conference of the Seventh-day Adventist Church. "It is hard to judge from what others have brought just what is the policy of the General Conference. . . . I sent Pearce a list of a few things that we will need; some of the furniture she already had, and I trust you will feel free in arranging for her to bring the same along with her. I do not expect to furnish a house like I would if I lived in the States, but I do want to have everything as comfortable as possible."[24]

Using the term "comfort" to describe material living standards, as Varney does, was relatively new. For centuries, comfort "had primarily referred to moral, emotional, spiritual, and political support in difficult circumstances."[25] It is only from the beginning of the eighteenth century onward, especially in the Anglo-American world, that the word had come to suggest a type of material well-being found in a space between "necessity" and "luxury."[26] By the first decades of the nineteenth century, the aspiration toward material comfort had become, as the French philosopher Alexis de Tocqueville observed, a central feature of the U.S. middle class.[27] The idea of comfort set apart the middle classes from those believed to be "uncomfortable," namely the working class and the elites.[28] The first were uncomfortable because of their physical living conditions, and the latter, due to their constant attempts to maintain a social facade.[29] Comfort, therefore, tied middle-class consumption patterns to wider notions of respectability and moral values.

Gender also played an important role, since the arrival of white women to overseas colonies also contributed to setting the standard for respectable living.[30]

Thus, for missionaries, living without "the conveniences of the States" and overcoming "the longing for physical comforts" did not simply mean adapting to conditions in the Andes.[31] The meaning of this act ran deeper, pointing to the kind of sacrifices that the mission field required: leaving behind the material well-being to which their new middle-class position supposedly entitled them and accepting reduced conditions. Belle Wilcox, Harry Wilcox's wife, for example, pondered aloud if the two would be living in a bamboo hut without electricity once in the field.[32] Her exotic fantasies, sure enough, reek of a kind of orientalism, particularly since she and her husband were moving from the small frontier town of Clovis, New Mexico, to the city of Lima. However, her imagining also exposes the general convention that proselytizing required significant compromises, in this case regarding living conditions. Hence, although missionaries had published reports about their lives in South American cities, and while information about conditions in different parts of the field was available, images of life in one of Lima's upper-class neighborhoods were not the first that came to mind. Rather, forsaking modernity, living instead in a basic, even primitive way, was the image that came to mind.

Self-denial, in this case manifested through material compromises, attested to the missionary's moral standing. Hence, paradoxically for young Seventh-day Adventists, reaching occupational white-collar status by becoming a professional missionary, meant choosing to forgo some of the material benefits that were supposed to accompany this status. Achieving social mobility through the Adventist Church was therefore complex and contradictory. While secular occupations offered social prestige as well as a higher living standard, a missionary career offered the former but not necessarily the latter. In other words, although social mobility was an outcome of missionary work, the benefits could hardly be reduced to that, as missionaries' spiritual commitments often undermined their prospective gains.

Thus, Varney, by now impatiently waiting for his fiancée, could not expect his home to be as it would have been in the States, nor could he, for that matter, complain about it. What he could do was attempt to make the best of the existing circumstances or, as he put it, have "everything as comfortable as possible."[33] Yet, as Varney's words imply, a degree of comfort was necessary, and no one could expect him to live in completely unsuitable conditions. Ignorant of the General Conference's policy on furniture but assuming no one would possibly expect him to live without any, he openly inquires about it. Other missionaries believed that the General Conference would cover, or at the very least participate in, furnishing costs.[34] Sacrifice had its limits, and apparently it did not mean living without a table and chairs.

Yet, one cannot but wonder why missionaries were prepared to live without Western medical care, but no missionary could possibly imagine his home without furniture, his children sleeping on the floor, and his wife preparing meals over a fire. After all, missionaries and, on occasion, their wives spent months out of the year away from home, wandering around the open lands, sleeping on the cold ground, and cooking outdoors. They regularly huddled together with natives and farm animals while visiting faraway mission posts or canvassing among prospective converts.[35] They were, undoubtedly, able to get along without furniture; they were even quite proud of it, relating their experiences outdoors to emphasize commitment to the cause as well as manifest a kind of "manliness," extinct in places conquered by cities, industries, and bureaucracy.[36] Yet, furnishing a home was one of the missionaries' top priorities and usually their first relatively large consumer transaction.

The importance of furniture was connected to the separation of the "home" from what "lay beyond it," which was prevalent in Victorian-era America.[37] Stepping out of the front door, missionaries, already stationed in secluded areas, entered the realm of the unknown and uncultivated, where animals reigned and courtesy and culture were left behind. Once outdoor endeavors were concluded and missionaries returned home, they reunited with civilization; home had become a civil outpost amid the uncivilized.[38] The process of civilization, as Norbert Elias argues, consists of creating a distance from "animal"-like behavior.

The fact was, as Orley Ford obliquely stated, that some missionaries were willing to do practically anything to avoid sleeping among Indians: "If it is your lot to sleep there [in an Indian home] you must lay down with a dozen Indians and a half dozen dogs and more flees, lice and other varmints. . . . If you should be able to doze off you would probably be awakened before long by the snout of one of the Peruvian razorback hogs rutting you in the face. . . . There is never such a thing as a chair or a table."[39]

Packed in small huts, sleeping on the ground, barn animals breathing into his face—so far from "civilization"—Ford was clearly "uncomfortable." The racial dimension here is so salient that it is almost banal: the white man, in danger of contamination by the dark man and his dirty habits, never lets down his guard. Uncomfortable indeed. Equally conspicuous was the sexual aspect of a sleepover where everyone, including animals, shared a common space. Scholars have already suggested that the compartmentalization of middle-class homes into separate rooms, according to activities, was rooted in notions of "respectability" and intended to control sexuality.[40] Beds, in this regard, played a particularly important role, demarcating a precise and permanent place of sleep for different family members and prospective guests. In a sense, they served as a kind of surveillance tool, putting order into sleeping arrangements, making any attempt to move around or change one's sleeping location just a little more complicated. In other words, they set men apart from the ground and the wrong pillow partners.

It is easy to imagine, therefore, why Orley Ford felt so much more comfortable in the house of "one of the best to do men in Puno," where he and his wife were shown their room.[41] This man's house, as he describes it, did not "compare very well with an American house, but was very comfortable and had lots of very nice furniture."[42] Thus, professing bluntly his U.S.-centrism, Ford proclaims that not only did the house fail to live up to U.S. standards, it could not even be considered "American." From a cultural perspective, Peru was not in America. Yet, even so, it was a comfortable home. In fact, it was "very comfortable."

Ford's words evidence a clear correlation between the quantity of furniture and the degree of comfort: a home with no furniture was uncomfortable and a home with "lots of nice furniture" was "very comfortable." The first was a hut, providing very basic, animal-like conditions. The second provided suitable accommodation and respectable surroundings, even if it did not completely live up to U.S. standards. Furthermore, Ford's comment is especially interesting, as it implies that comfort was not uniquely tied to the United States nor did a product have to be produced in the United States to be comfortable. Certain "things" could fall below U.S. standards but still be considered comfortable. In this regard, although created in the English-speaking Atlantic, comfort had gained a life of its own, breaking out of national borders and undermining U.S.-centric attitudes.

Finally, when it came to notions of comfort, the interior carried more weight than the exterior. In 1916 Clinton Achenbach and his wife, Minnie, were sent from the main Adventist station in Platería to open a new station in the nearby Peninsula. The convoy that escorted them to their new home must have been a spectacle for local and foreign onlookers: a few men carrying an organ on two poles, one Indian with a rocking chair tied to his back, another carrying parts of a bed, and yet another, lamps and other appliances. At the rearguard, walking slowly, were two donkeys carrying mattresses and other bedding. Once they arrived, the furniture was unloaded and arranged in what was, in Achenbach's words, "a genuine Indian hut, but is far better than most of the houses of the Indians. It belongs to the Indian Chief of this section. It is a mud hut . . . and has a mud floor; but we have covered that with matting."[43] In other words, missionaries could live in an Indian hut, but they could not live in it *like* Indians, with a mud floor or without furniture. As the interior asserted notions of domesticity, it was what made the home respectable and hence could not be compromised upon.[44]

Yet, even a covered floor and a room full of furniture were not enough to make an Indian house respectable, and the Achenbachs had to make sure their friends and family in the States knew that it was "far better" than an ordinary Indian hut. What made it so much better? The only distinguishing characteristic mentioned in Achenbach's letter is ownership: the house belonged to an "Indian Chief"; since he was not an average

Indian, neither was his house. Perhaps the missionaries were referring to a supposedly superior economic status this Indian had, which would have enabled him to provide them with better living conditions. Yet references to the status of this residence also relate to historical and philosophical notions that date back to ancient Greece and associate politics with the capacity for reason and divide between the civilized and barbarians.[45] An Indian who attained a certain political standing in his community would be considered less animal-like than others; his social and political standing (or at least, what the missionaries understood his status to be) added to the house's prestige. The missionaries, therefore, claimed to be "very comfortably situated" in their new home despite the inferior living conditions.[46]

Paradoxically, similar notions associating comfort with respectability led missionaries to wander about the highlands in clothes that appeared to be anything but comfortable. Seventh-day Adventist missionaries—who were relatively tolerant about what neophytes chose to wear—were conservative concerning their own wardrobe and remained loyal to a Western dress code. Once more, the racial component played a prominent part— Indian clothes, even if clean, were still only appropriate for Indians. Furthermore, progress was woven into the missionaries' imported and ready-made suits and underclothes. As children growing up in the plains and prairies of the Midwest, in the 1880s and 1890s, perhaps some missionaries still dressed in homespun clothing. However, most dressed in ready-made clothes. With the advance of industrialism and mass production, homemade clothes became a thing of the past, representing the rural, underdeveloped farm life that people, and the nation, had left behind.[47] For young white-collar men, it had become "imperative not to look like some poor country person living on $300 a year. . . . The man who did not manifest progress in his sartorial habits was marked."[48] As a part of these larger trends, missionaries ascribed to a new dress code and fashions as well, preferring the ready-made over the homespun. Nevertheless, the fact was that they were stationed in a rural area, commuting by horse or mule rather than by train; walking in open areas and muddy ground, rather than paved sidewalks; engaging in agricultural tasks alongside paperwork. Their lives were everything that, in their appearance, they presumed to have left behind, but it was in this attire that they felt most comfortable. Thus, even though their wardrobe had few practical benefits, missionaries continued to dress, more or less, as other white-collar men.[49] Some things simply could not be sacrificed.

In sum, in keeping with prevalent discourse, sacrifice was an essential part of missionaries' identity and the means through which they constructed their own exceptionalism. From their perspective, evangelization was not meant for everyone; most would prove unable to carry its burden. In a kind of Darwinist manner, they would drop out, and only a few, those who were truly strong in spirit, would survive and prove themselves to be true light bearers. Nevertheless, there was a limit to what even the most dedicated man could bear. No man could live like those whom he had come to redeem. No missionary could conduct his life too close to the earth, living and dressing like an Indian. Moreover, had a missionary been found sitting on the ground, wearing old, homespun clothing, resembling an Indian just a little too much—"going native"—something had gone wrong.[50] Sacrifice, in this sense, was something to take pride in, but at the same time, it must be embraced with caution. An invisible, often pliable line distinguished a dedicated missionary from a lost soul.

In broader terms, stories of unselfish sacrifice and self-denial help set a standard for what was considered a modest, yet acceptable, material standard of living and differentiate it from what were completely unsuitable conditions. In this regard, the missionaries' stories disseminated through a wide range of church publications contributed to the construction of class, particularly the middle class and lower class, by defining the material well-being associated with each of these. If living without certain commodities was worthy of praise, if it deserved heavenly rewards, then this was no ordinary compromise. Furthermore, by describing life without these goods as a sacrifice, missionaries accentuated the essentiality of these "things," legitimizing their purchase to the readers back home. As a corollary, people who could not afford these items were considered poor and hapless.

Within the Adventist context, the relationship between sacrifice and middle-class material culture illuminates the tension between Seventh-day Adventism's unique characteristics and the ones it shared with other Protestant denominations. On the one hand, observing Saturday instead of Sunday impeded the entrance of devoted Adventists into the new middle-class secular professions and "pushed" them toward a career in the Adventist Church. On the other hand, missionaries' ideas about sacrifice, which correlated with wider Protestant tendencies and Victorian values, contributed toward the consolidation of middle-class consumption patterns. Paradoxically, Adventists contributed to the "moral imperative around which the northern middle class became a class" while limiting the Adventist Church members' ability to actually be employed in the new professions that were considered "middle class" professions.[51] In Puno, the fact that missionaries viewed certain middle-class commodities as necessary for a basic living standard had a particular implication: it shaped the way they interpreted Andean material culture. Although missionaries were aware of Andean racial hierarchies and able to make precise observations about them, they tended to misinterpret the cultural value attached to commodities, creating at times a sense of disproportionate sacrifice, and even of deprivation, among themselves.

Luxury or Comfort? The Meaning of Things in the Andes

Upon arriving at the mission field, missionaries hurried out to the markets and commercial houses in search of the goods they needed.[52] As required by their mission, they consumed modestly, only looking for those few goods that were necessary for living decently: a bed, a kitchen cabinet, a closet. Yet, they soon discovered that they could scarcely live on their earnings and that even modesty was expensive. Carefully broaching the topic with the General Conference in 1914, William Pohle, at the time stationed in La Paz, wrote: "We are having financial struggles here in La Paz. Bro. Stahl and his wife were drawing

$20 a week here . . . and they could scarcely live, the mission paying part of their rent. . . . The Union is paying me $17."[53]

Taking Pohle's observations at face value, one might be inclined to believe that missionaries were simply underpaid. Perhaps the General Conference was even taking advantage of their dedication and demanding unreasonable self-denial and sacrifice. Nevertheless, a meticulous examination reveals a much more complex picture. In absolute terms, missionaries earned relatively well, in comparison to what U.S. white-collar professionals were earning at the beginning of the twentieth century and, obviously, local middle classes. Seventeen to twenty dollars a week, an average of $960 a year, was no small amount in either place. In the United States, for example, an average male clerk working in Boston at the beginning of the twentieth century would have made $9.76 a week. If this man then decided to try his fortune in Pittsburgh, he would enjoy a raise, now earning $11 a week. Acquiring some expertise and experience also brought about an increase in salaries. Bookkeepers, for instance, who were among the best paid clerical workers, made an average of $9 a week.[54] An important comparison to make, since missionaries also engaged in medical work, is that physicians at the turn of the century earned an average of $730 a year in the city and $1,200 in the country, or about $15–$25 a week.[55] In other words, missionaries' salaries placed them in the upper sectors of the middle class, together with the more educated and experienced members of the new middle class. In this regard, the Adventist Church offered competitive wages that fit missionaries' level of education.

Turning to the Andes, missionaries' incomes exceeded by three to five times the salary of an upper-middle-class, well-paid Peruvian clerk. For example, Juan Antonio Rouillón, a high-level employee at the Compañía Recaudadora de Impuestos, a half-private, half-public tax collection agency, earned about 100 *libras peruanas*, or LP (1,000 soles), a month, equivalent to approximately US$20–$25.[56] This was more or less the amount that Stahl earned in a week or ten days. It was also equivalent to the church funding that Alvin Allen requested for Father Toalino, the Catholic priest who was considering converting—a sum that did not include living expenses, as the former priest was to live with Allen and his family. Compared with low-level white-collar workers, missionaries' monthly salaries could be forty or even fifty times higher. In this regard, Camacho, earning $8 a month, was well paid, even if he earned considerably less than U.S. missionaries.[57]

In comparison with peasants in Puno, missionaries were, of course, making a fortune. Yet what is even more interesting is that they were not running too much behind the income of some haciendas (and in some cases, they perhaps even surpassed that income). In 1909 hacienda Picotani in the Azángaro Province had net revenue of 7,500 soles (750 LP), meaning roughly $150 a year.[58] It would be a mistake to reach conclusions about the hacienda's economic output solely from cash income. Barter, reciprocal commitments, peonage, and forced labor were a crucial part of a hacienda's overall economic standing. As foreigners, missionaries incurred expenses that the hacienda did not concern itself with. Missionaries did not have the same kind of networks and had to resort to cash payments in places where locals relied on other kinds of transactions. For example, Stahl commented that one of the reasons for their high expenses was not just the high tariffs but also the agents, the people who delivered the goods. Local authorities, by contrast, enjoyed the free service of a *propio*, a position within the politico-religious hierarchy whose duties included deliveries.[59] The Andes was not an open labor market, and finding available working hands was hard for anyone, even more so for unwanted foreigners. Hiring such workers was therefore costly. The economic significance of reciprocal networks, therefore, surpassed in many cases that of revenue. Due to these dynamics, statistics documenting income cannot be juxtaposed simplistically. Even so, a rough comparison between missionaries' earnings and their surroundings does provide us with a general impression of where missionaries stood vis-à-vis other people in the Andes.

Although missionaries were far from underpaid, and while their followers lived on much less, they still found life in the Altiplano to be an economic burden. The problem, however, stemmed not from the amount of money they made but rather from its purchasing power. The fact was that items missionaries considered to be essential, those they could not sacrifice in the name of the cause, were either out of their reach or very expensive. As Curtis Varney explains, "An ordinary bed here that would not cost more than $20 in the states, will cost about $50. An oil stove that you could buy in the States for about not more than $20, will cost . . . $45 in American money."[60] Similarly, Orley Ford observed that "there is nothing we have in the U.S. that you cannot have here if you have a long pocketbook. . . . It is very expensive to live as we would in the States, and our workers here do not even try to—but they are fixed up quite comfortable."[61]

From the missionaries' vantage point, they were not seeking luxury, nor were they attempting to live "as they would in the States." Becoming a missionary entailed a sacrifice, as we have seen, and as missionaries seemed to have accepted this as an inherent part of their mission, they therefore "do not even try" to change their circumstances. They did try to achieve a basic degree of comfort, the "ordinary," that would allow them to maintain respectability. Nevertheless, missionaries tended to treat commodities in absolute terms, ignoring the fact that what was "ordinary" in the United States was hardly "ordinary" in a place where the majority of the population slept in beds made of earth. Missionaries misinterpreted the social value attached to certain goods, treating them as the overpriced necessities that they were for them rather than the luxuries that they had become in the local context.

An abundance of imported goods had been circulating in different regions of the Andean countries from the beginning of the nineteenth century.[62] There was also a growing market for these items as a result of the burgeoning ranks of white-collar *empleados*. Imported items, especially clothing, were crucial for the Peruvian middle class as they attempted, like their counterparts in other places across the globe, to construct respectability or decency as they understood it.[63] Due to the limited transportation infrastructure and the small market for imported goods, the Altiplano lagged behind. Nonetheless, by the late nineteenth century, things began to rapidly change as a result of the railroad (1873) and the soaring demand for wool.[64]

Sacrifices and Experiences

Thus, by the time missionaries arrived in Puno in the 1910s, they found shelves stocked with a relatively wide variety of foreign goods. While peasants purchased cheap imported clothes or specific items such as scissors or a shovel, most goods were consumed by local elites. Commodities that were considered "ordinary" in Europe or the United States, such as beer and ham, were enthusiastically purchased by the upper classes.[65] Luis Valcárcel testifies that members of Cuzco's elite bought items that were considered luxurious and ranged from liquors and perfumes to expensive fabrics and jewelry, consuming them on special occasions.[66] Imported furniture played a similar role, although, due to its size and weight, it was not introduced into high-class parlors until the early twentieth century, after the railway reached Cuzco. Once unloaded from the train, however, furniture quickly became fashionable and a "must" for any self-respecting family.[67]

Puno, on the other hand, had been accessible by train for more than three decades. Yet, according to Orley Ford, even in 1918 furniture was "out of sight and generally of inferior quality."[68] Unlike Cuzco's elite, Puneños did not seem to be quite so taken with the idea of acquiring a French commode or an English armchair. Perhaps the lack of enthusiasm for foreign furniture had to do with the fact that Puno's elite was relatively new, made up of men who had only recently become hacienda owners and had little connection to any traditional aristocracy.[69] Additionally, Puno's hacienda owners were acquainted with, not to say integrated into, Indian communal life, and their networks among the Indians, as we have seen, were essential to their social and economic standing. Thus, while they reacted harshly against Indians who had "crossed the lines" by adopting Western dress, local elites also had to be careful with how their own consumption patterns could be perceived. Symbolically, ostentatious demonstrations of Western fashion could increase social distance to an extent that would undermine long-standing reciprocal relations.[70] In practical terms, consumption was embedded in local reciprocity, and furnishing a room thus entailed hiring local artisans.[71] Purchasing mass-produced furniture did not fit into this scheme and was potentially harmful to reciprocity.

It is perhaps for this reason that Ford saw little furniture on display while strolling down the streets of Puno. His comment, however, is perplexing, as it is quite difficult to understand how he could possibly assess the quality of commodities that were "out of sight." Most likely it was imported goods, especially those manufactured in the United States that could not be found in Puno, and local goods that he believed to be inferior.[72] But despite elites' reluctance to purchase imported furniture and Ford's disregard for locally produced goods, we have already met one man who owned furniture that *was* up to Ford's standards: "the well to do man in Puno" who had "lots of very nice furniture." While recognizing that this man was a member of the upper classes in Puno, Ford, as we shall recall, describes his material well-being in terms of comfort rather than luxury, tying his host to the middle class rather than upper-class elites. In this regard, the social and cultural meaning of things stayed the same. Even missionaries' own complaints regarding the high prices of presumably middle-class items did not change the symbolic value ascribed to these items. Nor did it change the basic assumption that these goods were meant for the middle class rather than people with deeper pockets.

To complicate this issue even further, missionaries did find a group of people whom they labeled middle class: "The Spanish people make up the highest class, as doctors, lawyers and officials and are very well to do," Stahl observed.[73] While "the cholos," which Stahl describes as "mixed people" in the biological sense, "are largely artisans, and could well be called the middle class; while the Indians are the laborers and the roustabouts—the poorest class."[74]

While modern scholars might debate whether a cholo artisan could be described as middle class, missionaries viewed them as such and not without reason. Accurately pointing to the interplay between race and class, Stahl describes the caste-like system that characterized the Andes, in which "mix-race" ranked higher than Indians.[75] Notwithstanding his categorization, it is very doubtful that Stahl, who had sent away for U.S.-manufactured clothes and furniture, would be willing to live the middle-class life of a cholo or anything similar. Both Stahl and

Ford did not apply their analysis of local society to themselves. They did not conclude, for example, that owning an oil stove in the Andes would put them among the elites. Thus, on the one hand, missionaries were able to analyze the local social structure. On the other hand, it made no difference to the value they ascribed to material commodities or to their self-perception as people engaged in ongoing sacrifice and self-denial.

Furthermore, missionaries assumed that Indians believed them to be rich, commenting, "Although all the people [missionaries] have very simple houses but to the Indians, they are the grandest palaces. They like to come and even look in."[76] Missionaries had recognized the deep material gap between themselves and the vast majority of the local population. But the missionaries believed that the Indians were misinterpreting their economic status. In the eyes of the missionaries, it was the Indians who mistakenly thought missionaries to be extremely rich, living in grand palaces, rather than the simple homes they owned. The symbolic essence of commodities, therefore, did not change even though missionaries recognized that tables, beds, and ovens were not consumed in the same manner or by the same class of people as they were in the United States. In a sense, missionaries were living in two places at once: in their host countries and their place of origin, and sacrifice was conceptualized as what one could have "there," back at home, but does not have "here," in the mission field. By the same token, the cultural essentialism of material artifacts enhanced the commonalities between North American missionaries. Looking to the northeastern and midwestern new middle class, they shared an understanding as to what each missionary, no matter his or her denomination, had sacrificed for God and the salvation of humanity.

Furthermore, while missionaries may have addressed their needs mostly in terms of the new concept of comfort associated with middle-class identity, race played a decisive role as well. Race was a major criterion for comparisons and a way to justify differences in standards of living or access to funds. Hence, while no white Seventh-day Adventist teacher would be expected to live in a home with a dirt floor, for an Indian teacher it was deemed to be sufficient.[77] On the one hand, missionaries could not sacrifice so much as to be reduced to Indian living standards. On the other hand, an Indian, no matter how civilized, was still an Indian and as such could spend his life close to the earth. Race set different standards, one for a brown, cholo member of the middle class and another for white foreign men. Conversion, in this regard, may have turned an Indian into a civilized Indian, but it did not turn brown into white. Missionaries often belittled Andean elites, too, making condescending remarks that disregarded factors such as education and social prestige.[78]

Discipline, Obedience, and Sacrifice

While living in the field altered missionaries' material life significantly, it did provide opportunities to maintain some middle-class comforts or even elevate their living standards. One area in which this is salient is that of domestic service. Missionaries often hired local Indians to help with housekeeping. Employing domestic service was a crucial element of elite life and a status symbol in Latin America dating from the colonial era.[79] In the United States, the idea of domestic service was relatively new, emerging in the late nineteenth century and strongly tied to the increase in immigration, urbanization, and the growth of a new middle class. With the outbreak of World War I and the soaring demand for women's working hands in factories, domestic service plummeted, and modes of employment of domestic workers changed, often shifting from a live-in mode to a live-out mode. It was still, however, a prevalent and important part of new middle-class lives.[80]

Hiring domestic workers was a common practice and not something anyone with the missionaries' level of income and social standing would necessarily view as a luxury. Nevertheless, missionaries often seemed uncomfortable admitting that they had hired help, apologetically claiming that they were so busy with their religious duties and that they had no choice.[81] At least in part, missionaries' uneasiness with the idea of domestic service stemmed from the values associated with the old middle class in which "help" was usually of a more egalitarian mode and the "helper," a neighbor or family friend.[82] Yet, the uneasiness also stemmed from the notion of sacrifice and the fact that missionaries were expected to live without such comforts. To live up to expectations, missionaries tended to depict the presence of an "untrained" and uncivilized domestic servant as a demanding mission in itself: "When the potatoes were finished . . . the Indian girl was greatly puzzled about what to do with the grease left in the skillet. Finally, she settled the matter by dumping it on the floor . . . so [Belle Wilcox's] work of teaching the simplest tasks continued."[83] Thus, rather than providing immediate relief from house chores, the Indians first proved to be additional work and in need of training. Employing them, teaching them about "our ways," was therefore made to fit into the larger civilizational narrative.[84] Having domestic help was not about missionaries' comfort, as it was for the new middle class in the United States, but was discussed as a way of uplifting the Indians, and part of the exacting chores of missionaries. Ferdinand Stahl had even written to the General Conference, complaining, "Another thing I have found out as far as my family and I are concerned we cannot buy much from the States as we are under too heavy expense here. For years, Mrs. Stahl and I have taken in natives to train even paying them some so that they could get clothes, etc. We have no allowance here for this part of the work and have felt that this was important."[85]

In his own eyes, Stahl was not even employing domestic service but rather "training natives"; the fact that the training included housework was irrelevant. The money he paid them, therefore, was not compensation for work but almost a kind of charity, given to the Indians so they could buy clothes. Further, rather than removing part of the workload, having Indians in the Stahl's household was portrayed as an economic burden for the family, which now could not purchase essential commodities, sacrificing perhaps just a little too much. Missionaries had therefore converted comforts (the household help) into inconveniences and presented them as part of their sacrifices for the cause. In the field, employing domestic staff was no longer a practice through which one identified as a member of the new middle class and asserted their white-collar status; it had become a manifestation of religious dedication and was implemented to help save souls. As a result of the strong social convention relating to the sacrificing missionary, it had become illegitimate to maintain certain comforts in the field. Furthermore, and perhaps more significantly, the requirement to conform to such an ideal made it difficult to discuss certain issues without risking admonition and losing face. After all, no one wanted to be seen as a failure or as one who did "not run well," in the words of Elder Maxwell.

Bringing up complaints regarding material conditions, for instance, was a delicate manner. It was not taboo, and missionaries often discussed it, but it had to be done in a specific way. Missionaries always weighed their words carefully to avoid being perceived as unworthy for the field: "We are having financial struggles here in La Paz. Just today, I wrote to bro. Westphal about the matter of wages. Something will have to be done if they wish to keep us here in Bolivia. . . . I might call your attention to other workers, but do not care to worry you about these matters. I know that all the workers in South America are not on equal footing. What can be done, I do not know but I felt that I ought to say something about how we feel."[86]

In communicating his situation to the General Conference, William Pohle showed ambivalence: at first glance, he rather confidently stated that wages would have to improve in order to keep the mission going in La Paz. But just a few sentences below, his firmness gives way to appeasement, and he does not claim to have answers or, more important, he does not put forward direct demands to the authorities. Pohle, therefore, ends up simply raising the issue. Frank Varney, while corresponding over the issue of his prospective furniture, had a similar attitude: requesting help to make his home "as comfortable as possible" but refraining from stating any clear demands or expectations. The entire issue, a very intimate aspect of life—the building of a home—was left to the "good judgment" of those sitting in faraway Michigan.[87]

Such a stance, of course, was enmeshed with general notions of politeness, as well as respect for authority and the policies

Sacrifices and Experiences

decided upon by the Adventist Church's governing bodies. In general, missionaries did not want to be perceived as rebellious or disrespectful. Notwithstanding the importance of etiquette, the idea of sacrifice limited missionaries' ability to broach issues concerning their material conditions. As missionaries were supposed to do without comforts, any questions about such comfort put one's image at risk, as they might be seen by colleagues or superiors as unfit or, worse, unworthy. Moreover, one's work and the threat to quit, the most important element that a worker could leverage in any negotiation with employers, diminished in power when it came to missionaries. Leaving the field was nothing like leaving a job; it was tantamount to acknowledging defeat, manifesting unworthiness, failing the cause; it meant returning to one's community of brothers as a failure. Resigning because a missionary could not overcome his yearnings for comforts and conveniences was an even greater shame. Such social sanctions had to be taken into consideration.

Nevertheless, not everyone succumbed, and the few, like Bro. Amundsen in La Paz, who had made demands and threatened to leave the field, were quickly reprimanded:

> Now, bro. Amundsen, I want to speak a few words to you regarding your suggested resignation in case the rate of wage which you stipulated is not paid. It may be that you do not mean this as strongly as indicated in your letter. We appreciate that you have made a sacrifice in going to the mission field and necessarily expect to put up with inconveniences and losses which would not be yours in the homeland. This is the experience of our missionaries world around. It is not good for a young man to assume that attitude towards the governing committee where he is working. . . . In the meantime, we sincerely hope you will hold steady in your work. . . . We are counting on loyal workers, there, every man, to stand by his post and do his part. In some way I believe the Lord's spirit will guide and direct you in the future as he has in the past, to lean heavily upon him believing that though you cannot understand the treatment which you have received you will hold on to the work.[88]

Bro. Amundsen's sacrifice, as is clear, did not give him any grounds to argue for higher wages. It was part of being a missionary; it definitely did not give him the right to threaten to leave the field. Even if unsatisfied or experiencing economic distress, this young man was expected to "stand by his post," and never succumb to the difficulties and contribute to the dissemination of the message. In other words, Amundsen was to follow in the footsteps of Jesus Christ. Specifically, he was to follow an image of Christ that had become popular at the end of the nineteenth century: the muscular Jesus. Tenaciously tied to the industrialization and corporatization of the United States, muscular Jesus was an entrepreneur and a leader. This Jesus decisively overcame setbacks and hardships in pursuit of his lofty goal, and so should Amundsen. There was nothing "Adventist" about this image, and it was common to mainline Protestantism and inherent to the Student Volunteer Movement's perception of Christ and his mission.[89] In other words, the General Conference admonished Amundsen for not living up to prevalent Protestant perceptions of Christ.

The General Conference had an obvious interest in keeping as many missionaries as possible in the field for as long as possible. First, since the General Conference had decided on placement, a man who was quick to leave the field reflected poorly on them. Second, a missionary leaving the field was an economic loss, since the General Conference participated in travel expenses, primary living expenses, and so forth. It also meant that the General Conference would now have to spend time and money searching for a replacement. Training a new missionary for the foreign field took time and demanded resources from others stationed in that field. Simply put, the General Conference and mission superintendents in the field all had an interest in ensuring that missionaries stayed in the field. Social stigmas, the idea that a person was a failure if he did not overcome the difficulties of the foreign field, helped keep missionaries in their posts.

In practice, of course, missionaries still asked to leave the field, yet to avoid sanctions they usually based their request on other grounds: "Lawrence will be 18 years old and Ernest will be 16 lacking a few months. We would like to place them in one of our schools where they could work some to help pay their

Sacrifices and Experiences

expenses. We are not asking to return because we are dissatisfied or care to leave the field, but because we feel like we ought to place our boys where they may have better school advantages for a few years."[90]

In 1915, after nearly eight years in South America, William Pohle asked for a furlough of a few months in the United States. It was not an uncommon request, and missionaries did return to the United States for vacations after an extended time in the field. Yet, even so, Pohle seems apologetic, emphasizing that his request is unrelated to his terms of service. The point here is not whether or not he was in fact content with his post. What is important is that he obliquely stated that the entire issue of "satisfaction" was irrelevant.

Pohle believed it possible that someone in the General Conference would think that his reason for departing the field, even for a short time, had to do with conditions. Since he wished to avoid any such perception, he turned the spotlight toward another, completely different direction—his children's education. Pursuing a proper Seventh-day Adventist education for children, making sure they would be fully prepared as faithful Seventh-day Adventist adults, so it seems, was considered a much more justifiable reason to leave the field than "dissatisfaction." In this regard, we are presented once more with the limits of sacrifice: sacrificing the material well-being typical of the new middle class was one thing, but sacrificing the entrance card into the ranks of the white-collar class, not to mention the younger generation's spiritual well-being, was another.

Missionaries, therefore, had to portray themselves as if they were giving up too much. Through such a maneuver, they attempted to achieve their goals without jeopardizing their position or exposing themselves to disciplinary measures. In doing so, however, missionaries enhanced the General Conference's authority over the idea of sacrifice. The final word concerning its "limits" was left in the hands of those sitting miles away from the field. Furthermore, missionaries were also exposed to various kinds of disciplinary measures from their peers in the field. In one notorious case, Edgar Maxwell, as head of the

Inca Union Mission at the time, complained to the General Conference about Stahl and wrote:

> Brother Stahl is owing over 3,200 soles or over $1600 U.S. currency. . . . Bro. Stahl is selling off a lot of furniture and has intimated that he expects to replace it with new goods that he will bring along with him from the States on his return. . . . I am quite sure that Bro. Stahl expects the General Conference to pay the excess or freight and the duties on his new furniture. If such is the case I should like to know it as I would like to get some things myself which I would not get unless the freight would thus be paid.[91]

After spending nine years in the field, Stahl had accumulated a large debt, and in 1918 his economic deficit was a major reason behind a series of conflicts and quarrels in the Titicaca mission. Some missionaries openly demanded his replacement as superintendent of the mission. I will delve deeper into these frictions in the next chapter. For now, it will suffice to discuss Maxwell's reaction to the idea that Stahl was selling old furniture to buy new goods. Why was it that he decided to focus on this issue rather than the circumstances under which Stahl had accumulated such a large debt? Stahl argued that he had covered, out of pocket, certain missionary expenses for years.[92] Perhaps he felt the mission was indebted to him? Why was Maxwell so bothered with the idea that the General Conference should cover Stahl's freight expenses with funds that would not be taken out of the budget allotted the mission? I would like to suggest that Maxwell found the circumstances of the debt no less disturbing than the fact that a man in debt—no matter how long he had served, what sources he put into the work, and what his current living conditions were—would spend money on furniture. Buying new furniture in this context was considered both extravagant and disrespectful toward others, two qualities in conflict with the behavior of a true missionary. This is not to say that there were no justifiable reasons to be unhappy with Stahl's conduct, particularly since others did not receive salaries due to the mission's economic burden. My point here is that consumption was policed by peers, and individuals were expected to behave in a manner that emphasized personal sacrifice rather than comfort.

That Maxwell points a finger at Stahl is, however, particularly noteworthy. Stahl was the most renowned missionary in the field, with a magnitude of converts attesting to his unselfish conduct and true love toward the Indians. He was depicted as a man who was willing to sacrifice all, let alone furniture, for those who followed him into Adventism. Furthermore, his sacrifices, real or imagined, were fruitful: more and more Indians had begun to observe the Sabbath. In 1919 over two hundred of them sent a letter in protest when he was moved out of the Platería mission, and hundreds more "loved their unselfish leader; they followed him, they obeyed him," as another missionary put it.[93] Adventist officials in the highest levels were truly impressed by him and his unprecedented success, earning him the title of "apostle to the Aymara Indians."[94] Contending that he was acting selfishly, preying on the mission, rather than contributing to it, was an attempt to undermine his reputation, to insinuate that perhaps this missionary had not sacrificed all that much, or, simply, that he did not necessarily live up to the ideal of the sacrificing missionary, as had been commonly thought.

Two years after these events, in 1920, Ferdinand Stahl left the Lake Titicaca Indian Mission and pioneered work among the Indigenous peoples of the Amazon region. Nevertheless, accusations against him continued, only now Harry Wilcox, who had come from Lima to take charge of the mission, accused him of being lax about Adventist doctrines. The accusations against Stahl reflect yet again the two main tendencies within Seventh-day Adventism: Maxwell's accusations against Stahl are based on ideals of self-denial and sacrifice that were prevalent among the white middle class and upheld by mainline Protestantism. By contrast, Wilcox's accusations center on what he perceived to be a failure to Seventh-day Adventism. For him, it was not enough that the Indians had left the Catholic Church in favor of those who were interchangeably called Evangelicals, Protestants, and Adventists. Converts also had to be knowledgeable about the unique features of Seventh-day Adventism.

In previous chapters, I discussed how Indians were compelled and coerced into conforming to hegemonic notions of Indian-ness. While the historical conditions and power structure of the ideal of the sacrificing missionary are extremely different, as a method, it functioned similarly. It provided a hegemonic notion as to who could, and who could not, be considered a true bearer of the cause. Men who fit the model, who sacrificed without complaining, yet at the same time kept a respectable home and living standard, were lauded and rewarded. Those who did not, who found that the field demanded too much and were not shy about saying so, were quickly disregarded or reprimanded. Yet, true success in the field, turning sacrifice into yield, was not a matter for missionaries alone. It hinged on their reception. Converting souls required more than the willingness to pay a price for the redemption of another person. It involved creating alliances and networks of support. It required resources and the ability to come to terms quickly with a disparate political environment. Above all, it demanded local cooperation, and the dynamics of relationships that missionaries established with converts, particularly the leaders among them, dictated, in many ways, the successes and failures of the mission.

PART 3

The Mission

8

Building an "Indian" Mission
on the Top of the Andes

FERDINAND STAHL, THE "APOSTLE TO THE AYMARA," CON-
verted to Seventh-day Adventism in 1901. He was twenty-eight
and would be one of the few Puno missionaries who had converted to Seventh-day Adventism as an adult. Although the circumstances of his conversion are unknown, it is known that the
Adventist Church was a path for social and occupational mobility: Stahl had been a steelworker in Milwaukee until 1902, when
he and his wife, Anna, enrolled in a nursing course at Battle
Creek Sanitarium. Afterward, the couple operated in treatment
rooms in Cleveland, and in 1909 they volunteered for the foreign mission field and were sent to La Paz.[1] Tellingly, 1909 was
the year in which Arthur Daniells, the president of the General Conference, established the Medical Missionary Council
as part of a wider reorganization of the Adventist Church, and
thus tied the Adventist medical enterprise to its growing foreign missionary interests.[2]

Once in La Paz, Stahl, his wife Anna, and their two children
settled in the center of the city and offered medical and spiritual care to the city's residents. After a few months, however,
the family decided to leap over a deep social chasm, moving
from the center of the city to the "great Indian neighborhood
called Challapampa."[3] Together with the district of Pura Pura,
Challapampa, today a part of El Alto, was the highest, cold-
est, and the most Indian zone of the city.[4] The Stahls' relocation was, undoubtedly, a statement. They had clearly decided
to focus their evangelizing efforts on the Indians, of whom, in

keeping with the greater narrative of Stahl's memoir, the family had been enamored from the very first day.[5]

The neighborhood's residents were not particularly impressed by the new people next door. While there were a few positive and negative encounters between the Stahls and the Indians, the couple's presence had little impact in garnering converts.[6] Nonetheless, their experiences in the area, together with Ferdinand Stahl's travels to other parts of Bolivia and Peru, turned what was a general tendency toward "Indian work" to a conclusive decision that informed missionary policy: "The persons that work for the Indians cannot work for the Spanish people," Ferdinand Stahl reported to the General Conference. "The Spanish people do not like it[;] when I returned from Puno, people here in La Paz found out that I had treated Indians and they did not want treatments from me, they look down upon the Indians very much, and still they do not say so in words, it is all in actions."[7]

Stahl had recognized that crossing racial lines in the Andes was no small thing, and the mission would eventually have to choose sides. Missionaries from other denominations were certainly aware of Andean social stratification as well. It is also likely that at times they too chose to side with the Indians over other segments of society. The U.S. Catholic Maryknoll mission in Puno, for example, allied itself with Indians during the 1940s, often at the expense of its relationship with local elites.[8] Nevertheless, in Peru, as in most countries in Latin America, missionaries did not distinguish their work in racial or ethnic terms. They did not identify as an "Indian mission," as Stahl would eventually do in Puno. Rather, they preferred to use geographical terms and appeal to as large a population as possible. Bolivia was unique in this sense. Perhaps due to the location of La Paz, numerous Protestant missions incorporated racial or ethnic terms into their official names. The first to do so were the Canadian Methodists who arrived in 1891 and decided to name their mission "the Bolivian Indian Mission." Other churches followed, including the Seventh-day Adventists.[9]

As it turned out, characterizing the mission as "Indian" was crucial for cooperation between veterans and missionaries.

As long as the Indian converts and the U.S. missionaries, each for their own reasons, envisioned the mission as an "Indian mission," cooperation flourished and the two sides developed a mutual, even if hierarchical, dependence on one another. Once the missionaries decided that the mission would no longer be an "Indian mission," prominent converts, such as Manuel Camacho and Juan Huanca, left or were forced to leave. As a result, the mission's character profoundly changed, even if most converts were still Indians.

The Quest for an Indian Mission

Ferdinand Stahl first became acquainted with Camacho and the Adventists in Chucuito when he, Eduardo Thomann, and Alvin Allen visited the area in late 1909.[10] For almost two years, Stahl frequently crossed the Peruvian-Bolivian border while traveling from La Paz to Puno and back again. Only in 1911 did the General Conference permit him to move the core of his activities to the Peruvian side of the lake permanently. At first, the General Conference suggested that Stahl move from La Paz to the town of Puno, until an adequate home for him and his family would be built in the rural district of Chucuito, where Camacho and the other Adventist Indians lived and studied.[11] Stahl refused. Instead, he and his family moved in with Manuel Camacho and lived in an Indian home with an Indian family until their own house was built. Not every Adventist missionary ended up residing in a room in an Indian home. But all lived in Indian villages rather than nearby towns, thus professing where their racial commitments lay.[12]

Interestingly enough, while the missionaries were settling among the Indians, efforts were made to restrict Indians' presence in provincial towns. Tarma, a prosperous provincial town in the central highlands was known for its colorful market. For as long as anyone could remember, every Sunday, Indians from the countryside would fill the town's main square, selling their produce. By the beginning of the twentieth century, however, voices among the local elites demanded the reordering of the town's space. In the name of progress, hygiene, and public health, the town's political authorities restricted the Indigenous presence in Tarma because they believed that the Indians brought in dirt and disease. In a "proper" town, "decent" people did not live among Indians. Boundaries were set in an attempt to keep each member of society in their "right" place, and missionaries moving in with Indians undermined that attempt.[13] Consequently, missionaries threatened the fragile boundaries of a racial geography in the making. They had also disregarded other types of racial boundaries established to preserve order and social status, leaving bystanders astounded.[14] In doing so, they had manifested a commitment to the Indians that served as a faith-building step in a polarized society.

Notwithstanding the Stahls' authentic fascination with the Indigenous peoples of the high Andes and their sincere intention to help bring them closer to God, they did have additional reasons to focus on the Indians. For one, the upper classes of La Paz, as in Lima, were securely ensconced within the Catholic Church and had little interest in the religious Protestant message.[15] With few exceptions, they chose to either stay within the boundaries of Catholicism, which was historically connected to ideas about decency, or completely leave religious life by "converting" to the popular secular ideologies of the time.[16] In this regard, a "progressive" religion was useful to civilize the Indians but not an actual option for already enlightened men. Secondly, working among the "Spanish people," as Stahl referred to upper-class creoles, created complexities and ambiguities, particularly concerning racial hierarchy, class, and social status.[17] From a white Anglo-Saxon and Protestant perspective, local elites were racially inferior: they were of Spanish descent, a mongrel race of oriental Jews and Muslims, which historically cast doubt on their "European-ness."[18] Throwing the "Indian" element into this racial mixture made elites' claims to whiteness even more problematic. Thirdly, the fact that missionaries came from industrialized and economically advanced nations also contributed to their sense of superiority over local elites.

Yet, while missionaries may have believed themselves to be racially superior, in terms of economic outreach and education, they were in an inferior position. In other words, since class and race overlapped, constructing whiteness vis-à-vis Latin

American elites became complicated and conflicting. Missionaries had moved into the professional new middle class via the Seventh-day Adventist educational system. In general, they had an above-average education, but it did not compare to the university education that Latin American elites had received, sometimes in Europe's finest institutions.[19] In fact, missionaries' professional education was at times belittled by Latin American colleagues in the field, as was the case with nurses pursuing work in La Paz.

Among the Indians, by contrast, missionaries were in a clear position of superiority: white, formally educated, "progressive" foreigners, with access to economic and political resources that were unavailable to Indians. Their high social standing vis-à-vis the Indians reflected on the credibility of their religious messages as they came out of the mouths of men with authority. Becoming a teacher, or even better, a redeemer like Stahl, was much easier from this position than from an inferior, or at the very least conflictive, status, such as that which missionaries had among the elites. Moreover, working among the Indians in meager conditions, literally exposing themselves to death and disease to save "poor ignorant souls," was a much more obvious sacrifice than spending time in the fancy homes of the elite.[20] If missionaries wanted to manifest devotion and show true dedication by sacrificing a new-middle-class material standard, then working among Indians carried much more weight than attempting to attract converts in the centers of La Paz or Lima. In this context, at least from the missionaries' perspective, there was an inherent connection between their discourse of sacrifice and the personal and collective regeneration of Indian converts: the one's sacrifice was the price of the other's atonement. If Indians were to be uplifted, purified of their sins, and regenerated in the warmth of the Lord, someone had to sacrifice for them.

Finally, working among the wretched and oppressed, giving up worldly comforts for the sake of their salvation, carried a special meaning: "Somehow, it seems to me, brother Stahl, when the day of coronation of the son of God takes place, that some of those nearest to Christ, about his throne, will be some of these poor people like this who through oppression of long years of papal rule, held down in ignorance and superstition, have been rescued by this last glorious truth of the everlasting gospel, who will demonstrate above all others the glory of Christ, what his power has been able to do for the children of men."[21]

The connection between poverty, both spiritual and material, and "purity of heart," the willingness to see God's truth, has a long history in Christianity.[22] During certain periods, poverty was treated as a spiritual value rather than a social condition; it was glorified and seen as a path to salvation. The first Christians lived frugal lives and were often persecuted. Such conditions were viewed as those of a model lifestyle and hence brought those who lived like this closer to God.[23] In other words, Indians, both spiritually oppressed by the lies and deceptions of the Catholic Church and materially deprived by rapacious landowners, shared a kind of intimacy with the Lord that others did not have or had lost. Platería was compared directly to Capernaum, with Stahl imitating the Savior's method for evangelizing and redeeming. Thus, by choosing "Indian work," the missionaries became closer to God and were able to realize their aspirations as to who they were and what they wanted to become. Of course, such holy work would be duly rewarded in both heavenly and earthly terms: being judged with the righteous upon the Lord's return and lauded within the Adventist Church. Stahl specifically became a legend among Adventists. In other words, choosing sides by establishing an "Indian mission" was more than just a measure through which missionaries gained Indians' trust. It played into missionaries' own self-perception and was a way for them to fulfill the ideal of sacrifice.

From the Indians' perspective, the creation of an exclusively Indian space was crucial. For them, it was not simply about testing the missionaries' commitment; it was necessary for conversion, as they understood the process. Duplicating Andean power structures inside the mission would have given them little room for racial regeneration, since they would have still been subjected to preexisting ideas concerning Indian-ness. The emergence of the regenerated Indian required a degree of autonomy from long-standing power structures, as those

Building an "Indian" Mission

were invested in the notions of Indian-ness that converts were rejecting.

In this regard, the difference in attitudes toward race between Anglo America and Latin America played an important role. In Latin America, race was constructed through cultural traits, and Lamarckian ideas about the inheritance of acquired characteristics were particularly popular. According to the French naturalist Jean-Baptiste Lamarck (1744–1829), the environment could alter human qualities, and these altered qualities would then be passed down to offspring. Thus, external forces had the power to change human biology, which could either elevate or demote individuals, families, nations, or races. From a Lamarckian perspective, public education, for example, was essential and had the power to biologically improve segments of the population.[24] By contrast, in the United States, Mendelian notions of inheritance gained prominence. Gregor Mendel (1822–84), a German-speaking scientist from Moravia, disregarded the idea that the environment altered people's biology and instead held that human features were passed down from parents to children with no external interference. Mendel's ideas were expanded to include moral and intellectual abilities, which could not be learned or improved by one's natural surroundings. Consequently, the key to a better society ran not through social initiatives such as public education but through breeding.[25]

The culturalist approach to race allowed fluidity between racial categories. But it also meant that to preserve social and racial hierarchies, cultural traits, such as the style of dress and language, had to be regulated. In this reality, mestizaje was an option for individuals who were willing to pay a personal price, usually in terms of their relationship with their native community. But it was not a valid option for those who wanted to change the "environment" that supported the existing racial hierarchies—that is, by implementing wide-ranging social initiatives and policies that would improve living conditions for Indians. Or worse, for those who refused to pay the price of mestizaje, insisting that being an Indian did not exclude certain traits that were crucial for social mobility, such as education.

Missionaries, however, did not need to police cultural characteristics to construct, or preserve, their racial superiority, because they were influenced by Mendelian theories, according to which race was inherited, was unchangeable, and had nothing to do with the social, cultural, or economic environment.[26] Indians, no matter what they wore or which language they spoke, were nothing but Indians. Biological notions of race also enabled the missionaries to accept the Indians as Indians, no matter which cultural characteristics that they had adopted. An Indian might be more civilized and closer to God, acting in one way rather than the other, but he was still an Indian. Missionaries refrained from regulating Indians' cultural attributes because they did not have to. In their eyes, race and their superior racial position were based on a completely different set of principles.

Since biology was so important, sexuality and sexual conduct were under severe scrutiny. The fear of miscegenation was partly why missionaries were usually married by the time they left for the field. It is also why they sent their children back to the United States when they got older.[27] Nevertheless, at this point, the converts were mainly interested in redefining how Indian-ness was understood in the Andes and in reforming the power relations practiced in these parts. The hierarchy within the Seventh-day Adventist Church was of less interest. Hence, by ignoring cultural characteristics, yet never doubting—or worse, slandering (e.g., "little mistis")—converts' Indian-ness, missionaries fostered precisely the environment that converts needed for regeneration. Moreover, missionaries provided converts' version of Indian-ness with religious legitimization, an essential component of Andean notions of community and sovereignty. Oddly, Mendelian notions of race became a harbor from Lamarckian accusations of mestizaje.

Constructing Dependence

Heavily invested in the idea of an Indian mission, both converts and missionaries found themselves in a complex relationship. They were mutually dependent, each side relying on the other, creating an apparent equilibrium. Missionaries had also introduced democratic practices, and certain issues, such as the admission of new church members or investment in infrastructure, were put to a vote. As a result, additional spheres of equality between the two sides took shape.[28] Yet, at the same time, these spheres were structured and hierarchical, with missionaries in an unquestionably superior position. In fact, in a way, missionaries' superiority had benefited both sides, insofar as the relations of power did not interfere with (and even protected) Indians' own goals.

The mutually dependent relationship between the sides was also shaped by mundane factors. For one, missionaries, especially Stahl, who pioneered the mission's efforts, needed local guidance. Stahl was a stranger; he was unfamiliar with the land, its customs, and its language. Manuel Camacho acted as a translator, of both language and cultural codes, and as a travel guide who made sure Stahl reached the right places. While doing so, however, Camacho also set standards for the mission's future conduct. The Seventh-day Adventist missionaries reached Puno, in the first place, because Camacho was exposed to their teaching while in Chile or Arequipa and invited them to come to Puno. Camacho's initial invitation quickly turned into a mission practice. The Seventh-day Adventists opened missions and schools only after being requested to do so, and only if the request had enough local support to establish a school and provide a home for the teacher. In many cases, even the initial evangelizing efforts were coordinated in advance and sometimes even sponsored by local Indians:

> I had observed that each time we started out for a new district, we had different mules to ride. The mule brought to me this time appeared to be very nervous. I told the chief that I was quite content to use the one I had come in on and asked if I might not retain him throughout my visit in this province. "No . . . that would be impossible, we have arranged for you to visit eleven districts here. Each district has to help furnish the mounts and the food and bear expense of this visit."[29]

Stahl, it appears, had little knowledge or involvement in the logistics of his visit; the Indians had arranged it, deciding where he should visit and when. In other words, they had significant influence, and at times even complete control, over patterns of missionary expansion, directing them according to their own interests.[30] Sources shed little light on the methods that Indian converts implemented and the connections that they forged to expand the mission's influence. But familial connections likely played a part in this expansion, as did relationships created in the military or while Indians had spent time in the cities. Concerning this last possibility, Camacho himself recounts how he had befriended other Indians from Puno during his time on the coast.[31] Around 1917, Indians in Lima were already engaging in the creation of migrant associations (*asociaciones de migrantes*), which would later become the basis for the Comité.[32] Such friendships, between young men from the same area, who had met each other in a completely different environment, detached from the traditional power structure, were likely to have played a part in the expansion of the mission.

Moreover, even if the missionaries knew whom to contact in a specific Indian community and how to approach him, they would still need to gain that person's trust.[33] Being introduced by a trustworthy native was a major advantage. Stahl himself testified that hostile attitudes often softened once a local Indian vouched for him.[34] Thus, missionaries relied on converts for connections, logistics, and legitimacy. This reliance enhanced the Indians' negotiating position and enabled them to exert a major influence on the way the mission was constructed in the area. Furthermore, Indians also enjoyed a significant degree of autonomy, because missionaries had little reason to interfere with their decisions. For missionaries, the success of evangelism rested on the number of Indians who responded to the message, beginning to keep the Sabbath and preparing for conversion. Whether they came from this community or that community—names of places that missionaries and church officials never heard of before—was of less importance. Simply put, if Camacho's efforts were fruitful, there was no reason to interfere. Thus, to an extent, converts shaped the geographical expansion of the mission.

Finally, although missionaries had power over Indians, they

Building an "Indian" Mission

were also entangled in additional networks that curtailed and limited their room to maneuver. Leaving the field was a complex issue. It was not that missionaries were physically constrained to the field, or that they could not leave because they lacked the financial means to do so, as was the case for converts. But there were issues of prestige and social status to consider. Leaving the field too soon, without sufficient reason and without making the necessary sacrifice, came with a price that people, especially religiously devoted people, did not always want to pay.

Converted Indians were also highly dependent on missionaries, if only because the missionaries protected and supported them during bitter conflicts with communal and district functionaries. Authorities often harassed Indians without thinking twice. When it came to white foreign men, with real and imagined connections in the capital of the country and around the world, however, things were different: "We told the authorities that if we get justice we will not have our minister take it up. So they are doing up to now the right thing," wrote Stahl during one of the many clashes between converts and district authorities in 1916.[35]

To obtain justice for Seventh-day Adventist Indians, missionaries threatened to "take the issue up" with the U.S. embassy. Missionaries, therefore, had flexed their political and diplomatic muscles in an attempt to intimidate local authorities. Their threat was grounded in reality: as a white U.S. citizen, Stahl could count on the embassy to intervene on his behalf and enjoyed a degree of immunity that granted him power and extended his room to maneuver in negotiations with authorities. Yet, it is rather doubtful that the U.S. embassy would use its influence to protect Indian converts, as he declared. From this perspective, missionaries' arm-twisting was as much a spectacle for the viewer as a demonstration of actual strength.

Such a spectacle was enhanced by the fact that during Leguía's first presidential term (1908–12), he invited U.S. citizens to fill government ranks as part of his border-modernizing efforts. Men such as Albert Giesecke, the distinguished rector and reformer of San Antonio Abad University in Cuzco, were sent to the sierra. Appointed by the president in 1910 and fulfilling roles in local politics, Giesecke would have had direct access to high places that were closed off to the average missionary.[36] Nevertheless, the fact that there were men like him in these roles contributed to the making of an image of U.S. citizens as powerful, which helped the missionaries even if they did not have the same kind of political outreach.

It is safe to assume that the U.S. embassy had little direct interest in the evangelization efforts of a small, unconventional church, which was treated with suspicion in the United States itself. As mentioned, in Peru, Seventh-day Adventists were excluded from joint evangelical platforms, leaving them relatively isolated.[37] Additionally, due to their interpretation of the First Amendment, Seventh-day Adventists refrained from taking government positions, making it highly unlikely that any of the embassy's officials belonged to the Adventist Church.[38] But for local authorities and Indian converts, who were unaware of North American interreligious dynamics and politics and viewed Adventists as "Protestants," uttering the threat was sufficient. The fact was that even without the embassy's backing, missionaries were in a position of superiority simply by being white, and both missionaries and converts knew it. When conflicts between Indian converts and other community members heated up, the presence of a white missionary did much to secure the physical well-being of both converts and the mission's infrastructure.[39] Thus, if converts were encountering difficulties promoting their agendas, having a foreign missionary stationed in the area could work to their advantage. Moreover, even if the embassy had little interest in the Seventh-day Adventists' enterprise, missionaries' political and financial outreach still exceeded that of the Indians by far.[40]

The ability to raise funds and provide a more or less steady influx of cash was also a major advantage from the Indians' perspective. One of the biggest challenges faced by local Indigenous teachers was keeping their schools open and functioning. In most cases, schools closed after a year either because of issues with teachers' salaries or due to other problems they encountered and were unable to solve by themselves.[41] Authorities in Lima were well aware of the problems rural schools faced.[42] Nevertheless,

Building an "Indian" Mission

the progressive elements within the Civilista government did not have the powers to overcome objections from the ranks of conservatives or the sierra landlords. Allowing Protestant missionaries to open schools was a way around this problem, as they did not depend on national resources and were free from local political pressures.[43] The mission, therefore, stepped into the void created by the state, with the blessing of the state itself. They provided the necessary support and a safety net that was missing from Indian schools: teachers received a regular salary that came both from the tuition that the mission collected and from other funds, including overseas donations. During the summer vacations, teachers had the opportunity to attend advanced courses, enriching their knowledge and acquiring tools to cope with pedagogical issues.[44]

Finally, Indians' understanding of politics was premised on verticality. They were used to working within unequal reciprocal relations to achieve their goals. Engaging in politics without a local patron and as an individual, rather than as part of a larger network of reciprocity, was not only foreign to Andean political culture but virtually impossible. Conceptually and practically, being a "good citizen" meant working along vertical lines, rather than against them, to prove their patriotism and legitimize demands of citizenship. To put it differently, in their political imagination, converts depended on a patron through whom they could realize their aspirations. Considering political culture in the Altiplano and the Indians' practical limitations in terms of outreach, missionaries offered Indians access to higher places, natural or supernatural. As competition over resources grew, intracommunal fragmentation intensified and intrafamilial and communal rivalries were exacerbated. Segments of the Indian population, such as the veterans, were left without traditional patronage and sought alternatives to fill that void. These alternatives were not exact duplications of existing power relations, nor did they have to be (in fact adjustments and changes were probably necessary). Nevertheless, to be viable, they did have to correspond with an established or known way of "doing things."

Entering into a pact with foreign missionaries to strengthen one's position in local politics is hardly a novelty in the history of missionary-native encounters. In British Columbia, Shuswap chiefs sought the help and protection of Catholic missionaries to "bolster their own authority and enact harsh measures of social control."[45] In other words, contrary to the Seventh-day Adventist mission in Puno, in this particular case study, the Shuswap used the mission as a reservoir of traditional leadership. Similarly, in the first decades of the nineteenth century, the Chiriguano leaders in Bolivia accepted a Franciscan mission to preserve their land, status, and culture. These two examples demonstrate how missions helped preserve traditional leadership, whereas the case of the Seventh-day Adventists points to the opposite pattern, but the basic principle is the same: disparate fragments of local communities believed that having a foreign missionary "on their side" would prove an advantage. In fact, they believed it to be so even if their interests conflicted with those of the missionaries.[46]

Thus, once veterans had decided to eschew the traditional politico-religious hierarchy, to become regenerated Indians who did not drink, chew coca, or participate in fiestas, and attempted to step out of traditional reciprocity networks, a vacuum had emerged. To become viable political actors with an actual ability to execute their agenda, they needed to replace the lost political networks. One way to do this was to contact the Seventh-day Adventist missionaries. But this was not the only strategy. Camacho, Juan Huanca, and Marcos Miranda are only some of the Indians who had developed strong contacts with the Asociación Pro-Indígena or with local indigenistas like Encinas. Yet the missionaries were willing to live among them (something that even devoted indigenistas did not do), and they could provide converts with the religious legitimacy that was embedded in Indigenous political thought. In other words, the Seventh-day Adventist missionaries were at the right place at the right time, and, as time would soon tell, they also had the right man—Ferdinand Stahl.

"Apostle to the Indians": Considering Ferdinand Stahl's Role, 1911–1920

One can only imagine the personal charisma and political shrewdness that a steelworker from Michigan needed to become the "apostle to the Indians." Ferdinand Stahl became a legend among the Indians, unlike any other Seventh-day Adventist missionary who arrived after him. In the center of what is now the town of Platería stands a statue of him together with Camacho, and songs lauding his character appeared in local publications.[47] On the other side of the hemisphere, a center named after him was established at La Sierra University, California. He did, of course, have Camacho on his side, and much of the Seventh-day Adventists' success should be credited to this insightful man. Nonetheless, Stahl's ability to listen, adapt, and follow Andean cultural codes should not be underestimated nor overlooked. He seemed to have learned (likely from Camacho) local codes of respect and used them to his advantage.[48] More significantly, he understood his position within the local hierarchy and adjusted relatively quickly to it. In other words, Stahl felt comfortable playing the role of "generous patron." During his first visit to Chucuito in 1911, Elder Westphal had observed, "While he gets very near to them [the Indian], will pat them on the back or head, or will put his arm about them and give them a special endearing embrace as the situation may require, he is not one to let them run over him. He seems especially fitted to labor for them, but he is equally fitted to labor for the whites of every class."[49]

On the one hand, Stahl treated the Indians with a combination of unbounded affection, not even recoiling from close, practically intimate, physical contact. On the other hand, he did so with a degree of firmness, expressing power and asserting his superior position. Perhaps what best symbolizes Stahl's relationship with converts was the way he greeted them: "With the handshake or embrace always comes the 'Como sake hermanito?' How are you brother?"[50] But "hermanito" did not mean "brother," as Elder Westphal had translated incorrectly. It means "little brother," and embracing one's little brothers perfectly describes the power relations in the mission during these years. Rather than the relationship between a father and son as implied in *padrinazgo*, the Seventh-day Adventist mission offered a relationship between siblings. Such a relationship was much more horizontal and much less formal than the Catholic padrinazgo.[51] In this regard, it offered a way out of a domineering power structure. Yet, at the same time, it preserved a clear hierarchy, the older and mature brother guiding his younger, much more naïve little brother in the right direction. It was a caring and mutually devoted relationship. But it also demanded respect and obedience from one side more than it did from the other.

Secondly, Stahl's relationships with the Indian converts appear to be highly personal, and in that regard, they correlated with the way daily interactions were conducted in the area. Unlike relationships in an individualistic market society, especially one that was becoming highly technocratic, in the Andes personal relationships were crucial for just about anything from buying land to military recruitment. For example, business interactions rarely took place without the two sides having a previous long-standing acquaintance.[52] The idea that things could be done through standardized procedures that treated people more or less as anonymous equals—without the identity of the two sides involved in the transaction playing a part in the outcome—was a far cry from the way things got done in the Andes. Stahl's very personal attention to the Indians through his medical practice allowed him to create the necessary relationships with prospective converts. A careful reading of the memos and letters from the Seventh-day Adventist Archive reveals that Stahl despised bureaucracy and often ignored "paperwork," misused funds, and generally did as he pleased:[53] "Bro. Stahl," wrote his nominal superior, Brother Edgar Maxwell, in 1914, "is a man of marked individuality, who does the strangest things and tells about them afterward. I should not be surprised to learn at any time that he had gone to Argentina or the States, or some other part of the country, without saying a word to anyone beforehand."[54]

Maxwell was the head of the Inca Union Mission and, officially at least, Stahl's supervisor. Yet Stahl did not seem to attach particular importance to the mission's chain of command. His lack of regard for procedures and his general attitude that he could do as he wished (especially with mission funds) was a cause of great tensions between Stahl and the other missionaries. They blamed him for being "quite German," wanting "all the workers to feel who is 'in the saddle.'"[55] Nevertheless, while the other missionaries contested his lack of respect for "proper administration," the metaphor of the "man in the saddle" corresponds to aspects of Andean reality. Not only does the image remind one of the *caudillo* on a horse, but it also emphasizes Stahl's personalist style. His successors, as we shall see, attempted to run the mission in a much more orderly, bureaucratic, and impersonal manner.

In sum, during the 1910s, the Adventist community was fashioned by relationships of mutual, albeit unequal, dependence between missionaries and converts. Veterans, who had been in the barracks for a long time, returned to their communities only to find themselves facing challenges and obstacles to their political, economic, and cultural integration. Veterans' quest for a new home led them to help establish the mission and to convert to Seventh-day Adventism. The mission was a space in which Indians could reconstruct the racial notions and the practices that were built on hegemonic ideas about Indian-ness. The mission also provided the logistics, economic support, and political patronage that converts needed to secure Indigenous schools as well as to fill the political void ensuing from their rejection of the traditional community authorities.

Missionaries, for their part, reached the Andes with the expectations of the white-collar new middle class. Sacrificing these expectations in favor of the wretched Indians was a way to manifest religious devotion as well as their success as missionaries. Furthermore, Seventh-day Adventists were scattered across the globe, and many made sacrifices. At that time, however, in no place were efforts greeted with such enthusiasm from locals as they were at Lake Titicaca. From this perspective, God seemed to be particularly responsive to the sacrifices and efforts these missionaries were making, shining on them a special light that distinguished them from other men and women in the foreign field. Practically, missionaries relied on Indians for connections, guidance, and information about local politics in the Andean communities. Missionaries provided Indians with access to "higher places," outreach they could not obtain on their own, especially after rejecting traditional networks. Both sides needed one another. Recognizing the superior position of the missionaries was part of the deal and stemmed not only from the missionaries' passion to save souls and their belief in North American and Protestant superiority but also from local Andean power structures. Historiography has tended to focus on the first of these two elements, emphasizing Eurocentric attitudes and domineering practices among missionaries. This is, of course, true. But a fuller understanding of the way power manifested itself must also consider the local political mechanisms that supported it. In this regard, missionaries were incorporated into a preexisting power structure, filling a vacuum created by others.

9

From the Lake Titicaca "Indian Mission" to "the Lake Titicaca Mission"

IN 1920, AFTER A DECADE IN THE ANDEAN HIGHLANDS, Ferdinand and Anna Stahl bade goodbye to their faithful followers and began a journey that would take them first to Lima and then to the Campa Indians in the Amazon. Stahl's departure from the Titicaca Indian Mission took place under stressful circumstances: his health had been deteriorating for some time, and he often had to leave the mission headquarters in Platería to spend time in lower altitudes to recuperate.[1] "I have broken down completely up in this high altitude," he wrote the General Conference in 1920, asking to be stationed among the "North American Indians in the West until it would be thought wise to enter Mexico."[2] Illness and fatigue, after long years of labor, had undoubtedly taken their toll. Yet, other issues seemed to have sparked the Stahls' desire to leave, or perhaps even pushed them out the door. Stahl did not get along very well with his coworkers. The tension culminated around 1918, when the majority of missionaries submitted a petition declaring, "We individually do not care to continue in our present positions unless . . . Bro. Stahl shall be restricted by the action of the local committee and that future policies of the mission shall be planned and shaped by actions of the local committee."[3] In other words, they requested that Stahl be relieved of any authority as superintendent.

Stahl's financial conduct and what his subordinates believed to be a lax attitude toward doctrine and baptism were at the core of this deep-seated distrust.[4] The General Conference, for its part, did not seem to be convinced by these accusations.

Perhaps the petition submitted by over 250 Indians requesting that Stahl, and no one else, stay among them, secured his position. Stahl had requested to return to the United States and labor with the Indians in California, perhaps moving to Mexico later.[5] Instead, however, he remained in Peru, first in Lima and then in the Amazon. The General Conference wanted him close to his "old Indian field," telling him "that now and again you could run through, giving a helping hand and letting your Indian believers know that you are still a part of the little band looking after them."[6] Obviously, the General Conference did not think Stahl was as dispensable as some of his coworkers did. Even more so, they feared the impact that his departure might have on the work, and therefore wished him to remain relatively close.

Finally, Stahl made plenty of enemies during his time in Puno, among them men of high standing. In addition to his involvement in incidents such as the attack on the school in Platería, a few legal suits were filed against him. In one case, a court ordered that he and Ezequiel Urviola be put in preventive custody, accusing them of causing Indigenous unrest and heading uprisings.[7] Urviola was a well-known activist, considered to be immersed in radical political activism on behalf of the Indians.[8] The exact nature of the relationship between the two men, as well as Urviola's connection to Seventh-day Adventism, is unknown. But the mere fact that they were defendants in the same lawsuit indicates how the local elites perceived Stahl. He had sided with the Indians, and the worst among them: those who were vigorously striving for social change. Perhaps Luis Valcárcel had stories of Stahl in mind when he imagined the figure of Karl Lamp, a German-speaking missionary who set out to resuscitate the Inca and earned the everlasting love and devotion of the Indians.[9]

The man chosen to fill Stahl's big shoes was Harry Wilcox, who had been stationed in Lima since 1916. Interestingly, both Stahl and Wilcox began their mission among the Indians during Leguía's presidency: Stahl, in 1911, at the end of Leguía's first term, and Wilcox, in 1920, at the beginning of the Oncenio, Leguía's eleven-year rule. Yet the nine years that had passed were crucial. World War I unleashed social forces and changed global and national politics. During this time, the curtain had finally gone done on the "Aristocratic Republic" and the order it represented. The twenty-five families who held power through the Civilista party, refusing to share it with other elements of Peruvian society, were now losing their grasp. These old actors were forced to make way for new ones who were eager to find a place on the political stage. Moreover, from afar, missionaries witnessed the opening of the political arena in their homeland. Women's suffrage (1920), for instance, changed the elector- ate and, consequently, the issues that candidates addressed. In contrast, the Seventh-day Adventist Church enjoyed rela- tive stability with Arthur Daniells as president for over twenty years (1901–22). From 1910 to the mid-1950s, Adventist mis- sions expanded rapidly, turning what was a small offshoot of U.S. Christianity into a global church.

As with any two men, we can see many differences in the biographies of Stahl and Wilcox. Yet in the context of the Indian mission, two of these differences deserve our attention: their career choices and the geographical location in which they first encountered Latin America. Unlike Stahl, Wilcox was not a medical missionary. In fact, according to his memoir, while he had toyed with the idea of becoming a doctor, eventually he preferred to stick to "pure" missionary work.[10] The difference between "medical missionary" and "missionary" at the time was more than just a personal career choice: the Seventh-day Adventist medical missionary enterprise, especially at the end of the nineteenth century and beginning of the twentieth cen- tury, was identified with larger trends in Christianity that called for greater involvement in social issues on the part of differ- ent denominations.[11] Under the auspices of Dr. John Harvey Kellogg, the Adventist Church offered poor city dwellers clean housing and basic medical care alongside educational and occu- pational opportunities.[12] Not everyone, however, subscribed to medical evangelism or these social projects. Many claimed that such social initiatives blurred what should be a missionary's first priority—personal redemption—and called for the return to traditional methods of evangelism such as selling religious literature and revivals.[13] As Stahl studied at Battle Creek Sanitarium and ran a medical social operation in Cleveland before leaving for Peru, he was much more likely to prefer public initiatives to doctrinal principles than Wilcox, who had received a more traditional education as a missionary.[14]

The second difference is that Wilcox came to Puno from Lima, rather than La Paz. "Whereas guano-driven Lima might turn its back on the Indian highlands, Bolivia's major cities were located in the very midst of Aymara and Quechua communities."[15] A half-decade later, after the War of the Pacific, the rise of indigenismo, the Asociación Pro-Indígena activism, and a much larger physical presence of Indians in the capital, it might have been harder to ignore the Indians. Still, Lima was not La Paz. Learning about the Indians miles away from any center of Indigenous culture, even if visits were conducted here and there, could not have given Wilcox the same wealth of experience and insight Stahl gained from living in Challapampa.

In addition to these personal differences, Wilcox's role in the mission was defined differently from Stahl's original role. Stahl was sent to "penetrate" into a new area and create a solid base of converts; Wilcox was expected to keep conversion on track but also "to reorganize the mission and put it on a more self-supporting basis."[16] There was nothing particularly new or unusual about this aim, and the standard expectation was that after a few years, a mission would become more or less self-sufficient.[17] From the General Conference's perspective, it was about time that the mission, which by now included numerous educational and medical institutions, generated enough revenue to finance its activities. Thus, less experienced in social religious initiatives and with a task that inherently meant prioritizing bureaucratic procedures and conduct, Wilcox had to make his way into the hearts of men and women whose language he did not speak and whose reality was relatively unknown to him.

According to his reports from the field, Wilcox sought from the very beginning to promote a "better" and "more efficient" conduct within the mission: "Our work is becoming more organized and the directors, putting better systems in their work, bring more results."[18] Clearly, Wilcox put much thought into these reorganizational programs, and he probably spent some sleepless nights wondering and worrying about the mission's future. He was not alone in his concerns. The fear of wasting resources had been haunting young corporate America during the first decades of the twentieth century. "Scientific management" aimed at reducing waste was widely discussed in offices and conference rooms.[19] In other words, the Adventists participated in the greater currents of developing corporatist culture, adopting a new discourse and setting new standards for success. For Wilcox, therefore, it was about saving *soles* as well as saving souls, and doing so in a "productive" manner. This meant taking actions that did not necessarily depend on Indians' responses to evangelizing efforts, and sometimes even contradicted Indians' interests.

The most salient example that comes to mind in this regard is the reorganization of the Seventh-day Adventist school system in Puno around 1921. In an effort both to reduce the influx of requests for schools and teachers, and to move the mission toward financial independence, a series of stipulations transferring a greater amount of the economic burden onto Indians' shoulders was enacted.[20] Aside from building the school and a home for the teacher, and providing equipment, Indians now had to pay a tuition of two soles per student per term, a sum that was the equivalent of ten days of work.[21] By his testimony, Wilcox knew in advance that the Indians would not accept these changes easily and therefore persuaded them by explaining that "good things cost money."[22] Then, by comparing paying for education to paying for farm animals, he exposed the changes that defined his generation: the transformation of Adventists from farmers and artisans of the old middle class to a new middle class of professionals did mean paying for education rather than investing in a farm. In addition, it also indicates that a "Christian education" that "would prepare for living with Jesus" was at least partially understood as a commodity to be purchased rather than a religious vocation.[23]

How was this comment understood in a place where tensions over "traditional" modes of production, such as land and animals, were reaching a climax? It is hard to know. According to

Wilcox, the Indians first complained and then "wholeheartedly" complied.[24] Perhaps some of them did relate to Wilcox's reasoning. Others may have believed that the missionaries were breaking out of what was already a fairly well-established relationship of reciprocity. Either way, however, in instituting that fee, missionaries had weakened one of the links that bound Indians to them.

As mentioned earlier, access to funds funneled from overseas in support of local Indigenous schools was one of the advantages of working with foreign missionaries as well as a way to secure Indians' dependence upon the mission. Turning the mission into a more self-supporting enterprise meant losing that advantage or, at the very least, making it less attractive, since missionaries continued to collect donations. Self-sufficiency also meant reducing Indians' dependence on the mission. In other words, Indians now relied more on their own resources for schools, which could, in turn, lead them to reassess their cooperation with the missionaries who controlled these funds.

Another of Wilcox's changes involved the requirements for baptism. Seventh-day Adventists practiced baptism by immersion, and a candidate was supposed to have a satisfactory understanding of Adventist fundamentals before he was baptized. What was satisfactory, however, is open to interpretation, and it does not appear that the General Conference had strict guidelines on this topic. The issue of baptism, however, was subject to debate. In Adventism's early years, James White proposed that converts should be baptized relatively quickly because of the fear of death. In the late 1890s, leading figures in the Adventist Church, such as Ellen White, called for greater emphasis on faith or conversion of the heart and radical change in lifestyle, and downplayed adherence to doctrines and laws.[25] Wilcox introduced new criteria for baptism that he described as much more rigorous than those implemented under Stahl. Although Wilcox does not specify what he demanded of candidates that Stahl did not, it appears that prospective converts had to demonstrate a higher level of proficiency in Adventist doctrines and rites before they were confirmed for baptism.[26] In other words, Wilcox seems to have had a more legalistic understanding of conversion than Stahl did. In one incident, Wilcox reported that he could have baptized an additional six hundred Indians, had his examination been less strict.[27] Therefore, in a subtle criticism of Stahl's work, Wilcox claims that the number of converts could have been much higher under his watch if he had been willing to compromise on doctrine as Stahl did.

Yet this strict attitude toward conversion had negative implications for the Indian leadership in the Adventist Church, especially those who were teachers. One of the factors that contributed to the Seventh-day Adventists' success was the fact that they downplayed doctrinal controversies: "Saturday worship and an end to idolatry . . . and the second coming were stressed, but more complex issues were for the most part overlooked. Instead, missionaries insisted on new standards of cleanliness and morality."[28] Consequently, the mission's doors were relatively open, welcoming most of those who wished to join.

For the Indian veterans that made up the Adventist Church's Indigenous leadership, this openness was a crucial factor. Doctrinal meticulousness enhanced the power of foreign missionaries at the expense of teachers and other local workers. The latter group was much less informed on theological particularities and had to depend more on missionaries to help them train prospective converts than they had in the past. Moreover, a teacher's leadership position within the community also had to do with the number of dedicated followers he had. Thus, once missionaries imposed strict criteria for baptism, excluding such large numbers of potential converts from the Adventist Church, they weakened the position of their intermediaries in the local communities. What made the situation even more precarious for these veterans was that while making it harder for Indians to convert, missionaries decided to actively court another kind of converts—mestizos.

Attracting Mestizos: Pioneering among New Populations

Stahl had barely reached Lima when Orley Ford, who was in charge of the Seventh-day Adventist mission station in Pomata, wrote that the mission had "dropped the word 'Indian'" from its name, thinking that "it may favor us some in the eyes of the officials and also help us in working for the cholo and Spanish class."[29] Dropping the word "Indian," as Ford soon explained, was intended to reduce the linkage between the mission and the Indians, in the hope that it would (a) change the attitude of local authorities toward the mission and (b) give the mission some kind of advantage in proselytizing efforts among the "non-Indian" populations.[30] Simply put, the mission decided to forgo its Indian uniqueness in favor of the more cosmopolitan approach that generally characterized Protestant missions. The Andean social and racial reality that led Stahl to "choose sides" did not carry the same weight with Wilcox. In fact, in his eyes, Spanish-speaking children were the ones deprived, since they did not have access to the "message" and a good Christian education, as Indians did.[31] Thus, to give Spanish-speaking children the "opportunities" that Indian children had, in 1924 the mission decided to open an "English School" in Puno that was specifically intended "for the children of Spanish speaking families." To attract students, the majority of the curriculum was in English, which was considered an important asset for business.[32] Although only a few of the students converted, the school had a good reputation and "helped to break down the wall that seemed to separate [Seventh-day Adventists] and 'Spanish speaking' Puneños."[33] The mission was no longer perceived as "Indian" as it had been in the past, and upper classes allowed themselves to take part in Adventist activities, even if, still bound to traditional notions of respectability, they chose not to convert.

The establishment of the school and the greater emphasis on converting members of the local elite also had to do with the attempt to make the mission self-supporting. While still in Lima, Wilcox observed that the Adventist Church's inability to secure converts from among "a better class of people" left it with few economic resources.[34] Converts with higher incomes made larger tithe payments, increasing the Adventist Church's revenue. Their political contacts could also shorten bureaucratic procedures, which could potentially reduce expenses. Moreover, if Adventism was to cease to be seen as hostile to the social order, perhaps its workers would not be a target of lawsuits, reducing legal expenses. Finally, the school's charging tuition that was higher than other schools' also contributed to the mission's financial stability.[35]

The case of the Puno English School sheds light on the intricate structure of imperialist power: promoting the English language in and of itself was not on the mission's agenda. To the contrary, Adventists spent significant time and money translating its publications, building local publishing houses, and supporting other initiatives in local languages to advance evangelism rather than have local converts learn English.[36] They soon recognized, however, that other aspects of imperial power, particularly business relations, created a local demand that they could meet. Thus, in this case, imperialism supported itself as one agent created a demand that another could supply.

Now, it is quite possible that Ford and Wilcox, under whose supervision this step was implemented, did not intend to make modifications to the time, financial resources, or devotion they gave to the Indians. Perhaps they even believed that a mission, which would include cholos or mestizos, would end up being an advantage for the Indians. But the Indians were never consulted, and unlike other decisions that Indians took part in, this "executive" decision was not brought to a vote. Thus, what was once a more or less exclusively Indian space no longer existed as such. Similarly, Wilcox chose to live in the town of Puno and conduct the mission from there. Living among the Indians in Platería sent one message, while living in Puno and mingling with parts of its elite sent quite another.

Turning to new audiences did not necessarily mean that missionaries would now be inclined to adopt more traditional notions concerning Indian-ness or impose a more "racially appropriate" behavioral code on their Indian convert. An equally strong hypothesis would be that the families who had decided to enroll their children in the Puno English School belonged to parts of the elite that shared some of the ideas concerning the regenerated Indian, for example, that he would be a much more effective worker in a market-oriented society. One could even take this argument a step farther and contend that the mission was now actively engaged in adapting the racial hierarchy to a new economic setting rather than changing it. While the Puno English School offered curricula that would prepare young men for the global market, the Indigenous training school had focused on farming and other crafts.[37] Here were the managers, and there was their workforce.

In both cases, though, the adoption of a more cosmopolitan approach meant introducing additional interests and agendas into the Adventist Church. Missionaries would now have to take into consideration the reaction of other parts of Puno's society when deciding on policy. Indians would no longer have the same degree of control over the mission's expansion and its demographics. Furthermore, sharing a space with mestizos and cholos, losing the identification between the mission and the Indians, played into the hands of those who were claiming that converts were not Indians at all but rather "little mistis." Attempting to create a regenerated Indian in a mongrel space was much more difficult. Simply put, by changing their name and going after new audiences, missionaries were undermining the Indians' interpretation of what it meant to convert. Interestingly, though, while missionaries were strengthening their ties with local elites, some prominent Seventh-day Adventist converts were becoming more vocal in their demands and radical in their outlooks. Tensions between the sides were deepening specifically as a new actor emerged on the southern highlands— the aforementioned Comité.

Breaking Ties: Missionaries and Indians at the Crossroads

In 1917 the Asociación Pro-Indígena, the first indigenista organization to advocate Indigenous rights, was dissolved as tensions between its members brought its operations to a standstill. One reason for the impasse was that most of the organization's members disagreed with Pedro Zulen's legitimization of the use of violence during the Rumi Maqui uprising in 1915. Another was that the scandal caused by Dora Mayer's alleging a love affair with Zulen (which he denied) had profoundly damaged the organization's reputation. No longer able to function, the Asociación Pro-Indígena met its demise, leaving a vacuum for all those who relied on it to promote various causes.[38] Into

The Lake Titicaca Mission

this void, a new organization, the Comité Pro-Derecho Indígena Tahuantinsuyu, was born in 1919. Little is known about the early history of the Comité, including how exactly it was founded. Researchers have found, however, that Indian peasants who migrated to Lima played a decisive role in the Comité's early formation and activities.[39] And the participation of Indian peasants, who voiced their own needs, distinguished this organization from the dissolved Asociación Pro-Indígena, which had been composed of city-based mestizos and creoles.

Structurally the Comité resembled Peru's state apparatus: the body's headquarters sat in Lima, and departmental committees were subordinated to it. In turn, these departmental committees oversaw the activities in provinces, and the representatives in the provinces then supervised the representatives in the districts, who were in charge of subcommittees that included one or more communities. The organization was promptly endorsed by the Leguía administration, a move that has generally been attributed to the new president's attempts to weaken the traditional Peruvian oligarchy from whom he had just wrested power.[40]

In 1921 the Comité held its first Indigenous conference in Lima, gathering 145 delegates from all over the country. On the agenda were topics such as rural schools and access to education, a minimum wage, and the dispossession of Indian peasants from their land.[41] Despite political pressures, particularly from hacienda owners, to dissolve the Comité, it continued to operate throughout most of the 1920s. Moreover, it enjoyed governmental support until 1927. For example, during the second Indigenous Congress, in 1922, Leguía hosted a delegation at the governmental palace. Both the fifth and sixth conferences received government subsidies to cover delegates' travel and living expenses, and, during the latter conference, August 29 was officially declared "Indian Day" in a symbolic act commemorating the assassination of the last Inca emperor, Atahualpa, by the Spanish conquistadors.[42] Things had changed, however, toward the end of Leguía's first term. The Peruvian president recalculated his steps, confronted the Comité, and eventually declared their activities illegal in 1927.[43]

Turning to the organization's social structure, we can roughly distinguish between different groups: one group was made up of left-wing indigenistas, including some former members of the Asociación Pro-Indígena. Another included anarchists who had "developed an idealistic approach towards the Andean peasants and the Inca past" and were mainly urban mestizos.[44] The final group consisted of Indigenous delegates who were either migrants living in the city or community representatives, "messengers," as they were called, who reached Lima to put forth a variety of requests and demands on behalf of their communities or, more precisely, on behalf of certain sectors of their communities. Among this last group were numerous Seventh-day Adventists, Manuel Camacho being the most salient example.[45]

These men were part of a larger phenomenon of growing Indigenous political activism in the 1920s and 1930s. The Peruvian messengers in the Comité, for example, closely resembled the Bolivian *apoderados*. Both groups were Indians who felt comfortable in urban settings and forged ties with intellectuals and labor organizations. In both cases, Indians demanded recognition and protection of their lands as well as access to education.[46] Another important group of Indigenous political activists in the Bolivian highlands was Alcaldes Mayores Particulares. The AMP emerged in the 1920s out of the apoderado movement and out of frustration with failed attempts to secure land rights by obtaining titles. Instead, they demanded the reenactment of colonial law and, in effect, the resurrection of the Republic of the Indians. The Alcaldes Mayores emphasized Indigenous religiosity, spirituality, and their special connection with the earth. In other words, like the Seventh-day Adventists, these political activists turned to a religious alternative to Catholicism as a means of legitimizing their demands and leadership.[47] The AMP, however, was a project of decolonization that included detachment from white-mestizo law and culture. It is for this reason that some of the movement's leaders objected to Indians learning Spanish or wearing mestizo clothing, calling them to religiously remain loyal to Indigenous clothes, the Aymara language, and gods.[48] These demands contrasted with those of the Comité and those of Adventist converts, who demanded access to mestizo cultural capital to enable social mobility. Furthermore, they contrasted with the vision of the regenerated Indian who remained an Indian even though he spoke Spanish. Returning to the occurrences in Puno, I can identify only one person, Camacho, who proudly admitted to membership in both the Seventh-day Adventist mission and the Comité, until he was excommunicated from the mission in 1921 because of his activities in the Comité. In other cases, finding direct links was much more complicated for both technical and ideological reasons. The technical reason has to do with archival material (or, rather, its nonexistence). I was unable to find any membership list for the Comité, since the location of its archive is still unaccounted for. From an ideological standpoint, both the Adventist Church officials and Comité activists preferred to blur the connection between their organizations. The mission wished to safeguard its image as apolitical and did not want to expose any possible connections its members had with an organization that was considered radical. The Comité activists, some of whom in later years developed an anti-imperialist consciousness, wished to blur any past connection to North American imperialists. Nevertheless, a meticulous reading indicates that some of the prominent names among the Comité activists had adopted habits that were distinctly associated with Seventh-day Adventism, and some notable converts acted and sounded as if they were a part of the Comité.

Carlos Condorena, for example, was a major figure in the Comité. He was not only one of its founding members but also its executive secretary during 1922–23, as well as a delegate from the province of Huancané and a leading figure in the uprising there in 1923. According to the testimony given by his granddaughter, Condorena had spent time reading the Bible and using it to resist labor exploitation. He had even unapologetically declared that the Bible did not mention slavery or free labor and that everyone was equal in the eyes of God.[49] Reading the Bible in general, especially viewing it as a source of authority that exceeds human authority, is profoundly Protestant. Additionally, according to Mariano Larico's testimony, Condorena regularly walked around with a book in which "the statutes, the commandments" were written.[50] In other words, he walked around with a Bible, which in Puno was a distinctive Seventh-day Adventist marker of identification. Another example is Rita Puma, a teacher and a Comité activist who used the Bible in school to teach children to read and write, which was a Seventh-day Adventist method.

Among those known as Seventh-day Adventists with ties to the Comité were Marcos Miranda and Juan Huanca. Both were veterans, among the first converts, and teachers who had previously been active in the Asociación Pro-Indígena.[51] Huanca had reached the position of missionary licentiate and seemed to have a promising career in the Adventist Church, yet he decided to leave around 1922, at more or less the same time that Camacho was excommunicated and any connection with the Comité prohibited.[52] The same seems to be the case with Pedro Pauro, who was a teacher in Pallalla, although his connections with the mission might have been looser in the first place. Together with Camacho, these men were central to the Seventh-day Adventists' endeavors at their inception and were considered essential Indigenous leaders. Others include Andrés Mamani, Juan Salas, Julián Arpasi, and Agustín Mamani, all converts from Camacho's original community, Potojani. According to one complaint, they were all involved in the kind of activities the Comité promoted: blowing the *pututus* and organizing mass meetings in which they called Indians to abandon all forced labor, handing out various publications, and demanding greater access to land, including land that was part of local haciendas.[53]

The fact that Comité activists were affiliated, or at least sympathetic, with Seventh-day Adventism is not surprising. Both organizations appealed to relatively young men and women who spent time away from their communities or were familiar with an urban way of life.[54] There were also common features in the agendas that both organizations promoted: education, hygiene, and an end to Indigenous exploitation. Furthermore, the Comité promoted an idea of Indian-ness that was compatible with the one fostered by converts, countering "the dominant vision of Indian-ness as equated with illiteracy and instead, envisioned Indian citizens empowered by literacy."[55]

Finally, the Comité even declared that freedom of religion was one of its official goals, a stance that led the Peruvian historian and intellectual Alberto Flores Galindo to state that the Seventh-day Adventist Church had directly influenced the formulation of the Comité's aims.[56] At this time, it was legal to exercise any religion publicly, due to the constitutional revision put into effect in 1915. In other words, at least formally, Protestants should have been able to conduct their missionary efforts peacefully. Stating that freedom of religion was one of the Comité's goals could have resulted from the central government's incompetence in ensuring its implementation. Seventh-day Adventist schools were attacked well into the 1920s. From the missionaries' perspective, it is very likely that freedom of religion and the separation of church and state were still objectives to be achieved. The Catholic Church was still formally recognized as having a special place in the nation, and it enjoyed a variety of social, cultural, and economic prerogatives, some of which still exist.[57]

Considering commonalities between the aspirations of the Comité and those of the Seventh-day Adventist mission in Puno, we see that the former supported freedom of religion and could potentially open new fields for the missionaries.[58] Why ban them rather than seek cooperation? What is even more intriguing is that the mission decided to "keep members clear of it [the Comité]" in 1923. At that time, the Comité enjoyed the patronage of Leguía's government, and another four years would pass before it was declared illegal.[59] An attempt to avoid confrontation with the central government cannot explain the mission's reaction. The mission's attempts to win the sympathies of the elites played a part in this stance, as the Comité was at that time the hacienda owners' nemesis. From the local hacienda owners' perspective, the organization was engaged in a racial war aimed at depriving white men of their properties, and probably their lives, as well as reestablishing the legendary Inca state Tahuantinsuyu.[60]

Accusations that Indians were conspiring against creoles and mestizos, that they were planning to overthrow Spanish or Peruvian rule and reestablish in its stead their long-lost ancient empire, had a long history in the Andes. Specifically, the Andean Utopia tied Indigenous redemption to the return of the Inca.[61] The most salient example is that of José Gabriel Condorcanqui, an Indian nobleman, who took the name Túpac Amaru II and rebelled against colonial rule by linking himself to the Inca and Tahuantinsuyu. The rebellion lasted two years and ended in the rebels' defeat but left a deep imprint on Andean society.[62] The notion that Indians were fighting to reinstall their long-lost Inca empire resurfaced in the decade of 1915–25. The constant encroachment on Indigenous lands spurred peasant unrest and unleashed Indian rebellions on a scale that had not been seen since Túpac Amaru's defeat.

One famous case is that of Teodomiro Gutiérrez Cuevas. Gutiérrez Cuevas was a midlevel army lieutenant who had reached Puno, occupied various administrative posts, and ended up leading an Indian rebellion. In December 1915, hundreds of Indian peasants attacked haciendas in several districts in the province of Azángaro. Gutiérrez, who organized the rebellion, adopted the name Rumi Maqui, Quechua for "Hand of Stone," and the title "General and Supreme Director of the Indigenous villages and armed forces of the Federal State of Tahuantinsuyu," and presumably declared that he had come to restore the Inca empire of Tahuantinsuyu.[63] Moreover, some scholars have attributed the expectation of *pachacuti*, an Andean notion of the cosmic order being turned upside down and those on the bottom are put on top, to the Indian rebels. What exactly Gutiérrez meant by restoring Tahuantinsuyu and whether he was caught up in a millenarian mode of thinking or simply aimed to supplant the gamonales is debated.[64] What is clear, however, is that Gutiérrez invoked memories connecting his present acts with a mythic image of the Inca empire and used this image to mobilize Indian peasants. The rebellion was eventually suppressed, and Gutiérrez was captured. But the discourse of the restoration of Tahuantinsuyu lingered on, and although it is unclear whether Indians rebels did have millenarian expectations and were attempting to reestablish the Inca empire, they are often described as having held such intentions.

What about the Indian converts? Were they looking to restore a mythic past? After all, they did adopt a discourse of redemption that looked to the past as a model. Furthermore, Seventh-day Adventism was a millenarian and messianic movement in its own right, and it is quite easy to imagine how the return of Christ could be interpreted as the return of the Inca in some manner. Indians had expressed millennial beliefs, particularly in their premillennial shape and form: "he [Ferdinand Stahl]," wrote a group of converts to the Seventh-day Adventist General Conference, "has suffered many tribulations in the name of Christ's love and for this we would like him to stay with us until Christ returns."[65] Stahl's difficulties at the top of the Andes had become "tribulations," a key concept in premillenarian thought, referring to a short period of intense suffering and pain, after which Jesus will return to earth, punish the wicked, and establish his just kingdom.

In one case, an elderly Indian, recently converted, expressed this Andean understanding of death, heaven, resurrection, and afterlife by saying that his "days were few in this earth, but I have joy in my heart of meeting you in the new earth." The term "earth," *pacha*, is common in Andean thought, signifying both "place" and "period."[66] An epoch, for example, with a certain social order, in a certain geographical place, could be considered a "pacha"; a new earth would thus be a place and a time with a different order of things. Would this include some sort of return of the Inca Empire? Was it simply a way to refer to the thousand years of Jesus? We find no direct references to an Inca past that were part of "Andean utopias" in other places or other times. In fact, during the first years of the mission, converts entirely refrained from making any direct references to a concrete event or person in the past. Perhaps this has to do with the nature of the sources themselves, letters and police reports, which required one to choose their words carefully. Nevertheless, even with this reservation in mind, it appears that while converts shared the general restoration ideal that characterized Andean utopias, the exact nature of that past was rather amorphous, and not without good reason. Converts, after all, did see themselves as devoted Christians for whom redemption depended on the realization of a fundamentally

Christian event—the second coming of Christ. They cried out against Catholic idols and blamed priests for having taught them to worship a false god. What kind of utopia, from this perspective, could come from restoring the "heathen" past of an empire in which people worshipped the sun? This is not to say that other Andean utopias were necessarily intent on reviving Andean religion, relieving themselves of all things Christian. Rather, within the Seventh-day Adventist framework, with the emphasis on "purity" and the rejection of Sundays as a Catholic change of the scriptures, tensions became too acute, leaving less room for interpretations. Hence it appears that while Seventh-day Adventists shared the general discourse of regeneration and redemption, they had neglected to paint a picture of what it was exactly that they wished to restore, leaving space for a wide range of interpretations. At least such was the case until the emergence of the Comité.

Although there are contrasting views on the role of millennial expectations among Comité activists, recent scholarship tends to play it down, pointing to their reformist social and political goals.[67] Such an interpretation, however, does not account for the Adventist influence among Puneño activists and representatives that may have fused Adventist messianic eschatology with Incaic myths and images. Indeed, a later religious movement, the Israelites of the New Universal Pact, which emerged in the 1960s, blends Adventist elements with Andean mythology and other religious components to create its doctrines.[68] The idea that Adventist members of the Comité had some kind of millennial expectations is speculative, and hard to sustain due to the lack of sources. Nonetheless, the presence of Adventist Indians in the Comité as a possible source for some kind of millennial attitudes should at least be considered.

Missionaries, for their part, did believe it to be the case. Even more so, they adhered to the conception prevalent among Andean elites according to which the restoration of Tahuantinsuyu meant caste war and the extinction of whites. The Comité, simply by incorporating the word "Tahuantinsuyu" into its title, put the North American millenarian expectations of "resurrection" into historical context. From the missionaries' perspec-

The Lake Titicaca Mission

tive, the Comité offered a vision of redemption that competed with their own: rather than Christ, the Inca, and instead of a Christian kingdom, an idol-worshiping empire. The binaries in their own consciousness had made missionaries blind to a long-standing Andean tradition that combined Christian millenarian thought with Andean symbolism. The fact that the Comité had included some of the missions' indigenista allies and that the organization openly supported freedom of religion did not quell missionaries' fears. They were convinced that one of the Comité's goals was to "put an end to the white Peruvians, the evangelist pastor, and mission whom they considered a hindrance to the furtherance of their case and the final establishment of the old Inca Empire again."[69]

Missionaries were suspicious also of the anarchist element in the Comité. Indian activists, it is true, were exposed to these ideas and perhaps even adopted elements of the Andean discourse. But none of the leading Indigenous peasants in the organization identified themselves as anarchists, and as far as sources can tell, neither did any of the leading Seventh-day Adventist converts who took part in the Comité.[70] Despite the lack of evidence, missionaries viewed it as a "Bolshevik society."[71] What is even more intriguing is that during these years, until the late 1920s, the Seventh-day Adventist Church was prospering in Russia and enjoyed greater freedom than it had ever enjoyed under the czar. Seventh-day Adventists even received land there to form their own religious communities.[72] Yet, the image of an antireligious, anti-private-property fundamentalist ideology set the tone more than concrete reports from missionaries laboring in the Russian fields. Thus, in the missionaries' eyes, the Comité activists were perusing two utopias: attempting to restore a sun-worshiping empire and creating a society without religion or private property at all.

Finally, the Seventh-day Adventist Church, as it had developed in the United States, encouraged political passivity in general, arguing that its members should stay out of "state issues." Seventh-day Adventism developed a tradition of political passivity as a result of adherents' radical interpretation of the First Amendment that "led the leadership to believe that the Church was outside of state authority."[73] For instance, the Adventist Church did not think that state or federal courts had the jurisdiction to judge them, as religious issues were separate from state laws. The other side of this coin was that the Adventists also believed that they had no right to meddle in state affairs, the two institutions being independent of each other. Adventists, therefore, rarely sought positions within the state apparatus.[74] Yet this logic did not apply to issues concerning the First Amendment. When and where freedom of religion was at stake, the Adventists believed that they have the right, and even the obligation, to intervene. Thus, as long as the missionaries perceived the Indians' confrontations with authorities as a struggle for religious liberty, they could easily support it. Paradoxically, the fact that Peru forbade the practice of other religions before 1915 smoothed the mission's way into local politics. Yet the Comité had a broad political agenda, one that could not be reduced to a struggle over religious liberty; it also encouraged political mobilization to strengthen the Indigenous voice in Peru's public sphere, while the mission believed that converts should do quite the opposite.

From the Indians' perspective, however, political activism in the framework of the Comité was not necessarily a break from religious conversion. Rather, the two went hand in hand. For Indian converts, conversion had always been about resisting the local political structure. The separation between state and church, or between religious and secular authority, was a foreign concept and unrelated to the political reality in the Andes, where the two were deeply interwoven. From this standpoint, one could easily understand Camacho's surprise when the Adventist missionaries called him to order because he was involved in "what was for them a political organization," as if all he had done up to that point in time had not had any political meaning.[75] Thus, while in the past, missionaries' ideas about the separation of church and state created a space for Indigenous political activism, which was never labeled as such by the missionaries, now this space had been significantly limited and subject to the interpretations missionaries had of indigenous politics (or no politics). Under these conditions, with missionaries limiting their steps and censuring their actions, key figures such as Camacho and Huanca, who were committed above all to the "regeneration" of the Indian, chose to leave the Adventist Church.

The establishment of the Comité not only induced missionaries to show the door to some Indians in the mission, but it also provided the Indians with a place to go. Indians relied on outsiders to open certain doors for them and to provide access to places and power from which they were generally excluded. Missionaries, with all their foreignness, filled this role; Indians engaged in politics through them. The Comité provided an alternative, becoming the principal coordinator between the local and national levels. The Asociación Pro-Indígena also contributed toward this cause but not in the same magnitude. Among some of the Comité's supporters were indigenistas who held different posts in the Leguía administration, giving the organization access to decision makers as well as actual influence over policy. Moreover, the Indians were encouraged to assume leadership positions, undermining traditional paternalistic politics and transferring greater responsibilities to the Indians themselves.[76] In this regard, the democratic practices that the mission introduced had also "trained" Indians toward a disparate form of political participation. Finally, Leguía's general tendency toward greater integration, in an effort to promote modernization, created a climate, at least during his first term, in which the Indians found more ears attentive to their demands than in the past. Consequently, Indians did not need missionaries to act as intermediaries as they had in the past, and leaving the Adventist Church did not come at the same cost as it may have in the past.

A Path toward Reintegration:
Converts and the Local Political System

Aside from participation in the Comité, it looks as if another political path was slowly opening for young army veterans. In 1918 a group of peasants from the community of Pallalla submitted a complaint to the subprefect of the department against the acting lieutenant governor, Don Genaro Ayahunca. According to the complaint, Ayahunca was "authoritative, against the wellbeing of the Indian, aggressive, alcoholic. . . . His atrocities against the education of the Indian race are well known, he is determined to harass anyone that is engaged in popular schooling."[77]

As the accusations against Ayahunca show, it appears that being an "alcoholic" who was opposed to the education and the "well-being" of the Indian race had become legitimate grounds to demand the dismissal of a district authority. Yet, what is even more interesting in this case is that the plaintiff's proposed alternative men for the job were all Indians whose names all appeared in the military registry.[78] Five years later the community members of Pallalla submitted another complaint, this time against the lieutenant governor whom they had previously recommended. Once again, they offered three different names to replace him; the man that was chosen, Pedro Pauro, was an army veteran, activist, and former Seventh-day Adventist.[79] In other words, military service had become a steppingstone from which one could reach office. Veterans who had been contending for years that their service was a manifestation of "good citizenship," instead of, or in addition to, taxes or free labor, were finally seeing the fruits of their efforts. They were now able to bypass the hierarchy that had impeded their reintegration.[80] From their new positions, veterans could establish new networks and foster numerous relationships that were inconceivable in the past: Elias Cordoba, for example, the governor of Pallalla who recommended Pauro and two other Adventists for the position of lieutenant governor, participated in the 1913 attack on the Platería mission and school. It is clear, therefore, that at least some of the veterans found a way to integrate into local district politics and develop alliances with former enemies. They were no longer little mistis subject to abuse by communal and state authorities but had become part of the power structure.

The fact was that the mutual dependence between this group of Indians and the missionaries had been unraveling. Stahl's departure was a significant turning point. Stahl saw himself as an apostle to some of the most wretched people on the face of the planet. For him "redeeming" the spiritually and physically miserable Indians, sacrificing to save their fallen souls, was especially glorious in the eyes of God and the church. Wilcox had to prove himself worthy in other ways. Redeeming the Indian was still important, but no less important was offering salvation to another part of the society and making the mission substantial. Preserving the mission's Indian uniqueness was a necessity for Stahl and an obstacle for Wilcox. As one person replaced the other, bringing with him a new vision, the mission's character changed, leaving Indians to redefine their places within it under a disparate set of circumstances.

Practical conditions had changed as well. Missionaries were no longer rootless strangers, and the mission had matured and became a part of the local scenery.[81] Indians were also empowered through the education they received and the organizational skills they acquired. Years of work and advocacy had brought about certain changes in the way they were perceived by those around them, and while they had lost some battles, there were others they won, such as recognition of military service as a parameter of "good citizenship." The emergence of the Comité provided an alternative mediator, giving veterans an additional option, maybe even a better option, once missionaries decided to set an ultimatum. Thus, faced with a choice, men such as Camacho, Huanca, and Miranda decided to leave the mission and pursue the regeneration of the Indian on their own terms.

The departure of these men was not without consequences. While some missionaries claimed that numbers of Indian converts continued to rise, the rate of conversion declined during the 1920s. Stahl and Camacho began their endeavors with only a handful of followers, probably around twenty converts. By 1920, the year Stahl left, the mission included 2,255 believers, a growth of 1,127 percent. Hence, on average, during the decade Stahl spent in Puno the mission doubled each year. Between 1920 and 1925, membership had increased and now included 6,881 brothers and sisters. Total growth had been about 300 percent at an average of 60 percent per year. In other words, the growth rate had declined almost by three-quarters. From 1925 to 1928, membership practically stagnated, with only about one thousand new members in three years.[82] Even the General Conference was aware of the deteriorating religious zeal among Indians. They claimed, "The former enthusiasm has worn off, and the propaganda work of today necessarily rests upon new workers."[83]

Yet, while converts could have opted to stay in the mission, and although their reactions to the missionaries' ultimatum had an impact on the mission they were in fact reacting. Indians were forced to choose, and the choices they were presented with were based on preconceptions that resulted from traditions, values, and cultural outlooks generated in another place. Furthermore, leading converts paid a high personal price for their choice: Camacho lost his position (and salary) as an interpreter.[84] Juan Huanca gave up a career as an Adventist missionary, and others lost their jobs as teachers or the mission's auspices over their schools.[85] These sacrifices had immediate effects, not to mention that they left behind a spiritual community they believed in. Missionaries also paid a price, but it was an institutional price. Their living conditions and occupational security were not jeopardized, nor were they faced with the difficult choice of leaving their spiritual home. In other words, although there was a large degree of dependency in the relationship between missionaries and converts, it was a hierarchical relationship. Ultimately, missionaries set conditions for Indians, not the other way around. Missionaries also made decisions from a more secure place, and these decisions did not come with the same personal cost that the converts paid.

Nonetheless, the rupture between the veterans and the missionaries in the early 1920s should not lead us to the sweeping conclusion that there were no longer Seventh-day Adventist Indians among the Comité activists. Mariano Larico mentions the presence of converts in Comité activities at least twice: once when describing the committee's assembly meeting and again when naming the members of the delegation to meet with President Leguía, headed by Carlos Condorena, after the bloody events in the province of Huancané.[86] Even after the Comité had been outlawed and dissolved, Seventh-day Adventists were involved in various political activities that resonated with the

The Lake Titicaca Mission

discourse and actions of the Comité. Perhaps the best explanation for this phenomenon is provided by Julio Mendoza Díaz, an activist from Huancané, in an interview with the historian José Luis Ayala: "Condorena was convinced that the Adventists would take the movement off track. . . . However, Carlos Condorena was also a very good friend of the Methodists, Adventists and was acquainted with prominent members of the Puno freemasonry, he knew very well who would attack him and who could offer protection."[87]

In other words, Condorena knew exactly who in the mission would help him and who would not, which meant that certain segments of the Adventist Church still sympathized with the Indians' cause. It is possible that in some cases, specific missionaries turned a blind eye toward Indian political activities, or that certain converts kept a low profile. And in many cases there was no mission station nearby, the Indian teacher being the only Seventh-day Adventist representative around. In such cases, Comité activists may have remained within the mission's framework, going about their own business right under the missionaries' noses. Moreover, we should not assume that leaving the Seventh-day Adventist Church meant converting back to Catholicism or renouncing their religious beliefs. These options were of course possible, but so was continuing to practice Seventh-day Adventism outside the official Adventist Church. After all, Indians had a long history of doing so, and the Catholic Church had been in a dire state for decades. Perhaps a new popular form of Seventh-day Adventism emerged, or maybe their beliefs blended in with other forms of devotion or even secular ideologies. In any case, the impact of the Seventh-day Adventists around one of the highest lakes in the world could not be erased and had become an integral part of the region's landscape.

Afterword

Reflections in Hindsight: Converts

IN THE MID-1970S A U.S. ANTHROPOLOGIST, TED LEWEL-
len, took interest, like myself, in a small Seventh-day Adventist
community situated on the shores of the Peruvian Titicaca Lake:
the Seventh-day Adventists of Soqa. Lewellen arrived in Soqa
during the twilight of the Velasco military regime, about forty
years after Camacho was excommunicated from the Adventist Church. In the decades since Camacho's excommunica-
tion, Indigenous peasants across the Andes witnessed a series
of military coups, joined unions, gained access to public education, and even participated in a revolution. After Vatican II and
the Second Episcopal Conference in Medellín, even the Catholic Church was singing a different tune. Amid these events
and transformations, the Adventists in Soqa became a political and intellectual elite.

On average, Lewellen found that Adventists were more educated than Catholics and that they were disproportionately represented in communal politics. Specifically, Adventists accounted
for a little less than 18 percent of Soqa's population but held four
of the six top political offices and filled 40 percent of all political positions in the community.[1] The president of the community was a third-generation Adventist. His grandfather, Pedro
Cupita, had opened an Adventist school in Soqa in the early
1910s. Hence, Adventism moved from the margins to the center, and Adventists held a considerable block of political power.
Significantly, this did not happen only in Soqa, and Adventists

have been disproportionately represented in local politics in other places in Puno.[2]

In the following pages, I use this body of anthropological research as a steppingstone to broaden the boundaries of this book. My purpose is not to give an in-depth analysis of the dynamics through which the marginalized Adventists became a political elite. That would be, and probably should be, a topic for more research. Instead, I intend to revisit some of this book's main themes and reflect on the ways they relate to other historical and contemporary developments in Latin American Evangelicalism in general and Adventism in particular.

For instance, from a historical perspective, it is not surprising that Adventists had more years of schooling than rural Catholic peasants in their community.[3] Almost all Protestant denominations opened schools, and many of these schools provided education to sectors of the population that had not previously had access to it. Victor Raúl Haya de la Torre, the founder and historical leader of the American Popular Revolutionary Alliance, for instance, studied at a Methodist school that served students from the growing petite bourgeoisie.[4] It therefore makes sense that Protestants would have a certain educational advantage and that this advantage would be particularly pronounced among Indigenous populations in faraway regions. In Puno not only did Indians have to wait years for public education but any attempt to establish schools was met with fierce resistance.

In the Andes, where race was constructed through cultural traits more than biological features, where it sat at the core of power structures and justified social hierarchies, teaching Indians Spanish was not simply an initiative to increase alphabetization. Rather, it was a demand for the redistribution of crucial cultural capital, and as such it was not only a profoundly political demand but also a socially subversive one. Indians were Indians precisely because they spoke Indian languages, not Spanish. Teaching them Spanish put their racial identity into question, which in turn also cast doubt on their social standing. Hence, it is hardly surprising that the first to object to the establishment of schools for Indians were the local hacienda owners and state authorities, or *gamonales*. But schools also intimidated segments of the Indian community, specifically Indians whose own prestige was accumulated through traditional mechanisms and whose power stemmed from their relationships with strong patrons. Shaking the system that supported their privileged positions was hardly in their best interest. Add to this the fact that the acquisition of new skills could come at the expense of traditional forms of knowledge, and it is clear why communal authorities were suspicious, not to say openly resentful, toward Adventists. Indigenous education, therefore, was a politically subversive demand, one that could undermine the social hierarchies, and it required devoted people who were willing to pay a high personal cost to achieve it.

Conversion was, in and of itself, an act of political defiance carried out against local community authorities. Communal authorities were responsible for both religious and "secular" duties, and Catholicism legitimized their political authority. Consequently, when converts rejected Catholicism they also renounced the authority of those who held power within the traditional religious political hierarchy. Simultaneously, conversion introduced new sources of authority, such as the Bible, constituted new paths toward leadership, and provided the ideological framework and logistical support for the establishment of a new community. Instead of sponsoring religious events, converts earned prestige by demonstrating their proficiency in Spanish, by keeping clean and refraining from coca and alcohol, and by teaching other Indians to do the same—or, as I have argued throughout this book, by "regenerating" themselves and their race. In this regard, Adventists were part of a larger discourse about the future of the Peruvian nation and the place of the Indians within it. Conversion to Seventh-day Adventism put indigenista ideas into practice: here was the clean and educated Indian that intellectuals in Lima had been waiting for. These future citizens would be able to carry the nation forward. Adventist converts were well aware of these discussions and openly claimed to be good citizens because they built schools, taught in them, and served in the military. Nevertheless, converts differed from indigenistas on one important issue: for indigenistas, regeneration was mainly social, while for converts, it was profoundly religious. Reading the Bible was a direct pathway to the sacred, hygiene was about purity, and becoming a "good citizen" was also about choosing the "true" form of Christianity.

Religious conversion played a significant role in manifesting and articulating political and national projects in other places in Latin America as well. For all its anticlerical history, Mexico serves as a case in point. Protestants were involved in labor unrest in the prerevolutionary years and then were disproportionately active in the Mexican Revolution.[5] These Protestants, as historian Jean-Pierre Bastian argues, "understood the revolution as a wave of morality and regeneration of a society, the Porfirian society, that gave too much room to the reinvigorated Catholic Church, impoverished the peasant and laborer masses, and prevented the rise of the petite bourgeoisie."[6] In the years after the revolution, Protestants believed that their version of Christianity was essential to the revolutionary project and the formation of a revolutionary state, whereas Catholicism bound Mexico to its colonial and prerevolutionary past.[7]

Conversion also played an important role in Paraguay during the 1960s and 1970s. The integration of Indigenous peoples was a crucial element in Stroessner's national project. In some cases, especially in the western regions of the Chaco, Indigenous peoples reacted to integration pressures from above by joining the Anglican or Mennonite churches. From the macro perspective, this is a puzzling choice, since all religious organizations cooperated with the regime, even if it was the Catholic Church that took on a leading role.[8] In other words, if Protestant missionaries were as committed to integrating natives as Catholic missionaries were, why was conversion a way of resisting these pressures? The micro level provides the answer. As René Horst argues, "Because surrounding Paraguayos were Catholic, Protestantism provided indigenous people in the Chaco clear religious and cultural barriers with which to distinguish themselves from other peasants."[9] Additionally, in these churches converts were also able to maintain and legitimize Indigenous social and political structures. What worried Indigenous peasants was not integration into an amorphous "nation" but the loss of cultural identity, economic resources, and whatever political autonomy they had to their mestizo neighbors. At least for a time, conversion to Protestantism offered a solution, or a partial solution, for this problem; it was a path toward national integration that on the local level allowed Indigenous people to preserve something of their cultural heritage and political structure. Hence, like the Adventist case, religious choices were deeply embedded in local politics, and conversion was just as much about these local power structures as it was an individual profession of faith.

Eventually, Protestant converts paved their way into local Indigenous politics, although the length of this process varied. In Colombia, for example, it was difficult to find Protestants conducting local Indigenous affairs before the 1980s.[10] In Mexico, by contrast, Protestants were serving in various political posts by the early 1920s. The revolution and the clientelistic ties between caudillos and specific pastors no doubt facilitated Protestants' entrance into local politics. In Lake Titicaca, the first Adventists to fill low-ranking positions in the district's political system were nominated in the late 1920s. Then slowly, but at an accelerating rate, the barriers that prevented Adventists from participating in local politics crumbled. Over time, people became accustomed to the Adventist presence and less suspicious of it. In this regard, the missionaries' efforts to "rebrand" the mission and present it as less "Indian," that is, omitting the word "Indian" from its title, bore fruit. In parallel, and more important, structural changes in the way Indian communities were administered were slowly unfolding. In Soqa, for instance, the *cargo* system, with its politico-religious hierarchy, ended in the mid-1950s. Population growth, coupled with other socioeconomic pressures, had made it too costly, and it was replaced with a secular system based on the elections of a mayor and a vice mayor. Without belittling the importance of Catholicism, it no longer played an official role in communal management. Consequently, Seventh-day Adventists could become leaders in their community without their own beliefs presenting an obstacle.[11] Similar changes, at a different pace, were underway in Indian communities across the region and provided Seventh-day Adventists with a way "back" into their communities.[12] By the 1970s they were overrepresented in the administration of various communities in the region.[13] Eventually and not without extreme efforts, Adventists integrated into the communal political fabric.

The discussion of the Seventh-day Adventist Indigenous converts could not be complete without also examining them as part of a wider social group: army veterans. While there is no official estimate regarding the number of discharged soldiers who had returned home, their numbers were likely to be counted in the thousands. For a few hundred, becoming teachers and joining the Seventh-day Adventist mission had provided a solution to their inability to reintegrate into the community. But not for all. Standing on the edge of the community, veterans found various solutions for their precarious situation. Some, in all likelihood, used their military experience as capital to negotiate patronships with local strongmen, basically offering their services as mercenaries. Such was perhaps the case of Justo Condori, an army veteran who served as a soldier for local mestizos during the 1923 Huancané rebellion. Condori, according to one testimony, worked alongside mestizos, arresting prominent Indians involved in the rebellion. His success, however, was rather limited, his mestizo allies "paying him poorly" and members of his own community treating him as a traitor.[14]

Another possible occupation for ex-soldiers was banditry. Eric Hobsbawm has discussed the topic of bandits at length from a global perspective, suggesting that former servicemen who found themselves on the margins of their home communities were historically a potential reservoir for outlaws. Hobsbawm specifically quotes one progressive Bolivian who wonders why Aymara ex-military men had returned to their villages only to become bandits' leaders rather than teachers or agents of civilization.[15] Hobsbawm disregards the question, stating that "ex-servicemen can act as leaders, educators and village cadres, and all socially revolutionary regimes use their armies as training schools for this purpose, but who would have really expected this in feudal Bolivia?"[16] They are both wrong: Hobsbawm, for presuming that the question was irrelevant, and the "progressive Bolivian," for believing that ex-soldiers were not involved in civilizing missions of any kind. Nevertheless, the progressive Bolivian's comment does provide additional evidence that some veterans had turned banditry into a career.

In any case, exploring issues of demobilization and army veterans' reintegration into communal and civil life might provide some important insights concerning the extent, character, and mechanisms of violence in the high Andes. As we have seen, some community members feared former soldiers, who were not always shy about using force. In fact, even the Seventh-day Adventists, a minority and supposedly part of a movement that preached pacifism, implemented violent methods when deemed necessary. They actively burned Catholic churches, did not hesitate to smash Catholic icons, and were willing to humiliate adversaries or men who stood in their way. These actions were not out of historical context and had deep roots in medieval Spain. Notwithstanding the historical precedent, the question of the military tactics implemented in such events still begs for an answer. Furthermore, there are plenty of accounts of military drills performed regularly in Seventh-day Adventist schools or during events the mission had organized.[17] What were the social implications that sprang from the fact that military rituals became part of a religious colloquium? In which other ways and through what other institutions were military practices and behavioral codes transferred and incorporated into civil life?

In this context, we should recall that Seventh-day Adventist army veterans were not only a part of the mission. They were also active members of other organizations such as the Asociación Pro-Indígena and later, of course, the Comité. In other words, army veterans were involved in the making of Andean civil society and participated in the creation of nongovernmental organizations, religious and otherwise (in this sense, the Seventh-day Adventist mission can also be analyzed as an NGO). Their role, in this regard, was two-sided; not only did they convey the Indigenous "situation" to Lima, but they also served as agents who helped such organizations enter rural Indian communities. From a broad perspective, this role provides a historical precedent for phenomena such as that which Ivan Degregori remarks on in his discussion of the role ex-soldiers (licenciados) played to help forge relationships between the army and local peasant communities in Ayacucho in an attempt to defeat the "Shining Path" (Sendero Luminoso) in the 1990s.[18] Even more interesting in this context, and specific to Puno, is José Luis Rénique's conclusion regarding the army's initiatives to "win over" the church and local NGOs in an attempt to defeat both the Shining Path and any "third way."[19] In other words, precisely the world that eighty or ninety years ago the military's former soldiers had helped establish was now a target for "conquest." Thus, without falling into historical determinism, examining the role of army veterans provides additional insights into issues of violence and military-society relations in the Andes, as well as set existing knowledge in a larger historical context.

Retrospective Thoughts: Missionaries

Establishing an alternative community on the outskirts of a small town in a remote area of the world was not accomplished by a group of Indians alone. With them were a few foreign missionaries, their spiritual "older" brothers, although they were roughly the same age. These men were not a part of Lewellen's study; in fact, they weren't even there when he arrived. By the time he had reached Soqa to conduct research, the Seventh-day Adventist churches and the large network of schools, hospitals, and clinics were in local hands. The Adventist Church, which already had a wide representation of Indians in relatively high roles, was completely nationalized. Perhaps the winds of time blew from the International Petroleum Company oil fields into the Adventist Church.[20] Yet, even in their absence, Lewellen's findings on education and political activism are a good starting point to reflect on the missionaries, their success, and what was, to my mind, one of their biggest blind spots.

Missionaries were no strangers to rural life and, for the most part, grew up on farms scattered throughout the Midwest of the United States. Their fathers had left family farms in established communities to build their own homes in less colonized areas, in keeping with the prevalent migration patterns at the time. They were relatively successful in their economic endeavors, ranking among the wealthiest upper 50 percent in their local communities. Nevertheless, when the sons came of age and were ready to seek out economic independence, they learned that following in their parents' footsteps would be costly: the price of land was rising, industrialism demanded high investments in machinery, and a globalized market expanded competition, leaving farmers practically at the mercy of external forces. To put it differently, reaching early adulthood at the beginning of the twentieth century, in a period of burgeoning capitalism, had significantly altered one's prospects. Hence, like their future converts, missionaries had to deal with the ramifications of a globalizing world. They did so, however, from a relatively comfortable position: their social status and economic outreach enabled them to pursue an education that opened numerous new opportunities to them.

Seventh-day Adventist missionaries were far from being part of the United States' social, economic, and cultural elite and had little direct influence on contemporary economic policy. Nor did their families necessarily gain from it. Furthermore, the missionaries selected for Puno were not even part of the Seventh-day Adventist elite, which was clustered in Battle Creek, Michigan. Most came from the periphery, and some were recent converts, without special connections or prestige. Notwithstanding these social disadvantages, missionaries were still part of the white northern European hegemony. Their families were well-established farmers in their local communities, "cultivators of the earth" and a symbol of a (North) American ideal. As such, a comfortable spot, at an obtainable cost, was reserved for them within the transforming socioeconomic system, even if they did not set its terms or directly hold the reins of power. With the economic ability to acquire new tools and to be considered socially "fit" to fill new "white-collar" positions, these men had a relatively good chance of being able to swim with contemporary currents, securing their place in a changing world. At a time when Protestant religious zeal had reached an apogee, leaving for the foreign field was one of the options these men had. Yet doing so, or fulfilling any other position within the Adventist Church, required an education.

Historically a movement of freeholders, Seventh-day Adventism had created a unique time cycle that encouraged its members to remain in control of their working hours. The importance of the Sabbath to this denomination, both in theological terms and as a part of its identity, cannot be overestimated. Yet Adventist leaders were aware of the challenges that modern time(s), quite literally, posed for the new generation of believers. The Adventist Church established educational institutions through which young men, who were essentially brought up to become farmers or artisans, now gained tools to practice various professions. Education had opened the door to the growing ranks of the new and professional middle class: farm boys and apprentices became nurses, doctors, accountants, teachers, and professional missionaries. In this sense, missionaries truly identified with the importance that Indians accorded to education, believing that a Seventh-day Adventist education could help them to transform and adjust. After all, their own experiences buttressed the notion that to be "born again" required spending time in front of a blackboard. Thus, the fact that Seventh-day Adventist Indians had an above-average education and tended to prefer it over other forms of profit making, as Lewellen found, indicates that missionaries had succeeded in transmitting their message. In the long term, Wilcox's claims that Indians should opt for a good Christian education over investment in farm animals did not fall on deaf ears.

What missionaries overlooked, or simply did not understand, was that the Indians' place in society turned their quest for education into a struggle over rights and access to power. From the geographical periphery and the bottom of the Andean racial hierarchy, they had limited means to seek better opportunities or acquire new skills. Furthermore, even those (or perhaps, particularly those) who possessed a higher level of education and aptitude found out that it was incredibly difficult for them to free themselves from the shackles of race. They may have gained knowledge, but they still lacked the social legitimacy and support to be anything but Indians or do anything other than what Indians were expected to do. By demanding education and insisting that they remain Indians, converts rejected hegemonic notions of Indian-ness and the racial order that was associated with it. Their demand was highly politicized. Likewise, missionaries failed to comprehend that conversion itself was a political act. Missionaries may have been well aware of the role that Catholicism played in Indians' daily lives, yet they were blind to the full implications of a political system that was embedded in religion. From their perspective, choosing Seventh-day Adventism over Catholicism was a matter of consciousness and had to do with freedom of religion. The fact that it also entailed repudiating communal authorities, shifting one's loyalties and patronage networks (and the importance of these relationships in the Andes), was overlooked or misunderstood. To state things clearly, they were blind to the implications that conversion had on the local political structure and to the political implications of their own presence. Proselytizing, in this context, contained an element of political propaganda, and while missionaries may have tried to stay out of politics as Stahl once claimed, their mere presence made this goal impossible.[21]

While the political nature of their religious activity was probably missionaries' most salient blind spot, it was not the only one. Missionaries tended to ignore the cultural value of certain material goods in the Altiplano, specifically those they were used to consuming in the United States. In other words, it made little difference to them that items such as an oil stove and imported furniture were to be found in Puno almost exclusively in the homes of the rich. Missionaries continued to believe that these were common commodities and that they should be accessible to any member of the middle class. Living without these goods, or obtaining them at extremely high prices was, therefore, a sacrifice expressed through the Christian ideal of self-sacrifice. Hence, a religious movement that was born out of the needs and necessities of freeholder farmers, the old middle class, and fostered among them, was now contributing to the formation of a new professional middle class.[22]

Paradoxically, Seventh-day Adventism that historically

excluded laborers through its exclusive time cycle and preserved its whiteness by the same means, had become, in the
second half of the twentieth century, one of the most ethnically
diverse churches, recruiting most of its converts from the lower
stratum of society. How this change came about, what its implications were for Adventists, and how it reflects more broadly
on modern U.S. society are topics for a separate investigation.
Nevertheless, the slow implantation of a five-day workweek (for-
malized by the Fair Labor Standard Act in 1938) that incorporated Seventh-day Adventists into the nation's time, removed
serious barriers. Another possible hypothesis may be found in
the historical connection between Seventh-day Adventism and
the new middle class. According to Gary Schwartz, Seventh-day
Adventists, more than Pentecostals, tend to believe in upward
social mobility via education and cultural adaptation.[23] There is
some historical continuity in the Adventist Church's relation to
the middle class, this time contributing to its ethnic and racial
diversity. In this regard, it is impossible not to mention former
Republican presidential candidate (2016) Ben Carson. Carson,
an African American born in Detroit, was raised by his mother
and grew to be one of the leading pediatric neurosurgeons in
the United States. His biography is contradictory but still exem-
plifies upward mobility among second-generation Seventh-day
Adventist minorities. His presidential bid is also intriguing in
the context of the Adventist Church, illustrating how politics
and church could coexist, namely, by presenting political activism as personal and unrelated to the religious beliefs.[24] How
such a discourse could be translated in other cultures with disparate political traditions is still open. What is clear, however,
is that Carson, unlike Camacho, or other Seventh-day Adventists across the globe, did not have to choose between politics
and religion.

Some Final Remarks on Power Structures

Throughout this research, I argue that both missionaries and
converts, who were vulnerable to the global social, economic,
and cultural turmoil of the time, found shelter in the walls of
a newly established religious community. For Indian converts,

the mission was a space for regeneration, a place where their version of Indian-ness was not only legitimate but the basis for communal cooperation. For missionaries, the mission was an arena of sacrifice where they could express their material expectations in religious and spiritual terms, giving it meanings that went beyond personal comfort. Both sides were embedded in power structures and subjected to punitive measures if they ignored or contested the general conventions upheld by the system. We have witnessed, for instance, how missionaries were expected to conform to the image of the "sacrificing missionary," remaining in the field even if they experienced intense personal hardships. Similarly, they had to weigh their words carefully when making appeals for changes in their terms of service. Any request considered "too demanding" was quickly treated as a "burden" to the cause and a manifestation of a poor missionary spirit.

Furthermore, missionaries oscillated between the ideal of sacrifice and that of respectability, carefully balancing the two. Respectability, in this context, may have shielded missionaries from harsher demands of sacrifice. It might have served as a counterargument against pressures originating from the General Conference or other authorities in the field for additional compromises in living conditions. Additionally, one could imagine that there was a degree of peer pressure from coworkers who may have worried that too much emphasis on the sacrifice one has made would possibly lead to a decline in the standard of respectability. In other words, ones' willingness to sacrifice more than the average could bring on new demands and create new standards, eventually degrading missionaries' material conditions and weakening their position vis-à-vis Adventist authorities.

Missionaries' vulnerability to the General Conference, however, was insignificant in comparison with Indians' subordination to local authorities. While missionaries worried mostly about their social and professional reputation within Adventist circles, converts feared for their lives. I mentioned earlier the ramifications that learning Spanish and adopting other mestizo characteristics had for converts. Incorporating new features into Indian-ness and shedding old ones was not a peaceful process of give and take. It was bloody and, in this case, resembled a battlefield more than any kind of unequal negotiations between authorities and their subordinates.

The fact that the converts were fighting for the regeneration of all Indians, rather than attempting to individually "pass" as mestizos, was one of the reasons why the reactions against them were particularly harsh. Nevertheless, even men like Gregorio Mamani who were simply returning home after their military service and had no pretensions for social change were subjected to sanctions. In this sense, mestizaje had limits. Personal histories and familial backgrounds did not simply disappear as one emerged as a mestizo in a specific social context. Relatives, family friends, and even local authorities were well acquainted with the Indians in their districts and had long memories. They did not easily accept or acknowledge changes in one's racial identity.

Moreover, while missionaries may have had disagreements and disputes with the General Conference at times, they were part of the system. Broadly, missionaries stayed within the boundaries that society had dictated for them, choosing what was considered a legitimate path for a young white man from a relatively well-off rural family. They adhered to the notion of the sacrificing missionary, and while they may have tried to limit the extent of sacrifice, they did accept it. Indians, in contrast, crossed borders and contested limits, demanding access to resources that society deemed to be out of their reach. Their vision of Indian-ness stood in direct contrast to contemporary hegemonic notions and entailed major shifts in power relations, if not the complete abolition of the system. In fact, it was precisely their rejection of the Andean hierarchy, and its religious framework, that led them to the doorstep of the Seventh-day Adventist mission.

The two, as we have seen, undoubtedly depended on each other. Missionaries were strangers in a land where one needed personal relationships and a network of loyalties for even the simplest daily tasks, such as receiving mail. Converts were in desperate need of protection and legitimacy from "higher" sources. Furthermore, at least from missionaries' vantage point, sacrifice and regeneration were deeply connected, the second depending on the first. In other words, it was their version of the "white man's burden"; missionaries had to sacrifice for Indians to be reborn. Doing so entitled them to heavenly rewards.

Mutual dependence, as crucial as it may have been, however, could not erase the deep differences between missionaries and Indians' starting points. Nor could it obliterate the fact that Indians were fighting to change Andean social hierarchies while missionaries were outsiders, complying, more or less, with their native home and Protestant religious and cultural values. Finally, missionaries, as white U.S. citizens, enjoyed a safety net that no Indian could dream of, which enabled them to support Indigenous demands and buttressed their authority over converts, also functioning as a potential threat. Missionaries' sponsorship could be removed easily, with converts having little direct say in such a decision but to pay its price. The most salient example of such a case was the banishment the Comité, which left long-time converts without the mission's protection.

One could argue that converts were the ones who had decided to leave the mission. They could have opted to stay, giving up their activities in the Comité instead. In this respect, the decision of converts to leave the mission exposes the weaknesses and strengths of the paradigm of cultural imperialism: as critics have pointed out, converts were not passive. They joined the mission of their own free will because it had much to offer them. They left when it no longer met their needs and did so from an improved position. Converts had obtained a relatively high level of education and recognition (even if contested) as leaders. They had made new friends and allies and expanded their social, political, and cultural outreach. Moreover, their choice to leave had significant repercussions on the mission. Although some missionaries claimed that numbers of Indian converts continued to rise, the rate of conversion actually declined during the 1920s. Yet, while converts certainly had options, the missionaries did set forth an ultimatum, and converts were forced to choose. Furthermore, leading converts paid a high personal price for their choice, while missionaries paid more of an institutional price and their own livelihood was never in jeopardy.

Missionaries and converts shared concerns over the challenges of the time, and neither side was immune to global currents as a group or as individuals. Although both groups had to cope with a new and insecure environment, missionaries enjoyed privileges that converts did not have. The advantage of being a young, white man, from a family with means, accompanied them throughout their travels and did not vanish in the Altiplanos. Missionaries' shortcomings such as being a stranger and relying on locals for support did reduce some of their advantages, creating a sort of equilibrium between them and their followers. But the social distance between these two sides was so great that it could not but manifest itself, even in a community of well-intentioned spiritual brothers. The fact was that missionaries and Indian converts operated in completely different worlds in terms of possibilities and outreach. Nevertheless, at the same time, both were very much embedded in a world where white meant more than brown.

Notes

Introduction

1. Evo Morales is popularly referred to as the nation's first Indigenous president, yet whether this is in fact the case is debatable and depends very much on who is considered an "Indian." For example, from 1829 to 1839, the incumbent president of Bolivia was Andrés de Santa Cruz. Santa Cruz's father was a Peruvian Creole, and his mother was an Aymara Indian. According to Cecilia Méndez, the Peruvian elite considered this man an Indian, and, according to Natalia Sobrevilla Perea, people remarked on his noble Inca lineage on different occasions. See Sobrevilla Perea, *Caudillo of the Andes*; Méndez, "Incas sí, indios no." Heated debates continue about the political nature of the events in Bolivia, specifically whether Morales resigned, was ousted in a coup d'état, or a little bit of both. At the time of writing, new information on these events and new interpretations about them are constantly flowing in. My present description of these events should therefore be taken with extreme caution.

2. General elections were held in Bolivia on October 20, 2019. The two leading candidates were incumbent president Evo Morales, representing the left-wing MAS-IPSP party, and former president Carlos Mesa, representing the right-wing Civic Community. According to Bolivian law, the candidate that received more than 50 percent of the vote or 40 percent of the vote with a 10 percent margin wins the election. If there is no such candidate, a second round is held. Furthermore, there are two types of vote counts: the quick count and the official count. The "quick count," which is not legally binding, does not process 100 percent of votes, and is done to provide the public with credible information about the results and voting tendencies. The second count is the official count, which takes a few days and is the only valid voting system. On October 21, after about 84 percent of the tally sheets were counted, MAS-IPSP received 45.71 percent of the vote and the Civic Community, 37.84 percent. These results meant that Morales won the larger number of votes but would still have to go to a runoff because his advantage over Mesa did not reach 10 percent. At this point the quick count stopped, leading to rumors and allegations of possible election fraud.

When the final results were processed, they showed that Morales achieved 47.08 percent of the vote over Mesa's 36.51 percent. In other words, there wouldn't be a runoff. For more information, see Long et al., "What Happened in Bolivia's 2019 Vote Count?"; Organization of American States, *Final Report of the Audit of the Elections in Bolivia: Intentional Manipulation and Serious Irregularities Made It Impossible to Validate the Results*, December 4, 2019, https://www.oas.org/en/media_center/press_release. asp?sCodigo=E-109/19.

3. Max Blumenthal and Ben Norton, "Bolivia Coup Led by Christian Fascist Paramilitary Leader and Millionaire with Foreign Support," The Gray Zone, November 11, 2019, https://thegrayzone.com/2019/11/11/ bolivia-coup-fascist-foreign-support-fernando-camacho/.

4. Ari Chachaki, *Earth Politics*.

5. MacCormack, *Religion in the Andes*, 59, 99.

6. Religious freedom was legally granted in Ecuador in 1905 and in Bolivia one year later, in 1906.

7. Until the liberal revolution and Eloy Alfaro's rise to power, the Ecuadorean government earnestly protected the Catholic Church from any kind of religious competition. See Kuhl, "Protestant Missionary Activity," 1.

8. On the relationship between liberals and Protestantism, see Fonseca Ariza, *Misioneros y civilizadores*; Garrard-Burnett, *Living in the New Jerusalem*, 1–21.

9. Kuhl, "Protestant Missionary Activity," 82–85.

10. Kuhl, "Protestant Missionary Activity," 404–6.

11. Kuhl, "Protestant Missionary Activity," 443–44.

12. Catholic officials continued to view Evangelicals as outsiders well after Vatican II. CELEM, for example, described the growth of Evangelical churches as the "invasion of the sects." See Gill, "Struggle to Be Soul Provider," 19.

13. In 1930 Seventh-day Adventists made up less than 1.5 percent of Puno's population and were not spread evenly across the department but were located mostly in districts close to Lake Titicaca, especially Chucuito and Acora. In these areas, baptized Adventists made up 10–15 percent of the population. For statistics about Puno's Adventist population, see "Sixty-Sixth Annual Statistical Report (1928)," GCASR. For data about the department's general population during the late nineteenth and early twentieth centuries, see Quiroga, "La evolución jurídica," 66–69; Jacobsen, *Mirages of Transition*, 24–27, 270.

14. "Relación incompleta de los sectos adventistas," Archivo Arzobispal de Cusco, caja 177, 1.12.ff.2–10. Adventist schools served adults as well as children, and it is unclear whether these adults are included in the numbers quoted in this report.

15. The most notable examples are Stoll, *Is Latin America Turning Protestant?*, and Martin, *Tongues of Fire*.

16. Jean-Pierre Bastian points to the historical ties between Protestantism and nineteenth-century reform movements, especially in Mexico, see Bastian, *Protestantismos y modernidad latinoamericana.*

17. Garrard-Burnett, *Living in the New Jerusalem*, 60. In comparison, in 1920 the Lake Titicaca mission had 2,255 baptized members. See SDAYR, 1921.

18. Berg and Pretiz, "Latin America's Fifth Wave"; Freston, "Pentecostalism in Latin America."

19. Drinot, "Historiography"; Orlando Melo, "De la Nueva Historia a la historia fragmentada"; Cataño, "La Nueva Historia y sus predecesores."

20. Drinot, "Historiography." For an in-depth historiographical review about scholarship on popular religion in Latin America, see Román and Voekel, "Popular Religion in Latin American Historiography."

21. See Armas Asín, *Liberales, protestantes y masones*; Ramos and Urbano, *Catolicismo y extirpación de idolatrías.*

22. Dan Hazen and Jean Baptist August Kessler have discussed the Seventh-day Adventist work in early twentieth-century Puno as part of their wider research. See Hazen, "Awakening of Puno"; Kessler, *Study of the Older Protestant Missions and Churches.* Ted Lewellen and Juliana Ströbele-Gregor have conducted anthropological studies among Seventh-day Adventist converts in Puno in the 1970s and in La Paz in the 1980s. See Lewellen, *Peasants in Transition*; Ströbele-Gregor, *Indios de piel blanca.*

23. Meethan, "Remaking Time and Space," 101.

24. Lambert, "Reclaiming the Ancestral Past."

25. Roniger and Sznajder, "Politics of Memory"; Olick and Levy, "Collective Memory and Cultural Constraint."

1. Wars, Indians, and the Nation

1. Leinaweaver, "On Moving Children," 164.

2. There are various versions of Camacho's biography. See Gallegos, *Manuel Z. Camacho*; Chambi, "Sección pedagógica," *Platería: Revista extraordinaria en homenaje al 51 de Platería, 1911–1961*, September 3, 1961, 5; Kessler, *Study of the Older Protestant Missions*, 228; Hazen, "Awakening of Puno," 36.

3. Gonzales, "Capitalist Agriculture and Labor Contracting"; Favre, "Dynamics of Indian Peasant Society."

4. Klarén, *Peru: Society and Nationhood*, 183–86.

5. Bonilla, "War of the Pacific," 100–103.

6. Mallon, *Defense of Community*; Manrique, "Campesinado, guerra y conciencia nacional."

7. Klarén, *Peru: Society and Nationhood*, 190–91.

8. Klarén, *Peru: Society and Nationhood*, 193.

9. Klein, *Concise History of Bolivia*, 107–9.

10. Klaiber, *Catholic Church*, 50–52.

11. Piel "Place of the Peasantry," 128.

12. Masterson, *Militarism and Politics*, 27–30.

13. Velásquez Silva, "Indios, soldados sin patria."

14. For the power struggles between Lima and regional elites, see Martínez Riaza, "Política regional y gobierno de la Amazonia"; Nugent, "Building the State, Making the Nation."

15. Davies, *Indian Integration in Peru*, 46.

16. Scholars have offered various estimations concerning the military's size at different points throughout the nineteenth century. For example, the numbers of enlisted soldiers during the War of the Pacific ranges between forty-five hundred and nine thousand, and the highest number of soldiers that Congress approved was thirty thousand during the Chinca Island War (1964–66). See Sater, *Andean Tragedy*, 47; Hunefeldt and Kokotovic, "Power Constellations in Peru," 53.

17. Hunefeldt and Kokotovic, "Power Constellations in Peru," 53.

18. On the Bolivian case, see Shesko, "Mobilizing Manpower for War," 319.

19. Masterson, *Militarism and Politics*, 18.

20. Valcárcel, *Ruta cultural del Perú*, 101.

21. Others have also taken specific note of veterans, often arguing whether their role in the community was positive or negative. See Roca, *Por la clase indígena*, 269.

22. Núñez-Núñez, "Presencia protestante en el altiplano peruano," 157–58.

2. Veterans Return to the Highlands

1. Burga and Flores Galindo, *Apogeo y crisis*, 38.

2. As well as around Lake Arpa. See Maltby, "Indian Revolts in the Altiplano," 48.

3. Quiroga, "La evolución jurídica," 67.

4. About fifteen thousand people were living in these two districts, which covered around 1,550 square kilometers. I calculated these figures from statistics compiled by Manuel Quiroga. See Quiroga, "La evolución jurídica," 64–67; and Guevara Velasco, *Apuntes sobre mi patria*, 701, 707. According to Quiroga, the average population density in 1905 was about five people per square kilometer for the entire department of Puno. In Chucuito and Acora, it was almost double that figure.

5. Gallegos, *Manuel Z. Camacho*, 35.

6. Masterson, *Militarism and Politics*, 18.

7. In this regard, Nils Jacobsen, in *Mirages of Transition*, noted that transactions in the Andes were usually conducted between people who were previously acquainted, often for most of their lives, and not between two anonymous parties who have only recently met. The fact that relationships in the Andes were highly personalistic leaves little room for arbitrary actions or technocratic procedures, including recruitment.

8. Hunefeldt and Kokotovic, *Power Constellations in Peru*, 70.

9. Hunefeldt and Kokotovic, *Power Constellations in Peru*, 76.

10. Méndez, "Militares populistas," 575–77.

11. Méndez, "Militares populistas," 576; Mallon, *Defense of Community*, 103; Hunefeldt, "La guerra y la reconformación del poder local," 157; Foote, "*Monteneros and Macheteros*," 86.

12. Méndez, *Militares populistas*, 576.

13. Celestino, *Migración y cambio*, 35.

14. See, for example, "Venta acciones en la estancia Calacata," September 11, 1902, FNT; "Venta de la estancia Calantacu y sus adyancentes," March 3, 1908, FNT. For Indian complaints against the Pinazo family, see "Memorándum de Mariano Istaña," 1912, APP, caja 236; "Queja de Mariano Polomino," 1906, APP, caja 213; "Queja de Hipólito Cruz Tevez," 1915, APP, caja 246.

15. "Queja de Hipólito Cruz Tevez," 1915, APP, caja 246.

16. See Boelens and Gelles, "Cultural Politics, Communal Resistance"; Gelles, *Water and Power in Highland Peru*; Isbell, *To Defend Ourselves*, 139.

17. Isbell, *To Defend Ourselves*, 139.

18. Tschopik, "Aymara of Chucuito," 156.

19. Similar conflicts between Indians who had climbed the traditional communal hierarchies and younger men, who had not, occurred in other places in the Andes. See Celestino, *Migración y cambio*, 35.

20. See, for example, "Queja de Caquira y Juan de la Cruz Chahuaris," 1980, APP, caja 223.

21. During 1916, clashes between Indians and members of the Pinazo family in the Chucuito Peninsula prevented Jorge Pinazo's entrance to the peninsula. During this time Pablo del Carpio ran the Pinazos' affairs in the area. "Memorandum de Pablo del Carpio (#70)," 1917, APP, caja 254. Del Carpio was related to Jorge Pinazo through the latter's wife, Isaura Carpio.

22. Such tactics had been implemented in the past. For example, in 1906, Salvador Gumaza, an Indian from the district of Acora complained that the governor was conspiring with José Cursi, another Indian and Gumaza's enemy, to expropriate his estancia. At the time, apparently, the governor was conducting a land survey in which he classified Gumaza's private property as belonging to the state. Gumaza requested protection from the subprefect and a guarantee that he would be able to cultivate his lands as he had done before. Whether he was granted the legal protection is unknown due to missing documentation, but this incident adds to the growing evidence concerning land-grabbing tactics. "Queja de Salvador Gumaza," 1906, APP, caja 213.

23. Manrique, *Yawar Mayu*.

24. Jacobsen, *Mirages of Transition*, 244. According to Ted Lewellen, the changes in inheritance began in 1825, when the population density was still low and there was enough land to distribute. See Lewellen, *Peasants in Transition*, 38.

25. Jacobsen, *Mirages of Transition*, 267; Guillet, "Land Tenure, Ecological Zone."

26. "Queja de Pedro Pauro, Juan Huanca y otros," 1912, APP, caja 254.

27. Méndez Notari, *Desierto de esperanzas*.

28. "Queja de Rufino Pilco indígena de Ilave," 1916, APP, caja 251.

29. Gallegos, *Manuel Z. Camacho*, 36.

30. Klaiber, *Catholic Church in Peru*, 182.

31. There is much dispute among scholars over the nature of trial marriage in the Andes. See Bolin, *Rituals of Respect*, 112.

32. Bolin, *Rituals of Respect*, 117.

33. Ayala, *Yo fui canillita*, 186.

34. See, for example, Fuenzalida et al., *El indio y el poder en Perú*; Van den Berghe and Primov, *Inequality in the Peruvian Andes*. Academic discussions over the usage of the term "race" or "ethnicity" were prevalent in the Andean countries, especially Peru. From a historiographical perspective, these discussions could be viewed as both a continuation of and a breaking away from indigenista discourse.

35. Flores Galindo, *In Search of an Inca*, 131.

36. De la Cadena, *Indigenous Mestizos*; Orlove, "Down to Earth"; Weismantel, *Cholas and Pishtacos*; Poole, *Vision, Race, and Modernity*.

37. Weismantel and Eisenman, "Race in the Andes," 121.

38. Setting forth the importance of race in the history of Peru, Flores Galindo contended, "Racism is more than contempt and marginalization. It is an ideological discourse that underpins social domination and accepts the existence of races and the hierarchical relationship among them. Racist discourse in Peru structured itself around the relationship between whites and Indians and then disseminated to other groups." Flores Galindo, *In Search of an Inca*, 132.

39. The idea of *mestizaje*, of course is not new, nor is it a product of scholars advocating the usage of race. It has long existed in research (as well as popular discourse) and was often discussed by the earlier generation of scholars who preferred the term "ethnicity" over "race."

40. De la Cadena, *Indigenous Mestizos*, 220.

41. Lesley Gill, for example, notes that urban Aymara women's clothing, which is considered quintessentially Indian, actually originated among Creoles. See Gill, "'Proper Women' and City Pleasures," 78. Rebecca Earle examines the way dress contributed to the construction of racial and ethnical identities in colonial Anglo- and Latin America. See Earle, "'Two Pink Pairs of Satin Shoes!!'"

42. Orlove, "Down to Earth," 214.

43. In this context Sarah Radcliffe and Sallie Westwood have argued that in the Andes, "race is regionalized and region is racialized." See Radcliffe and Westwood, *Remaking the Nation*, 111.

44. Orlove, "Down to Earth," 214.

45. Nunn, "Professional Militarism," 400.

46. "Queja de Hipólito Mamani, Mariano Vaca Mamani y otros," 1926, APP, caja 276. In another case, Juan Gómez signed a letter in the name of discharged soldiers from the fifth battalion. "Queja de Mamani indígena de Chucuito," 1918, APP, caja 257.

47. Condori Mamani et al., *Andean Lives*, 51.

48. Mamani testifies that some soldiers had in fact reached a relatively high degree of proficiency in Spanish. See *Andean Lives*, 53.

49. Condori Mamani et al., *Andean Lives*, 52.

50. De la Cadena, *Indigenous Mestizos*, 6.

51. On the role of liberal discourse in the Peruvian elites, see McEvoy, *La utopía republicana*.

52. Celestino, *Migración y cambio*, 35.

53. Condori Mamani, *Andean Lives*, 54.

54. Ayala, *Yo fui canillita*, 185.

55. Ayala, *Yo fui canillita*, 184, 186.

56. See, for example, Chambers, *From Subjects to Citizens*; Twinam, *Public Lives, Private Secrets*; Gotkowitz, "Trading Insults."

57. Nigerian World War I veterans displayed similar attitudes toward their peers. See Matthews, "Clock Towers for the Colonized," 268; Kingma, "Demobilization of Combatants after Civil Wars"; Dercon and Ayalew, "Where Have All the Soldiers Gone."

58. Gotkowitz, "Trading Insults," 97.

59. Condori Mamani et al., *Andean Lives*, 5.

60. Ayala, *Yo fui canillita*, 185.

61. "Queja de Santos Valdéz y Mariano Chahuaris indígenas del distrito de Chucuito," marzo 1913, APZC.

62. Weismantel, *Cholas and Pishtacos*, 45.

63. Larson, *Trials of Nation Making*, 197; Kristal, *Una visión urbana*, 182; Klarén, *Peru: Society and Nationhood*, 198–200.

64. Larson, *Trials of Nation Making*, 35–36.

65. Marcos Miranda a Pedro Zulen, 13 febrero 1912, ARPC.

66. Jacobsen, *Mirages of Transition*, 279–80.

67. Jacobsen, *Mirages of Transition*, 279–80.

68. Jacobsen, *Mirages of Transition*, 279–82.

69. Álvarez-Calderón, "Pilgrimages through Mountains," 44.

70. Webster, "Native Pastoralism," 126.

71. The economic burden of sponsoring fiestas caused some individuals to avoid filling positions of authority. See Stain, *Hualcan*, 249–51.

72. Sexton, "Protestantism and Modernization."

73. Willems, *Followers of a New Faith*; d'Epinay, *Haven of the Masses*.

74. Álvarez-Calderón, "Pilgrimages through Mountains," 15.

75. Known veterans who had become teachers include Juan Huanca, Pedro Pauro, Modesto Tarqui, and Mariano Luque. Erasmo Roca also notes that many of the Adventist teachers were army veterans. Roca, *Por la clase indígena*, 207.

76. Roca, *Por la clase indígena*, 207. Converts' military service was also mentioned in the press. See "Distrito de Chucuito," *La Unión*, 17 marzo 1913, APZDA, código 2000027183. My own research has confirmed that at least fifteen converts who joined the church between 1911 and 1920 were veterans.

Considering that it is extremely difficult to track the biographies of specific individuals, this is an impressive figure.

3. Conversion and Regeneration

1. I have been able to confirm that of these twenty-five students, five, or 20 percent, served in the army. Given the nature of sources, the fact that at this time men did not usually identify as veterans in petitions, and that we know close to nothing about Camacho's school before the Adventist missionaries became directly involved, this is an impressive number.

2. Hazen, "Awakening of Puno," 121.

3. Adventists reported that they had about two hundred schools at the time, although official church statistics indicate about eighty. Hazen, "Awakening of Puno," 122.

4. "Queja de los indígenas de Chucuito," 1912, APP, caja 238; "Queja de Máximo Naca, Manuel Yupanqui y otros," 1912, APP, caja 238; "Queja de Santos Valdéz y Mariano Chahuaris indígenas del distrito de Chucuito," marzo 1913, APZC.

5. Thurner, "From Two Nations," 380–85.

6. Chambers, "Little Middle Ground," 33–36.

7. De la Cadena, *Indigenous Mestizos*, 30.

8. García Jordán, "Iglesia y vida cotidiana en el Perú," 67–68.

9. Klarén, *Peru: Society and Nationhood*, 201.

10. Armas Asín, *Liberales, protestantes y masones*, 222–23.

11. Kuhl, "Protestant Missionary Activity," 272.

12. Armas Asín, *Liberales, protestantes y masones*, 133–34.

13. Clayton, *Peru and the United States*, 111–13.

14. Armas Asín, *Liberales, protestantes y masones*, 197–202.

15. "Denuncia de Manuel Z. Camacho y compartes por el delito de sedición y otros," 1914, ECP, 1.

16. "No es hay prisión arbitraria," *La Unión*, 10 marzo 1913, APZDA, código 2000027550; "Habrá justicia?," *El Día*, 10 marzo 1913, APZDA, código 2000027550.

17. "Denuncia de Manuel Z. Camacho y compartes por el delito de sedición y otros," 1914, ECP, 2–3.

18. Abercrombie, *Pathways of Memory and Power*, 355. On fiestas, see Klor de Alva, "Spiritual Conflict and Accommodation"; Randell, "Qoyllur Rit'I"; Manuel Marzal, *La transformación religiosa peruana*; MacCormack, "Pachacuti."

19. Allen, *Hold Life Has*.

20. Weismantel, "Maize Beer and Andean Social Transformation," 863.

21. Allen, *Hold Life Has*, 22.

22. "Curas de la diócesis," AOP.

23. Schmidt, "Fiestas Patronales in the Ecuadorian Andes," 54–60; Marzal, *Estudios sobre religión campesina*, 232.

24. Klaiber, *Catholic Church in Peru*, 180–84.

25. Bull and Lockhart, *Seeking a Sanctuary*, 128.

26. Knight, *Brief History*, 68–71. See also Numbers, *Prophetess of Health*.

27. Stahl, *In the Land of the Incas*, 128, 131.

28. Stahl, *In the Land of the Incas*, 86; Stahl to Spicer, January 20, 1914, SIGC, RG 21, box 61; Wilcox, *In Perils Oft*, 40, 105. For Indian comments about cleanliness, see Stahl, *In the Land of the Incas*, 140.

29. J. W. Westphal, "The Message among the Aymara Indians of Peru," *Advent Review and Sabbath Herald*, August 10, 1911, 12.

30. Langer, "Franciscan Missionary Enterprise," 173–74; Reed, *Pastors, Partners, and Paternalists*, 143; Comaroff and Comaroff, "Fashioning the Colonial Subject," 218–73.

31. Wilcox, *In Perils Oft*, 147.

32. Roca, *Por la clase indígena*, 205.

33. Roca, *Por la clase indígena*, 205.

34. Pohle to Spicer, September 2, 1914, SIGC, RG 21, box 61.

35. Ayala, *Yo fui canillita*, 77.

36. "Carta de Manuel Camacho al presidente de la República," in Kapsoli, *El pensamiento de la Asociación Pro Indígena*, 138.

37. "Denuncia de Manuel Z. Camacho y compartes por el delito de sedición y otros," 1914, ECP, 3.

38. Chambi, "Sección pedagógica," *Platería: Revista extraordinaria en homenaje al 51 de Platería, 1911–1961*, September 3, 1961, 3.

39. Komonchak, Collins, and Lane, *New Dictionary of Theology*, 437–50, 553–55, 836–51.

40. Wade et al., *Mestizo Genomics*, 4.

41. Flores Galindo, *In Search of an Inca*; Burga, *Nacimiento de una utopía*.

42. "Queja de Pedro Santiago y Juan de Dios Quispe y otros al Obispo de Puno," 3 abril 1920, AOP.

43. Szeminski, "Why Kill a Spaniard," 166–92.

44. Szeminski, "Why Kill a Spaniard," 168.

45. Dean, *Inka Bodies and the Body of Christ*, 112–13.

46. Prieto, *Missionary Scientists*, 31–33.

47. Arroyo Reyes, *Nuestros años diez*, 19.

48. Larson, *Trials of Nation Making*, 197; Cornado, *Andes Imagined*.

49. Kristal, *Una visión urbana*, 15.

50. Shesko, "Conscript Nation," 94–97.

51. Valcárcel, *Tempestad en los Andes*, 123–24.

52. Fonseca Ariza, *Misioneros y civilizadores*, 42. Monica Orozco notes a similar tendency for Mexican liberal elites. See Orozco, "Not to Be Called Christian," 182.

53. Valcárcel, *Tempestad en los Andes*, 123.

54. Roca, *Por la clase indígena*, 206.

55. See, for example, Erie, *War against Idols*.

56. "Oficio del Sr. Cura de la parroquia de Santo Domingo," 1910, APP, caja 228.

57. Stahl, *In the Land of the Incas*, 125.

58. On Protestant attitudes toward purgatory, see MacCulloch, *Reformation*, 580–81; Koslofsky, *Reformation of the Dead*. For the Adventist view: Knight, *Search for Identity*, 209.

59. Roca, *Por la clase indígena*, 205.

4. Conversion and Cohesion

1. Thurner, "From Two Nations," 85.

2. Thurner, "From Two Nations," 99.

3. Thurner, "From Two Nations," 107–8.

4. Larson, *Trials of Nation Making*, 57.

5. García Jordán, *Cruz y arado*.

6. 11 de abril 1925, oficios 1925–27, AOP.

7. Manrique, *Yawar Mayu*, 45–48.

8. Thurner, "From Two Nations," 311.

9. Van Young, "Popular Religion and the Politics of Insurgency," 92.

10. Armas Asín, *La invención del patrimonio católico*, 38.

11. Quoted in Fonseca Ariza, *Misioneros y civilizadores*, 225.

12. "Otra carta de Camacho," *El Día*, marzo 1913, APZDA, código 2000027183.

13. See Boelens and Gelles, "Cultural Politics, Communal Resistance"; Gelles, *Water and Power in Highland Peru*; Isbell, *To Defend Ourselves*, 139.

14. Orlove and Godoy, "Sectorial Fallowing Systems," 173.

15. Jacobsen, *Mirages of Transition*, 262.

16. Guillet, "Land Tenure, Ecological Zone," 144; Bourricaud, *Cambios en Puno*, 106.

17. Tschopik, "Aymara of Chucuito," 44.

18. Pesalozzi, "Sectorial Fallow System," 67.

19. Guillet, "Land Tenure, Ecological Zone," 144; Buechler, *Bolivian Aymara*, 11.

20. Bourque, "Developing People and Plants," 79.

21. Hazen, "Awakening of Puno," 233–42.

22. Álvarez-Calderón, "Pilgrimages through Mountains," 113.

23. Mark Thurner discusses this extensively in *From Two Republics to One Divided*.

24. Hunefeldt and Kokotovic, "Power Constellations in Peru"; Manrique, *Yawar Mayu*; Platt, *Estado boliviano y allyu andino*.

25. "Carta de Manuel Camacho al presidente de la república," in Kapsoli, *El pensamiento de la Asociación Pro Indígena*, 138.

26. Álvarez-Calderón, "Pilgrimages through Mountains," 116, 121–24.

27. "Queja de Manuel Camacho vecino del distrito de Chucuito," 1911, APP, caja 234.

28. "Queja de Manuel Camacho vecino del distrito de Chucuito," 1911, APP, caja 234.

29. "Queja de Pedro Pauro, Juan Huanca y otros," 1912, APP, caja 254.

30. Shesko, "Conscript Nation," 2, 82–85.

31. Hunefeldt and Kokotovic, "Power Constellations in Peru," 61, 63.

32. Thurner, "From Two Nations," 213–16.

33. Godoy, "Fiscal Role of the Andean Ayllu," 724–26; Abercrombie, *Pathways of Memory*, 119–21.

34. Platt, "Simón Bolívar, the Sun of Justice," 160; Platt, "Liberalism and Ethnocide," 13.

35. "Carta de los vecinos de Chucuito," *El Eco de Puno*, 1913, APZDA, código 2000027183; For similar examples, see "Denuncia de Manuel Z. Camacho y compartes por el delito de sedición y otros," 1914, ECP, 30; "Crónica de Puno," *La Unión*, 11 septiembre 1913, APZDA, código 2000027183.

36. Thurner, *From Two Republics*, 27.

37. Jacobsen, *Mirages of Transition*, 279.

38. Contreras, "Tax Man Cometh," 116–37.

39. Mallon, *Peasant and Nation*, 18.

40. Wilcox to Shaw, July 5, 1922, SIGC, RG 21, box 48.

41. Maxwell to Westphal, July 1, 1914, SIGC, RG 21, box 58; Wilcox to Shaw, August 31, 1920, GCSS, location 3559 (Treasury).

42. "Carta de los vecinos de la Villa de Acora," *El Eco de Puno*, marzo 1913, APZDA, código 2000027183.

43. Stahl, *In the Land of the Incas*, 53–56.

44. "Denuncia de Manuel Z. Camacho y compartes por el delito de sedición y otros," 1914, ECP, 29.

45. "Queja de los suscritos indios de Chucuito," 1912, APP, caja 238. See also "Queja de Florentino Ordeno y otros indios de distrito de Chucuito," 1912, APP, caja 238.

46. Davies, *Indian Integration in Peru*, 52.

47. "Queja de los suscritos indios de Chucuito," 1912, APP, caja 238.

48. "Queja de los suscritos indios de Chucuito," 1912, APP, caja 238.

49. Mallon, *Peasant and Nation*, 65.

50. Julián Palacios ran an Adventist School in Sandia that had been attacked. See Álvarez-Calderón, "Pilgrimages through Mountains," 121.

51. 3 mayo 1920, oficios 1925–27, AOP.

52. "Queja de Pedro, Santiago y Juan de Dios Quispe," 3 abril 1920, oficios 1925–27, AOP.

53. Poole, "Landscapes of Power in a Cattle-Rustling Culture," 337.

54. "Oficio del vicario capitular," abril 1920, oficios 1925–27, AOP.

55. MacCormack, *Religion in the Andes*, 57.

56. MacCormack, "The Heart has Its Reasons," 443–46.

57. "Queja de Pedro, Santiago y Juan de Dios Quispe," 3 abril 1920, oficios 1925–27, AOP.

58. Carlyle Haynes, "Call for Greater Evangelism," *Advent Review and Sabbath Herald*, November 24, 1927, 7.

59. Smith, *Livelihood and Resistance*, 31.

60. Smith, *Livelihood and Resistance*, 32.

61. Jacobsen, *Mirages of Transition*, 342.

62. Escobar, *Organización social y cultural*, 24.

5. Adventism and the Missionary Enterprise

1. Wilcox, *In Perils Oft*, 18.

2. Wilcox, *In Perils Oft*, 17.

3. On missionaries' narrative and socialization, see Wilson and Cornwall, "Powers of Heaven and Hell."

4. Parker, "Kingdom of Character," 172; Forman, "Americans," 54.

5. Handy, *Christian America*, 113.

6. On early missionary efforts, see Elsbree, *Rise of the Missionary Spirit in America*; Steves, *Poor Indians*; Salisbury, "Red Puritans."

7. Handy, *Christian America*, 113–15; Ahlstrom, *Religious History*, 733.

8. Porter, "Cultural Imperialism," 375; Dunch, "Beyond Cultural Imperialism," 308. Scholars have traced connections between missionary zeal and abolitionist causes, which often put missionaries at odds with other imperial interests. See Bridges, "Exploration and Travel," 55.

9. For a good discussion of the term "cultural imperialism," see Tomlinson, *Cultural Imperialism*, 1–34; Ortiz, "Revisitando la noción de imperialismo cultural"; Dorfman and Mattelart, *Para leer al pato Donald*.

10. Dick, "Millerite Movements, 1830–1845," 3–5, 20.

11. Dick, "Millerite Movements, 1830–1845," 3–5, 20, 27–29.

12. On William Miller and the Millerite movement, see Row, *Thunder and Trumpets*; Numbers and Butler, *Disappointed*.

13. Dick, "Millerite Movements, 1830–1845," 29–31.

14. On Seventh-day Adventist theology and fundamental beliefs, see Rasell, *Exploring the Heavenly Sanctuary*; "Fundamental Beliefs" (Silver Springs MD: General Conference of the Seventh-day Adventist Church, July 11, 2021), https://www.adventist.org/beliefs/fundamental-beliefs/; Anderson, "Sectarianism and Organization, 1846–1864," 39; Theobald, "From Rural Populism to Practical Christianity"; Conkin, *American Originals*, 125.

15. Observing the Sabbath on the seventh day of the week was not a new idea among Protestants. In the seventeenth century, a group of English Baptists, under the leadership of Dr. Peter Chamberlin, called believers to return to the scriptures, follow God's words, and observe the biblical Sabbath. From England the movement spread to the American colonies, eventually creating a new denomination: the Sabbatarian Baptists or the Seventh Day Baptists.

16. Morgan, *Adventism and the American Republic*, 15–17; Morgan, "Adventism, Apocalyptic, and the Cause of Liberty," 237–38.

17. Knight, *Brief History*, 47–49.

18. William Miller also preached notions of the shut door, believing that after the fulfillment of a prophecy, there would be no redemption for sinners and nonbelievers.

19. Morgan, "Remnant and the Republic," 71–73.

20. Butler, "Adventism and the American Experience," 179.

21. Morgan, *Adventism and the American Republic*, 86.

22. James White began to speak of an "open door" instead of a closed door as early as the 1850s.

23. Knight, *Brief History of Seventh-day Adventism*, 64–65.

24. Butler, "Adventism and the American Experience," 190.

25. Knight, *Search for Identity*, 107–8.

26. Knight, *Brief History*, 98–101.

27. Hunt and Bliss, *Religious Bodies: 1916*, 97; In the *Religious Bodies* report, the category of missionaries includes all those commissioned by the missionary societies and their wives. See also "1900 Statistical Report for the Seventh-day Adventist Church," *General Conference Bulletin*, 161–63, https://documents.adventistarchives.org/Statistics/ASR/ASR1900.pdf.

28. Hunt, *Religious Bodies*, 95.

29. Hunt, *Religious Bodies*, 95.

30. This data refers to church membership in the United States and U.S. missionaries. Native membership, missionaries, and local staff are not included. Hunt, *Religious Bodies*, 95.

31. Between 1916 and 1926, the gap between the growth rate of U.S. missionaries in the foreign field and foreign membership remained about the same or grew slightly. See "Sixty-fourth Annual Statistical Report (1926)," GCASR. Conversion is a complicated process that includes various stages. Not everyone who is an adherent has been baptized, and not all baptized are members of the church. Therefore, this comparison should be taken with caution. Conversion to other forms of Christianity, however, was no less complicated, and discrepancies between the missionary growth rate and membership growth rate are not as big as they were in the Seventh-day Adventists' case.

32. Parker, "Kingdom of Character," 176.

33. I have drawn the statistics for these calculations from the following sources: Nelson, *Fifty Years of History of the Ohio Wesleyan University*, 116; Findlay, "Moody, 'Gapmen,' and the Gospel," 332; Wheeler, "Alumni Echos," *Educational Messenger*, June 15, 1906, 2.

34. Morgan, *Adventism and the American Republic*, 67–70.

35. Bull and Lockhart, *Seeking a Sanctuary*, 167–71.

6. Adventists and Modern Times

1. Maxwell to Westphal, June 29, 1914, SIGC, RG 21, box 60.

2. Marty, *Righteous Empire*, 155–65; Stavely, *Puritan Legacies*; Stoll, *Protestantism, Capitalism and Nature*.

3. Butler, "Midwest's Spiritual Landscapes," 197. The Midwest has been and still is considered the most religiously diverse region in the United States.

4. Cayton and Gray, *American Midwest*, 3.

5. Graybill, "Millenarians and Money," 33–35. The prominence of rural population within the Adventist Church was also true of later periods. See Sahlin, *Demographic Profile*; Rowe, "Millerites: A Shadow Portrait," 9.

6. Graybill, "Millenarians and Money," 33.

7. Personal correspondence between the author and Robert Ford (Orley Ford's grandson), August 23, 2014.

8. Elder Ellis Howard's history by Hazel (Howard) Peters, Mark Peters's personal archive. On the creation of a rural middle class, see Kelly, "Well Bred Country People," 451–79; Barron, *Mixed Harvest*.

9. Kalbermatter, *20 años como misionero entre los indios del Perú*, 11–15.

10. For the sake of comparison, the Anchorena family, among the largest landowners in the history of Argentina, who had their holdings in the province of Buenos Aires, in 1864 owned 9,582 square kilometers of land with livestock that numbered in the thousands. Diego de Alvear, a large estancia owner in Santa Fe, possessed over ten thousand hectares of land. Nevertheless, in the cereal zones of Santa Fe, farms varied between 33 and 150 hectares, with only a few reaching up to 600 hectares. See Brown, "Nineteenth-Century Argentine Cattle Empire"; Solberg, "Peopling the Prairies and the Pampas." Also see Gallo, "Cereal Boom," 331–35.

11. Mills, *White Collar*, 3.

12. Mills, *White Collar*, 3.

13. Blumin, *Emergence of the Middle Class*, 8; also see Blumin's in-depth historiographical analysis on the formation of the middle class in the United States: Blumin, "Hypothesis of Middle-Class Formation"; Bledstein, *Culture of Professionalism*; Roberts, *American Alchemy*; Mahoney, *Provincial Lives*.

14. Graybill, "Millenarians and Money," 40.

15. D. H. Lamson, "Responsibilities," *Advent Review and Sabbath Herald*, January 13, 1874, 39.

16. "Sabbath-Breaking Partnerships," *Advent Review and Sabbath Herald*, March 21, 1854, 70.

17. The Seventh-day Adventist missionaries reached the southern U.S. states in the 1870s, and in 1886 the first all–African American Adventist church was established in Edgefield, Tennessee. In 1895 the Adventists established Oakwood College in Huntsville, Alabama, for African American Adventists. See Bull and Lockhart, *Seeking a Sanctuary*, 193–95.

18. Bull and Lockhart, *Seeking a Sanctuary*, 2nd ed., 273.

19. Jacque Le Goff has described tensions between "merchant time" and "church time" in the Middle Ages over whether one could charge money for time, since time, according to church theologians, did not belong to men and therefore was not theirs to profit from. See Le Goff, *Time, Work, and Culture*, 43–53.

20. On the constructing of the yeoman farmer class and its opportunities through the nineteenth century, see Kulikuff, *Agrarian Origins of American Capitalism* (especially chap. 2).

21. Engerman and Gallman, *Cambridge Economic History*, 282.

22. Lindert, "Long Run Trends in America Farm-Land Values," 45–85.

23. Engerman and Gallman, *Cambridge Economic History*, 275. See also Cox, "American Agricultural Wage Earner"; Kloppenburg and Geisler, "Agricultural Ladder," 60.

24. Argersinger and Argersinger, "Machine Breakers," 394.

25. On the historiographical debate over the agricultural ladder, see Atack, "Agricultural Ladder Revisited"; Cox, "Tenancy in the United States."

26. In 1820, for example, 80 percent of the produce produced in the U.S. rural North was consumed by people living in the rural North. Of the remaining 20 percent, about three-fourths was consumed by the northern urban population, a small part was sold in the South, and the rest (4 percent of the total) was exported. By 1870 rural communities were consuming 60 percent and the urban community was consuming 80 percent of the produce offered for sale (out of the remaining 40 percent). See Danohof, *Change in Agriculture*, 11.

27. Danbom, *Born in the Country*, 133.

28. For example, U.S. wheat exportation was thriving due to disastrous harvests in Europe in 1879–81 and in Russia and India in 1890–91. Rothstein, "America in the International Rivalry," 402, 404.

29. Engerman and Gallman, *Cambridge Economic History*, 282.

30. Barron, *Those Who Stayed Behind*, 93–97.

31. Henretta, "Families and Farms," 8.

32. Yoder, "Rethinking Midwestern Farm Tenure," 464–67.

33. Alvin Allen named his brother, Arthur Allen, as his next of kin to be informed in case of death, his address being the family farm. See file for Alvin Allen, General Conference of the SDA Church (Appointee files).

34. Untitled article, *St. Cloud (Minnesota) Journal*, August 20, 1874, 2.

35. History of the Ana Stahl clinic [in Spanish], http://www.clinicaanastahl.org.pe/nav.php?op=historia#/page/1 (page discontinued).

36. Mayer, "Midwestern Industrialization," 925.

37. These numbers refer to a farm operated by its owners. See Marriam, "Twelfth Census of the United States, Taken in the Year 1900," 148; Porter and Wright, "Report on the Statistics of Agriculture in the United States, Eleventh Census: 1890"; Sennett, *Families against the City*, 85. The variation in size, agricultural activity, and productivity of farms led to a wide array of possibilities for profit. And white-collar salaries ran a relatively wide gamut between low-ranking clerks to high-ranking managers and administrators. Without important statistical measurements such as the standard deviation and the median, not to mention indicators such as the costs of tuition, it is hard to provide an exact assessment of the economic advantages of white-collar professions vis-à-vis the economic advantages of agricultural enterprises

during this period. Nevertheless, the average income presented does illuminate, even if impressionistically, part of the appeal these new careers had.

38. Marriam, "Twelfth Census of the United States," 151.

39. Florey and Guest, "Coming of Age among US Farm Boys," 246.

40. Cram and Stebbins, *Official Map of Michigan, Railroad, Township and Sectional* (Chicago: Commissioner of Railroads, 1885), accessed February 19, 2022, via Library of Congress Geography and Map Division, Washington DC, https://www.loc.gov/item/98688499.

41. Knight, *Brief History of Seventh-day Adventism*, 76.

42. E. H. Morton "Maine," *Atlantic Union Gleaner*, April 22, 1907, 135.

43. Florey and Guest, *Coming of Age*, 240.

44. G. I. B., "Rural versus City Life," *Advent Review and Sabbath Herald*, January 7, 1890, 9.

45. "Tampa, Fla.," *Field Tidings*, April 21, 1915, 6.

46. "Tampa, Fla.," 6.

47. Thompson, "Time, Work-Discipline, and Industrial Capitalism."

48. Quoted in Hunnicutt, "Jewish Sabbath Movement," 197. See also "Sunday-Sabbath Movement," 75–89.

49. "Note and comment," *Advent Review and Sabbath Herald*, May 20, 1902, 6.

50. On the Jewish Sunday-Sabbath Movement, see Olitzky, "Sunday-Sabbath Movement."

51. "Note and comment," 6.

52. On the Christian discourse of truth and sacrifice, see Perkins, *Suffering Self*; Cohen, "Towards a History of European Physical Sensibility"; Hron, *Translating Pain*.

53. Bynum, "Violent Imagery in Late Medieval Piety," 3–36.

54. McCrossen, *Holy Day, Holiday*, 15.

55. Foster, *Moral Reconstruction*, 94–95.

56. "Why Christians Should Oppose Religious Legislation," *Advent Review and Sabbath Herald*, February 16, 1905, 4.

57. Bull, "Seventh-day Adventists."

58. Twelfth meeting, December 5, 1886, meeting transcriptions of the General Conference of the Seventh-day Adventist Church, 323, 63–88.

59. "Items," *Atlantic Union Gleaner*, July 21, 1915, 6.

60. For another example, see "Our President," *Columbia Union Visitor*, October 25, 1911, 5.

61. Knight, *Brief History*, 77.

62. Land, *Adventism in America*, 68, 124.

63. Land, *Adventism in America*, 124.

64. F. A. Painter, "Fear Thou Not," *Atlantic Union Gleaner*, March 30, 1904, 153; Arthur Wright, "A Living Guaranteed," *Indiana Reporter*, September 2, 1908, 16; J. W. Wilson, "I Can't Make a Living," supplement to *Advent Review and Sabbath Herald*, August 31, 1897, 8.

65. "Our Publishing Work," *Advent Review and Sabbath Herald*, July 12, 1906, 1; J. W. Hirlinger, "Elder J. W. Hirlinger Reports," *Advent Review and Sabbath Herald*, April 15, 1915, 24.

66. "The Conference," *New York Indicator*, February 4, 1903, 2.

67. This data is compiled from the 1916 Census Report on Religious Bodies. The statistical report on religious bodies includes the number of denominational hospitals, but it does not include the number of people employed in those institutions. Compiling this information from other source, in a way that would allow comparison with other denominations, is problematic and therefore not included in my calculation. Nevertheless, the reader should take into consideration that Adventists operated about twenty hospitals, which is a high number in both absolute and relative terms. Simply put, it is likely the number of Adventists employed by the church was more than 25 percent and probably closer to 30 percent. See Hunt and Bliss, *Religious Bodies*.

68. This number refers to Methodists that were members of the Methodist Episcopal Church as reported in the 1916 Census Report on Religious Bodies. Additionally, the percentage of Latter-day Saints employed by the church takes the number of members under the age of thirteen into consideration, since the number of children is especially high in that denomination.

69. Union College was one of the first Adventist institutions for higher education, founded in 1891.

70. Mertie Wheeler, "Alumni Echos," *Educational Messenger*, June 15, 1906, 2.

71. Bailey, "Professional Distribution of College and University Graduates."

72. On the bureaucratic expansion of the church, see Schwartz, "Perils of Growth, 1886–1905," 123.

73. "Statistics Show Growth," *Advent Review and Sabbath Herald*, September 9, 1915, 2.

74. Orley Ford quoted in Serns, "Why Not Try This . . . ?"

75. Gonzales and Gonzales, *Christianity in Latin America*, 184–90.

76. The British had established churches aimed at serving English speakers already in the 1810s.

77. Bahamonde, "Establishment of Evangelical Christianity in Peru," 139; Gonzales and Gonzales, *Christianity in Latin America*, 224–25.

78. Greenleaf, *Land of Hope*, 21–23.

79. In Puno alone, more than a third of the missionaries had German surnames.

80. In 1917 the Lake Titicaca mission, under the supervision of Ferdinand Stahl, became an independent entity under the direct supervision of the Inca Union Mission.

81. Greenleaf, *Land of Hope*, 190–92.

82. Maxwell to Westphal, January 4, 1914, SIGC, RG 21, box 62.

83. O. Montgomery, "Dedication of the Lanca Indian Church," *Advent Review and Sabbath Herald*, October 4, 1917, 13.

84. Bastian, "Metamorphosis of Latin American Protestant Groups," 40.

85. Greenleaf, *Land of Hope*, 192.

86. Fonseca Ariza, *Misioneros y civilizadores*, 341–43. The Evangelical Union of South America was the successor to a British mission named Regions Beyond Missionary Union.

87. Fonseca Ariza, *Misioneros y civilizadores*, 86–87.

88. F. L. Perry, "Peru," *Advent Review and Sabbath Herald*, April 25, 1907, 16.

89. E. L. Maxwell, "Blazing Light in Peru," *Advent Review and Sabbath Herald*, February 21, 1918, 11.

90. Maxwell to Westphal, January 4, 1914, SIGC, RG 21, box 62.

91. Maxwell to Westphal, January 4, 1914, SIGC, RG 21, box 62.

92. Allen to Spicer, October 14, 1910, SIGC, RG 21, box 49.

93. Allen to Spicer, October 14, 1910, SIGC, RG 21, box 49.

94. F. L. Perry, "In Peru," *Advent Review and Sabbath Herald*, August 16, 1906, 12–13.

95. Fonseca Ariza, *Misioneros y civilizadores*, 48.

96. Maxwell to Spicer, December 24, 1914, SIGC, RG 21, box 60.

7. Sacrifices and Experiences

1. "The Fifty-Sixth Annual Statistical Report (1918)," GCASR, 6.

2. Goslin, "Protestantism in Peru," 149–64.

3. Article 2 of the Argentine constitution of 1852 states that the "Federal Government supports the Roman Catholic Church." Hence, while Catholicism is not an official state religion, and practice of other religion was legal, the Catholic Church still enjoyed the support, including the financial support, of the government. See Jesús Méndez, "Church and State Relations," 225–26.

4. Armas Asín, *Liberales, protestantes y masones*, 430–31.

5. Klaiber, *Catholic Church in Peru*, 62.

6. "Denuncia de Manuel Z. Camacho y compartes por el delito de sedición y otros," 1914, ECP.

7. Sin título, *El Eco de Puno*, 17 marzo 1913, APZDA, código 2000027183.

8. Stahl to Spicer, January 3, 1913, SIGC, RG 21, box 58.

9. Westphal to Spicer, May 31, 1911, SIGC, RG 21, box 45.

10. Knight, *Search for Identity*, 70.

11. Morgan, *Adventism and the American Republic*, 53.

12. F. L. Perry, "Peru," *Advent Review and Sabbath Herald*, December 19, 1907, 17.

13. Maxwell to Knopp, July 12, 1915, SIGC, RG 21, box 64.

14. Maxwell to Knopp, July 12, 1915, SIGC, RG 21, box 64.

15. I. H. Evens, "A Day of Opportunity," *Advent Review and Sabbath Herald*, August 26, 1909, 5.

16. Parker, "Kingdom of Character," 186.

17. Parker, "Kingdom of Character," 171, 189–90.

18. See, for example, Pratt, *Imperial Eyes*, 18; Twain, *Innocents Abroad*, 456.

19. Herzig, *Suffering for Science*, 50–51. Social scientists also took part in this wide discourse; see Mizruchi, *Science of Sacrifice*, 29.

20. Knight, *Search for Identity*, 100–103. On the relationship between justification, sacrifice, and atonement, see Larsen and Treier, *Cambridge Companion to Evangelical Theology*, 79–92.

21. Knight, *Search for Identity*, 101.

22. Maxwell to Knopp, July 12, 1915, SIGC, RG 21, box 64.

23. Aside from prohibiting labor on Saturday, Judaism consists of a series of regulations and restrictions concerning if, how, and when one can consume or benefit from anything produced on Saturday, see Peninei Halakha, "Ma'aseh Shabbat and Lifnei Iver," https://ph.yhb.org.il/en/category/01/01-26/, accessed January 2022.

24. Varney to Spicer, June 12, 1917, SIGC, RG 21, box 16. The General Conference of the Seventh-day Adventist Church is the governing body of this denomination.

25. Crowley, "Sensibility of Comfort," 751.

26. Crowley, "Sensibility of Comfort," 750–52. Christine Adams has also demonstrated the prevalence of the notion of comfort among the French middle classes from the middle of the eighteenth century. See Adams, *Taste for Comfort and Status*.

27. Swedberg, "Tocqueville and the Spirit of American Capitalism," 48. "The passion for physical comforts is essentially a passion of the middle classes: with those classes it grows and spreads, with them it preponderates" (Alexis de Toqueville, *Democracy in America*, 600).

28. Horowitz, "Frugality or Comfort," 240–44; Grier, *Culture and Comfort*.

29. Horowitz, "Frugality or Comfort," 244.

30. Stoler, "Making Empire Respectable," 639; McClintock, *Imperial Leather*, 47–48.

31. Maxwell to Knopp, July 12, 1915, SIGC, RG 21, box 64.

32. Wilcox, *In Perils Oft*, 27.

33. Commenting on missionaries' living conditions, Orley Ford makes a similar observation, stating, "Of course it's very expensive to live as we would in the United States, and our workers here do not even try. However, they are fixed up rather comfortably." Ford quoted in Serns, "Why Not Try This . . . ?" I extend my gratitude to Robert Ford and Dan Serns for their valuable help.

34. On the crisis of manhood in the United States, see Kimmel, "Consuming Manhood."

35. E. H. Wilcox, "Nearly Two Hundred Converts Baptized," *Advent Review and Sabbath Herald*, September 19, 1918, 11.

36. See, for example, Stahl, *In the Land of the Incas*, 71.

37. Grier, *Culture and Comfort*, 5.

38. For an interdisciplinary review of relevant research regarding the conceptual and practical construction of the "home," see Mallet, "Understanding Home."

39. Ford quoted in Serns, "Why Not Try This . . . ?"

40. Marsh, "From Separation to Togetherness."

41. Ford quoted in Serns, "Why Not Try This . . . ?"

42. Ford quoted in Serns, "Why Not Try This . . . ?"

43. Elder and Mrs. C. V. Achenbach, "New Central Mission Station," *Field Tidings*, November 1, 1916, 2.

44. On domesticity in the United States, see Matthews, *"Just a House-wife"*; Kaplan, "Manifest Domesticity"; Fitts, "Archaeology of Middle-Class Domesticity," 39–62.

45. Coleman, "Ancient Greek Ethnocentrism," 189; Patterson, *Inventing Western Civilization*.

46. Elder and Mrs. C. V. Achenbach, "Peru," *Field Tidings*, January 5, 1916, 2.

47. Zakim, *Ready Made Democracy*, 102–5.

48. Zakim, *Ready Made Democracy*, 108.

49. Stahl to Spicer, August 8, 1916, SIGC, RG 21, box 64.

50. Cohen, "Missionary as Stranger"; Beidelman, "Contradictions between the Sacred," 85.

51. Johnson, *Shopkeepers Millennium*, 8.

52. Wilcox, *In Perils Oft*, 35–37.

53. Pohle to Spicer, September 2, 1914, SIGC, RG 21, box 61. Note that Stahl's presumed income includes his and that of his wife, while Pohle's income is his alone.

54. DeVault, *Sons and Daughters of Labor*, 61.

55. Starr, *Social Transformation of American Medicine*, 84.

56. Parker, *Idea of the Middle Class*, 91. For the conversion between currencies, see Pastor, "Peru: Monetary Exchange," 9.

57. Westphal to Spicer, May 11, 1911, SIGC, RG 21, box 45.

58. Jacobsen, *Mirages of Transition*, 313. The figure of $150 is a rough estimate, as the average exchange rate between the libra peruana and the U.S. dollar is missing for the year 1909. Marisol de la Cadena also provides insight into the earnings of Cuzco's elite: in 1906 the twenty wealthiest families in the city reported an annual income of 600–1,000 soles ($12–$20), which appears to be too low. It is possible that the numbers reflect partial income, or that "soles" actually refers to the libra peruana (thus making the annual income roughly $150–$200 a year). The source of this income is unknown, however; considering the amount, it is likely to be an income from the various professions these men practiced rather than their hacienda revenue. In other words, this figure most likely represents only part of their income. It does, however, give an indication as to where missionaries stood in comparison with local elites; see de la Cadena, *Indigenous Mestizos*, 313.

59. Tamayo Herrera, *Historia social e indigenismo*, 155, 157–58.

60. Varney to Spicer, June 12, 1917, SIGC, RG 21, box 16.

61. Ford quoted in Serns, "Why Not Try This . . . ?"

62. Kruggeler, "Changing Consumption Patterns and Everyday Life," 33–34.

63. Parker, *Idea of the Middle Class*, 58–60; Owensby, *Intimate Ironies*, 109.

64. Kruggeler, "Changing Consumption Patterns," 36.

65. Kruggeler, "Changing Consumption Patterns," 37–38, 48.

66. Valcárcel, *Memorias*, 35.

67. Kruggeler, "Changing Consumption Patterns," 36.

68. Ford quoted in Serns, "Why Not Try This . . . ?"

69. Encinas, *Un ensayo de escuela nueva*, 179–209; Leibner, "New Indians," 145 [in Hebrew].

70. Kruggeler, "Changing Consumption Patterns," 41.

71. Kruggeler, "Changing Consumption Patterns," 59.

72. At the time, European, especially British, commodities dominated the local market. See Valcárcel, *Memorias*, 36; Kruggeler, "Changing Consumption Patterns," 34–35.

73. Stahl, *In the Land of the Incas*, 62.

74. Stahl, *In the Land of the Incas*, 61, 62.

75. Stahl's understating of the term "cholo" is equivalent, more or less, to the term "mestizo." He does not differentiate between the two as modern scholarship often does. For a summary of scholarly approaches to the term "cholo," see Weismantel, *Cholas and Pishtacos*, 92; Bourricaud, *Cambios en Puno*, 202–4.

76. Ford quoted in Serns, "Why Not Try This . . . ?"

77. J. W. Westphal, "The Work among the Indians of Peru," *Advent Review and Sabbath Herald*, August 16, 1915, 10.

78. Maxwell to Knopp, July 12, 1915, SIGC, RG 21, box 64.

79. Francois, "Products of Consumption," 216–17.

80. Tinsman, "Indispensable Services of Sisters," 43; Katzman, *Seven Days a Week*.

81. Wilcox, *In Perils Oft*, 63.

82. Dudden, *Serving Women*.

83. Wilcox, *In Perils Oft*, 64.

84. Wilcox, *In Perils Oft*, 64.

85. Stahl to Spicer, August 8, 1916, SIGC, RG 21, box 64.

86. Pohle to Spicer, September 2, 1914, SIGC, RG 21, box 61.

87. Varney to Spicer, June 12, 1917, SIGC, RG 21, box 16.

88. Shaw to Amundsen, June 16, 1925, SAD, RG 21, box 28.

89. Parker, "Kingdom of Character," 130–35; Putney, *Muscular Christianity*.

90. Pohle to Spicer, August 23, 1915, RG 21, box 64.

91. Maxwell to Spicer and Knox, January 12, 1918, SGGC, RG 21, box 22.

92. Stahl to Spicer, August 8, 1916, SIGC, RG 21, box 64.

93. Meyers to Williams, May 13, 1924, SAD, RG 31; "Petition Concerning Stahl 1919," SIGC, location 3811, RG 21.

94. Westphal to Spicer, May 11, 1911, SIGC, RG 21, box 45.

8. Building an "Indian" Mission

1. Land, *Historical Dictionary*, 285.

2. Land, *Adventism in America*, 139–40.

3. Stahl, *In the Land of the Incas*, 68.

4. Leonard, "La Paz, Bolivia: Its Population and Growth," 452.

5. On Stahl's interest in the Indians, see Stahl, *In the Land of the Incas*, 104; Stahl to Spicer, November 23, 1910, SIGC, RG 21, box 49.

6. Stahl to Spicer, February 17, 1910, SIGC, RG 21, box 49. In 1911, the year Stahl officially moved to Puno, the mission in Bolivia had a membership of three converts and there was one man operating the church. See 1911 Yearbook, SDAYR, 219.

7. Stahl to Spicer, November 23, 1910, SIGC, RG 21, box 49.

8. Fitzpatrick-Behrens, *Maryknoll Catholic Mission in Peru*, 68–70.

9. Canessa, "Evangelical Protestantism," 21–40.

10. Álvarez-Calderón, "Pilgrimages through Mountains," 114.

11. Maxwell to Bowen, July 12, 1915, SIGC, RG 21, box 64.

12. Within the global Protestant missionary movement, there were other missions that attempted to identify themselves with the native population by adopting different cultural traits. One notable example is the China Inland Mission, whose missionaries dressed in traditional Chinese attire to present themselves as more accessible to the local population. See Semple, "Conversion and Highest Welfare," 29–50.

13. Wilson, "Indian Citizenship and the Discourse of Hygiene," 165–80.

14. Stahl to Spicer, January 5, 1914, SIGC, RG 21, box 61.

15. Canessa, "Evangelical Protestantism." For a general outline of the development of Protestantism in Bolivia, see Tapia, "Protestantismo y política."

16. Clorinda Matto de Turner was an example of one such exception, as she converted to Methodism.

17. Stahl to Spicer, November 23, 1910, SIGC, RG 21, box 49.

18. Kagan, "From Noah to Moses," 23.

19. Klein, *Concise History of Bolivia*, 150; Yeager, "Elite Education in Nineteenth-Century Chile," 79.

20. Spicer to Stahl, March 30, 1919, SIGC, location 3316, RG 21.

21. Spicer to Stahl, March 30, 1919.

22. Holms, *History of Christian Spirituality*, 17–22. Peter Brown has discussed the issue of poverty and the roots of the Catholic Church's attitudes toward wealth. See Brown, *Poverty and Leadership in the Later Roman Empire*; Brown, *Through the Eye of the Needle*.

23. Geremek, *Poverty: A History*, 21–22; Pullan, "Catholics, Protestants, and the Poor," 441–56; Kahl, "Religious Roots of Modern Poverty Policy."

24. Stern, *Eugenic Nation*, 14.

25. Stern, *Eugenic Nation*, 14; Kevles, *In the Name of Eugenics*, 40–45.

26. Kevles, *In the Name of Eugenics*, 40–45.

27. Maxwell to Knopp, July 12, 1915, SIGC, RG 21, box 64.

28. Phole to Spicer, May 6, 1914, SIGC, RG 21, box 61; Maxwell to Westphal, July 1, 1914, SIGC, RG 21, box 60.

29. Stahl, *In the Land of the Incas*, 227–28.

30. Andrew Porter suggests that missionary expansion often went with no particular logic, missionaries responding to local requests, personal rivalries, or fear of other denominations. See Porter, *Religion versus Empire?*, 162.

31. Gallegos, *Manuel Z. Camacho*, 31.

32. Pent, "Bridging the Rural-Urban Divide," 61.

33. In Indigenous imagination, strangers are tied to mythical creatures, one of which is popularly known as the Pishtaco. See Weismantel *Cholas and Pishtacos*; Olivar-Smith, "Pishtaco: Institutionalized Fear in Highland Peru"; Wolfenzon, "El 'Pishtaco.'"

34. Stahl, *In the Land of the Incas*, 196, 200.

35. Stahl quoted in Maxwell to Spicer, June 15, 1916, SIGC, RG 21, box 4.

36. On Giesecke's role in Cuzco, see Hiatt, "Flying 'Cholo.'"

37. Fonseca Ariza, *Misionaros y civilizadores*, 48.

38. On the Seventh-day Adventists' attitudes toward the United States, see Bull, "Seventh-day Adventists"; Butler, "From Millerism to Seventh-day Adventism," 50–64.

39. Elder and Mrs. C. V. Achenbach, "New Central Mission Station," *Field Tidings*, January 5, 1916, 2; Stahl to Spicer, August 1916, SIGC, RG 21, box 64.

40. Seventh-day Adventists had strong contacts with liberal Peruvian politicians, leading intellectuals, and other public figures like the chairmen of the Peruvian Temperance Society. See Maxwell to Spicer, July 1, 1914, SIGC, RG 21, box 60.

41. Álvarez-Calderón, "Pilgrimages through Mountains," 114.

42. Álvarez-Calderón, "Pilgrimages through Mountains," 136.

43. Álvarez-Calderón, "Pilgrimages through Mountains," 123; Hazen, "Awakening of Puno," 118.

44. Roca, *Por la clase indígena*, 205.

45. Furniss, "Resistance, Coercion, and Revitalization," 242.

46. Erick Langer, for example, demonstrates that while missionaries and Indian leaders shared a common interest in the preservation of Indian land, they were at odds when it came to preserving traditional leadership. See Langer, *Expecting Pears from an Elm Tree*, 170–73.

47. Unanchiri (pseudonym), "Homenaje a Platería," *Platería: Revista extraordinaria en homenaje al 51 de Platería, vocero de las inquietudes de nueva generación de campesinos puneños*, September 3, 1961, 13.

48. See, for example, Stahl, *In the Land of the Incas*, 198, 214–16.

49. Westphal to the brethren of the General Conference Committee, May 31, 1911, SIGC, RG 21, box 45.

50. Westphal to the brethren of the General Conference Committee, May 31, 1911, SIGC, RG 21, box 45.

51. Juan Ossio offers a structured analysis of the Andean social institutions of "compadrazgo" and "padrinazgo." See Ossio, "Cultural Continuity, Structure, and Context."

52. Jacobsen, *Mirages of Transition*, 226; Smith, *Livelihood and Resistance*, 170.

53. Howell to Bowen, September 16, 1916, SGGC, RG 21, box 3.

54. Maxwell to Spicer, December 24, 1914, SIGC, RG 21, box 60.

55. Maxwell to Spicer, November 13, 1917, SGGC, RG 21, box 13.

9. The Lake Titicaca Mission

1. See, for example, Stahl to Bowen, January 13, 1920, SIGC, location 3326, RG 21.

2. Stahl to Bowen, January 13, 1920, SIGC, location 3326, RG 21. At the time, the Mexican Revolution was in its final stages.

3. Varney to Spicer, May 9, 1918, SGGC, RG 21, box 26.

4. Maxwell to Spicer, November 13, 1917, SGGC, RG 21, box 26; Varney to Spicer, May 9, 1918, SGGC, RG 21, box 26.

5. Stahl to Daniels, Spicer, and Bowen, January 22, 1920, SIGC, location 3326, RG 21.

6. Letter to Stahl, March 8, 1920, SIGC, location 3326, RG 21.

7. Burga, "Los profetas de la rebelión," 474.

8. Rengifo, "Esbozo biográfico de Ezequiel Urivola y Rivero."

9. Valcárcel, *Tempestad en los Andes*, 40–43.

10. Wilcox, *In Perils Oft*, 22.

11. Historian Martin Marty argues that at the end of the nineteenth century and during the beginning of the twentieth, U.S. Christianity was divided by two major ecumenical trends: The first, which he calls "private," emphasized personal redemption and individual moral behavior. The second, which he named "public," tended to look at the wider social order and demanded Christian activism in this world. The "social Gospel" movement sprung out of the public trend. See Marty, *Righteous Empire*, 179–80.

12. Land, *Adventism in America*, 110–11.

13. Land, *Adventism in America*, 136–37.

14. "Business Notices," *Advent Review and Sabbath Herald*, February 13, 1908, 22.

15. Larson, *Trials of Nation Making*, 204.

16. Wilcox, *In Perils Oft*, 58.

17. It is unclear what proportion of missionaries' salaries was paid by the General Conference and how much was covered by tithes collected locally. It appears that the General Conference paid for missionaries' salaries and part of their travel and living expenses and tithes covered native workers and local expenses. But the balances changed, and various donations coming from conferences in the global north also help cover expenses.

18. Wilcox to Bowen, December 2, 1923, SIGC, location 3505, RG 21; Wilcox, *In Perils Oft*, 68.

19. Corwin, "Picturing Efficiency," 141. On the culture of efficiency in the United States during the first decades of the twentieth century, see Cobley, *Modernism and the Culture of Efficiency*; Alexander, *Mantra of Efficiency*.

20. Greenleaf, *Land of Hope*, 184.

21. Wilcox, *In Perils Oft*, 77.

22. Wilcox, *In Perils Oft*, 78.

23. Wilcox, *In Perils Oft*, 78.

24. Wilcox, *In Perils Oft*, 78.

25. "Pastor: When Is a Candidate Prepared for Baptism?," *Ministry: International Journal for Pastors* (July 1952), https://www.ministrymagazine.org/archive/1952/07/when-is-a-candidate-prepared-for-baptism; D. P. Wood, "The Test of Discipleship," *Ministry* 1 no.9 (September 1928): 12.

26. Greenleaf, *Land of Hope*, 184; Wilcox to Bowen, December 4, 1923, SIGC, location 3505, RG 21.

27. Wilcox to Bowen, December 4, 1923, SIGC, location 3505, RG 21.

28. Hazen, "Awakening of Puno," 111.

29. Ford to Bowen, December 2, 1920, SGGC, RG 21, box 48.

30. It may prove fruitful to compare Seventh-day Adventists' attitudes toward conversion with the French Catholic "White Fathers" mission to Rwanda, although the two situations are very different in scope and scale. The White Fathers had initially tried to convert the ruling Tutsi class, but they failed and turned to the underprivileged Hutus (who, like the Indigenous population in Peru and Bolivia, made up the majority of their respective country's population). The Hutus hoped, as did the Aymara Indians, that the Catholic Church would protect them against oppression and provide them with new opportunities. During the 1920s, the White Fathers once again directed their conversion efforts to the Tutsi, this time with great success (one that Seventh-day Adventists never achieved with mestizo populations). The cost of this achievement, however, was the decline of the Hutu Church, just as what happened, although less dramatically, with the Seventh-day Adventist missions to Indians in Peru. Even more intriguing in this context are the young Hutu men who were formerly educated in the Catholic Church and had become prominent activists in the 1959 revolution. Like Camacho and Juan Huanca, they were teachers and former members of the seminary. See Linden and Linden, *Church and Revolution in Rwanda*.

31. E. H. Wilcox, "The Puno English School," *Advent Review and Sabbath Herald*, April 3, 1924, 20.

32. Wilcox, "Puno English School."

33. Wilcox, "Puno English School."

34. Maxwell to Westphal, July 1, 1914, SIGC, RG 21, box 60.

35. H. M. Coulburn, "A School for All Classes," *Advent Review and Sabbath Herald*, July 26, 1923, 8.

36. Maxwell to Bowen, May 18, 1924, SIGC, location 3505, RG 21.

37. Walter E. Murray, "Australia Help Us," *Australian Record*, October 22, 1928, 4; B. L. Thompson, "Lake Titicaca Training School," *Advent Review and Sabbath Herald*, October 23, 1924, 11.

38. Arroyo Reyes, *Nuestros años diez*, 78–80.

39. Leibner, "Radicalism and Integration," 7; Pent, "Bridging the Rural-Urban Divide," 17.

40. About Leguía's Indigenous policy, see Davis, *Indian Integration*, 68–95; Klarén, *Peru: Society and Nationhood*, 247–48. For an additional interpretation, see Leibner, "Radicalism and Integration."

41. Kapsoli, *Ayllus del sol*, 236.

42. Hazen, "Awakening of Puno," 155–57; Kapsoli, *Los movimientos campesinos en el Perú*, 56–57; Kapsoli and Reátegui, *El campesino peruano*, 142–45.

43. On the confrontation between Leguía and the Comité, see Pent, "Bridging the Rural-Urban Divide," 153.

44. Leibner, "Radicalism and Integration," 7.

45. Gallegos, *Manuel Z. Camacho*, 59; Taiña, "Manuel Z. Camacho," *Platería: Revista extraordinaria en homenaje al 51 de Platería, 1911–1961*, September 3, 1961, 8.

46. Gotkowitz, *Revolution for Our Rights*.

47. Ari Chachaki, *Earth Politics*. For a long-term historical interpretation of Indigenous politics in the nineteenth and twentieth century, see Baud, "Indigenous Politics and the State."

48. Ari Chachaki, *Earth Politics*, 66.

49. Ayala, *El presidente Carlos Condorena Yurja*, 298.

50. Ayala, *Yo fui canillita*, 77.

51. On the political activism of Marcos Miranda, Pedro Ari Velásquez, and Aureliano Vasquez, all of whom were associated with the Seventh-day Adventist Church: "Queja de Marcus Miranda, Aureliano Vasquez, Nazario Mamani, Pedro Veláquez," 1922, APP, caja 266.

52. "Queja de Juan Huanca y Pedro," 1922, APP, caja 266. Additionally, Huanca appears in the Seventh-day Adventist yearbook as a missionary until the year 1921, after which he is no longer mentioned. See *1921 Yearbook*, SDAYR, 123.

53. "Queja de M. W. Delgao, vecino de este vecindad," 1921, APP, caja 265 A. The pututus are an Andean musical instrument made of bull or goat horns. Blowing the pututus had long been associated with a call for a community meeting and with possible rebellion.

54. For a social outlook on the Comité, see Pent, "Bridging the Rural-Urban Divide," especially chap. 3.

55. de la Cadena, *Indigenous Mestizos*, 88.

56. Flores Galindo, *In Search of an Inca*, 181.

Notes to Pages 181–187

57. Bureau of Democracy, Human Rights and Labor, U.S. State Department, *Peru 2014: International Religious Freedom Report*, accessed February 21, 2022, https://2009-2017.state.gov/documents/organization/238778.

58. Kapsoli, *Ayllus del sol*, 221, 226, 228.

59. E. H. Wilcox, "A Letter from South America," *Field Tidings*, January 31, 1923, 2.

60. For such a version, see G. A. Schwerin, "A Great Deliverance," *Church Officers Gazette*, May 1, 1926, 8. Due to the scope of this research, which focuses on the mission experience with the Indians, I will not expand on the conflictive and ambiguous relationships that the mission had constructed with Puneño elites. Yet, while I have not thoroughly investigated this aspect, my general impression is that while the mission did share the elite's general perception of the Comité, it did not necessarily agree with their interpretation regarding specific incidents that involved Comité activists, especially since some of these events included attacks on Seventh-day Adventist schools. Moreover, missionaries had also imagined a "Catholic" connection in which the Catholic Church had united with the Comité to "get rid" of the Seventh-day Adventists. See, for example, Wilcox, "Letter from South America."

61. Burga, *Nacimiento de una utopía*; Flores Galindo, *In Search of an Inca*, xxi; Manrique, "Historia y utopía en los Andes," 202.

62. Walker, *Tupac Amaru Rebellion*.

63. Historians have been debating what Gutiérrez's intentions were in the uprising, some claiming that the rebellion was an expression of Andean millenarianism that aspired to the resurgence of the Inca empire. Others have claimed that such accusations were made mostly by hacienda owners and that the rebellion had much more mundane causes. See Jacobsen, *Mirages of Transition*, 340–42; Tamayo Herrera, *Historia social e indigenismo*, 201; Ramos Zambrano, *Movimientos campesinos*; Arroyo Reyes, *Nuestros años diez*, 191–205.

64. On the concept of pachacuti, see Flores Galindo, *In Search of an Inca*, 22–23; Szeminski, *La utopía tupamarista*, 125–32; Tamayo Herrera, *Historia social e indigenismo*, 201; Rénique, *La batalla por Puno*, 53; Jacobsen, *Mirages of Transition*, 340–42.

65. "Petition concerning Stahl," sigc, location 3811, rg 21.

66. Szeminski, *La utopía tupamarista*, 99.

67. Jacobsen, *Mirages of Transition*, 346–49; Leibner, *El mito del socialismo indígena*, 177; Pent, "Bridging the Rural-Urban Divide," 136; Burga, "Los profetas de la rebelión."

68. De la Torre, "La utopía viva."

69. Schwerin, "Great Deliverance."

70. On Indigenous leadership, see Pent, *Bridging the Rural-Urban Divide*, 24; Kapsoli, *Ayllus del sol*, 203–4.

71. Wilcox, "Letter from South America."

72. Sapiets, "One Hundred Years of Adventism in Russia," 265–70.

73. Bull and Lockhart, *Seeking a Sanctuary*, 141.

74. Bull and Lockhart, *Seeking a Sanctuary*, 142.

75. Gallegos, *Manuel Z. Camacho*, 59.

76. Leibner, *El mito del socialismo*, 204–5.

77. "Queja de Pedro Pablo, Benficio Gómez," 1918, APP, caja 256.

78. "Queja de Pedro Pablo, Benficio Gómez," 1918, APP, caja 256.

79. "Al Sr. Subprefecto é intendente de policía se la provincial del cercado de Puno," 1923, APP, caja 268.

80. Researching the community of Compi, on the Bolivian shores of the Titicaca, Hans Buechler also notes that military service had become a key issue in the construction of citizenship, stating that "marriage takes place soon after military service. . . . Thus military service marks the beginning of the transition to full adult life status and at the same time acceptance as a Bolivian citizen. The importance of citizenship is apparent in the symbolism of the flags which adorn the ceremonial wedding tent." Buechler and Buechler, *Masked Media*, 110.

81. Langer, *Expecting Pears from an Elm Tree*, 6–10.

82. Information from the Seventh-day Adventist yearbooks, 1920–30; see SDAYR. In 1930, membership in the Lake Titicaca mission had fallen steeply, reaching a low of 4,376. But the reduced number may reflect bureaucratic reorganizations within the Latin American missions, and the reason for the decline requires further investigation.

83. Williams to Meyers, May 13, 1924, SAD, RG 31, box 20.

84. Gallegos, *Manuel Z. Camacho*, 59.

85. Juan Huanca's former affiliation with the Seventh-day Adventist mission is also reported in "Queja de Juan Huanca y Pedro Pauro," 1922, APP, caja 266.

86. Ayala, *Yo fui canillita*, 77, 88.

87. Ayala, *Celebración cósmica*, 123.

Afterword

1. Lewellen, "Deviant Religion and Cultural Evolution."

2. Ferguson, "Evangelical Religion and Social Instability."

3. On Adventists' level of education, see Ströbele-Gregor, *Indios de piel blanca*.

4. On Methodist education in Peru, see Bruno-Jofré, *Methodist Education in Peru*.

5. Vásquez Palacios, "Democratic Activity and Religious Practice."

6. Bastian, "Protestantismo y política en México," 1957.

7. McIntyre, "Contested Spaces: Protestantism in Oaxaca," 84.

8. Harder Horst, "Catholic Church, Human Rights Advocacy, and Indigenous Resistance."

9. Harder Horst, "Breaking Down Religious Barriers," 77.

10. Demera, "Trayectorias del protestantismo y redefiniciones étnicas," 114.

11. Lewellen, *Political Anthropology*, 88.

12. On changes in community structure, see Escobar, *Organización social y cultural*, 26–36, 41–44; Jacobsen, *Mirages of Transition*, 349.

13. Ferguson, "Evangelical Religion and Social Instability," 185–86.

14. Ayala, *Yo fui canillita*, 86.

15. Hobsbawm, *Bandits*, 38–39.

16. Hobsbawm, *Bandits*, 38–39.

17. "Pro-indígena," *La Unión*, 8 agosto 1913, APZDA, código 2000027183; Roca, *Por la clase indígena*, 205; Stahl to Bowen, December 12, 1915, SIGC, RG 21, box 54.

18. Deregori, "Harvesting Storms," 146.

19. Rénique "Apogee and Crisis of a 'Third Path,'" 327. See also Rénique, *La batalla por Puno*, 324–49.

20. Fernando Armas Asín notes that this transformation occurred in a number of Protestant denominations. He hypothesizes about the possible relationship between this shift and the anti-imperialist discourse that was part of Velasco's military regime. See Armas Asín, *Políticas divinas*, 27. A brief look at names in the Seventh-day Adventist books from 1962 and 1972 supports Armas Asín's hypothesis. See 1962 Yearbook, SDAYR, 229.

21. Stahl to Spicer, September 21, 1911, SIGC, RG 21, box 45.

22. This process did not go on without objections. Plenty of Seventh-day Adventists, who lamented the "loss" of young men lured from rural life into city temptations, warned against evils that, in their eyes, roamed around the bustling streets of the metropolis and criticized the new consumer patterns that professional Seventh-day Adventists were acquiring. See Mrs. E. G. White, "Shall We Colonize around Our Institutions?,"*Advent Review and Sabbath Herald*, June 2, 1904, 7; F. M. W., "Leaving the Farms," *Advent Review and Sabbath Herald*, April 27, 1911, 13; "A Word to the Girls," *Advent Review and Sabbath Herald*, August 9, 1898, 7.

23. Schwartz, *Sect Ideologies and Social Status*, 44–46.

24. "Adventist Church in North America Issues Statement on Ben Carson's U.S. Presidential Bid," *Adventist Review*, May 4, 2015, http://www.Adventist-review.org/church-news/story2602-adventist-church-in-north-america-is-sues-statement-on-ben-carsons-u.s.-presidential-bid.

Bibliography

Archives

AOP. Archivo del Obispado de Puno. Puno, Peru.

APP. Archivo de la Prefectura de Puno. Archivo Regional de Puno. Puno, Peru.

APZC. Archivo Pedro Zulen (correspondencias). Biblioteca Nacional de Perú. Lima, Peru.

APZDA. Archivo Pedro Zulen (documentación administrativa). Biblioteca Nacional de Perú, Lima. Lima, Peru.

Archivo Arzobispal de Cusco. Cuzco, Peru.

Archivo de la Presidencia de la Asociación Peruana Unión. Archivo de la Iglesia Adventista del Séptimo Día. Universidad Peruana Unión. Lima, Peru.

Archivo General de la Nación. Lima, Peru.

ECP. Expedientes Criminales de Puno, Archivo Regional de Puno. Puno, Peru.

FNT. Fondo de Notariales Públicas. Archivo Regional de Puno. Puno, Peru.

GCASR. Statistical Reports of the Seventh-day Adventist Conferences, Missions, and Institutions. https://documents.adventistarchives.org/Statistics/Forms/AllFolders.aspx.

General Conference of the SDA Church (Appointee files). Office of Archives, Statistics, and Research of the Seventh-day Adventist Church. Silver Springs MD.

Meeting transcriptions of the General Conference of the Seventh-day Adventist Church. Office of Archives, Statistics, and Research of the Seventh-day Adventist Church. Silver Springs MD.

SAD. South American Division of the General Conference of the Seventh-day Adventist Church. Office of Archives, Statistics, and Research of the Seventh-day Adventist Church. Silver Springs MD.

SDAYR. Yearbooks of the Seventh-day Adventist Denomination. Office of Archives, Statistics, and Research of the Seventh-day Adventist Church. https://documents.adventistarchives.org/Yearbooks/Forms/AllItems.aspx?_ga=2.6546546.1969059637.1627291560-20639998.1620194231.

SGGC. Secretariat of the General Conference of the Seventh-day Adventist Church (General Files). Office of Archives, Statistics, and Research of the Seventh-day Adventist Church. Silver Springs MD.

SIGC. Secretariat of the General Conference of the Seventh-day Adventist Church (In-coming letters). Office of Archives, Statistics, and Research of the Seventh-day Adventist Church. Silver Springs MD.

Manuscripts

Álvarez-Calderón, Annalyda. "Pilgrimages through Mountains, Deserts, and Oceans: The Quest for Indian Citizenship, Puno, 1900–1930." PhD diss., State University of New York at Stony Brook, 2009.

Bahamonde, Wenceslao Oscar. "The Establishment of Evangelical Christianity in Peru, 1822–1900." PhD diss. Hartford Seminary Foundation, 1952.

Ferguson, Michael. "Evangelical Religion and Social Instability in Southern Highland Peru." PhD diss., University of Michigan, 2005.

Hazen, Dan. "The Awakening of Puno: Government Policy and the Indian Problem in Southern Peru." PhD diss., Yale University, 1974.

Kuhl, Paul. "Protestant Missionary Activity and Freedom of Religion in Ecuador, Peru, and Bolivia." PhD diss., Southern Illinois University, 1982.

Maltby, Laura L. "Indian Revolts in the Altiplano: The Contest for Land, 1895–1925." Bachelor's thesis, Harvard College, 1972.

McIntyre, Kathleen. "Contested Spaces: Protestantism in Oaxaca, 1920–1995." PhD diss., University of New Mexico, Albuquerque, 2012.

Morgan, Douglas. "The Remnant and the Republic: Seventh-day Adventism and the American Public." PhD diss., University of Chicago, 1992.

Núñez-Núñez, Héctor Elías. "Presencia protestante en el altiplano peruano, Puno 1898–1915: El caso de los Adventistas del Séptimo Día." Bachelor's thesis, Universidad Nacional de Mayor de San Marcos, Lima, 2008.

Parker, Michael T. "The Kingdom of Character: The Student Volunteer Movement for Foreign Missions, 1886–1926." PhD diss., University of Maryland, 1994.

Pent, Steven E. "Bridging the Rural-Urban Divide: Mobilization and Citizenship of a Peruvian Peasant Organization." Master's thesis, University of California Santa Barbara, 2007.

Quiroga, Manuel. "La evolución jurídica de la propiedad rural en Puno." Thesis for doctorate in jurisprudence, Arequipa, Quiroz Perea, 1915.

Sahlin, Monte. "Demographic Profile: the Adventist Community in North America." Human Subject Research Archive. Book 39. https://digitalcommons.andrews.edu/hrsa/39.

Shesko, Elizabeth. "Conscript Nation: Negotiating Authority and Belonging in the Bolivian Barracks, 1900–1950." PhD diss., Duke University, 2012.

Thurner, Mark W. "From Two Nations to One Divided: The Contradictions of Nation-Building in Andean Peru; The Case of Huaylas." PhD diss., University of Wisconsin–Madison, 1993.

Published Works

Abercrombie, Thomas A. *Pathways of Memory and Power: Ethnography and History among an Andean People*. Madison: University of Wisconsin Press, 1998.

Adams, Christine. *A Taste for Comfort and Status: A Bourgeois Family in Eighteenth-Century France*. University Park: Pennsylvania State University Press, 2000.

Aguirre, Carlos. "Tinterillos, Indians, and the State: Towards a History of Legal Intermediaries in Post-Independence Peru." In *One Law for All? Western Models and Local Practices in (Post) Imperial Contexts*, edited by Stefan B. Kirmse, 119–45. Frankfurt: Campus Verlag, 2012.

Ahlstrom, Sydney E. *A Religious History of the American People*. New Haven: Yale University Press, 2004.

Albó, Xavier. *Raíces de América: El mundo aymara*. Madrid: Alianza Editorial, 1988.

Alexander, Jennifer K. *The Mantra of Efficiency: From Waterwheel to Social Control*. Baltimore: Johns Hopkins University Press, 2008.

Allen, Catherine J. *The Hold Life Has: Coca and Cultural Identity in an Andean Community*. Washington DC: Smithsonian Books, 2002.

Allen, Thomas M. *A Republic in Time: Temporality and Social Imagination in Nineteenth-Century America*. Chapel Hill: University of North Carolina Press, 2008.

Alomía, Merling B. *Breve historia de la educación adventista en el Perú, 1898–1996*. Lima: Universidad Peruana Unión, 1996.

Anderson, Benedict. *Imagined Communities: Reflections on the Origin and Spread of Nationalism Communities*. London: Verso, 2006.

Anderson, Godfrey T. "Sectarianism and Organization, 1846–1864." In *Land, Adventism in America*, 36–66.

Archer, Melanie, and Judith R. Blau. "Class Formation in Nineteenth-Century America: The Case of the Middle Class." *Annual Review of Sociology* 19 (August 1993): 17–41.

Argersinger, Peter H., and Jo Ann E. Argersinger. "The Machine Breakers: Farmworkers and Social Change in the Rural Midwest of the 1870s." *Agricultural History* 58, no. 3 (July 1984): 393–410.

Ari Chachaki, Waskar. *Earth Politics: Religion, Decolonization, and Bolivia's Indigenous Intellectuals*. Durham NC: Duke University Press, 2014.

Armas Asín, Fernando. *La construcción de la iglesia en los Andes*. Lima: Pontificia Universidad Católica del Perú, 1999.

———. *La invención del patrimonio católico: Modernidad e identidad en el espacio religioso peruano, 1820–1950*. Lima: Asamblea Nacional de Rectores, 2006.

———. *Liberales, protestantes y masones: Modernidad y tolerancia religiosa, Perú siglo XIX*. Lima: Pontificia Universidad Católica del Perú, 1998.

Armas Asín, Fernando, Carlos Aburto Cortina, Juan Fonseca Ariza, and José Ragas Rojas, eds. *Políticas divinas: Religión, diversidad y política en el Perú contemporáneo.* Lima: IRA, 2008.

Aron, Cindy S. *Ladies and Gentleman of the Civil Service: Middle-Class Workers in Victorian America.* Oxford: Oxford University Press, 1987.

Arroyo Reyes, Carlos. *Nuestros años diez: La Asociación Pro-Indígena, el levantamiento de Rumi Maqui y el incaísmo modernista.* Argentina: LibrosEnRed, 2005.

Asad, Talal. *Genealogies of Religion: Discipline and Reason of Power in Christianity and Islam.* Baltimore: Johns Hopkins University Press, 1993.

Atack, Jeremy. "The Agricultural Ladder Revisited: A New Look at an Old Question with Some Data from 1860." *Agricultural History* 63, no. 1 (January 1989): 1–25.

Axtell, James. "Some Thoughts on the Ethnohistory of Missions." *Ethnohistory* 29, no. 1 (January 1982): 35–41.

Ayala, José Luis. *Celebración cósmica de Rita Puma.* Lima: Editorial San Marcos, 2005.

———. *El presidente Carlos Condorena Yurja.* Lima: Editorial Sam Marcos, 2006.

———. *Yo fui canillita de José Carlos Mariátegui: (Auto) biografía de Mariano Larico Yurja.* Lima: Editorial Periodística S.C.R., 1990.

Bailey, Burritt B. "Professional Distribution of College and University Graduates." *United States Bureau of Education Bulletin,* no. 19 (1912). https://files.eric.ed.gov/fulltext/ED543043.pdf.

Barron, Hal S. *Mixed Harvest: The Second Great Transformation in the Rural North, 1870–1930.* Chapel Hill: University of North Carolina Press, 1997.

———. *Those Who Stayed Behind: Rural Society in Nineteenth-Century New England.* Cambridge, UK: Cambridge University Press, 1984.

Bashford, Alison. *Imperial Hygiene: A Critical History of Colonialism, Nationalism, and Public Health.* Basingstoke, UK: Palgrave Macmillan, 2014.

Bastian, Jean-Pierre. "The Metamorphosis of Latin American Protestant Groups: A Sociohistorical Perspective." *Latin American Research Review* 28, no. 2 (1993): 33–61.

———. *Protestantismos y modernidad latinoamericana: Historia de unas minorías religiosas activas en América Latina.* Mexico City: Fondo de Cultura Económica, 1994.

Bastien, Joseph W. *Mountain of the Condor: Metaphor and Ritual in an Andean Ayllu.* Prospect Heights IL: Waveland Press, 1985.

Baud, Michael. "Indigenous Politics and the State: The Andean Highlands in the Nineteenth and Twentieth Centuries." *Social Analysis* 51, no. 2 (2007): 19–42.

Beidelman, Thomas O. *Colonial Evangelism: A Socio-Historical Study of an East African Mission at the Grassroots.* Bloomington: Indiana University Press, 1982.

————. "Contradictions between the Sacred and the Secular Life: The Church Missionary Society in Ukaguru, Tanzania, East Africa, 1876–1914." *Comparative Studies in Society and History* 23, no.1 (January 1981): 73–95.

Berg, Clayton L., Jr., and Paul E. Pretiz. "Latin America's Fifth Wave of Protestant Churches." *International Bulletin of Missionary Research* 20, no. 4 (October 1996): 157–59.

Bledstein, Burton J. *The Culture of Professionalism: The Middle Class and the Development of Higher Education in America.* New York: W. W. Norton and Company, 1978.

Blumin, Stuart M. *The Emergence of the Middle Class: Social Experience in the American City, 1760–1900.* Cambridge, UK: Cambridge University Press, 1989.

————. "A Hypothesis of Middle-Class Formation in Nineteenth-Century America: A Critique and Some Proposals." *American Historical Review* 90, no. 2 (April 1985): 299–338.

Boelens, Rutgerd, and Paul H. Gelles. "Cultural Politics, Communal Resistance, and Identity in Andean Irrigation Development." *Bulletin of Latin American Research* 24, no. 3 (July 2005): 311–27.

Bolin, Inge. *Rituals of Respect: The Secret of Survival in the High Peruvian Andes.* Austin: University of Texas Press, 2002.

Bonilla, Heraclio. "The War of the Pacific and the National and Colonial Problem in Peru." *Past and Present,* no. 81 (November 1978): 92–118.

Bourdieu, Pierre, and Richard Nica. *Outline of a Theory of Practice.* Cambridge, UK: Cambridge University Press, 1977.

Bourque, L. Nicole. "Developing People and Plants: Life Cycle and Agricultural Festivals in the Andes." *Ethnology* 34, no. 1 (January 1995): 75–87.

Bourricaud, François. *Cambios en Puno: Estudios de sociología andina.* Lima: Instituto de Estudios Peruanos, 2012.

Bridges, Roy. "Exploration and Travel Outside of Europe, 1720–1914." In *The Cambridge Companion to Travel Writing,* edited by Peter Hulme and Tim Youngs, 53–70. Cambridge, UK: Cambridge University Press, 2002.

Brodkin, Karen. *How Jews Became White Folks and What That Says about Race in America.* New Brunswick NJ: Rutgers University Press, 1998.

Brown, Jonathan C. "A Nineteenth Century Argentine Cattle Empire." *Agricultural History* 52, no. 1 (January 1978): 160–78.

Brown, Peter. *Poverty and Leadership in the Later Roman Empire.* Waltham MA: Brandeis University Press; Jerusalem: Historical Society of Israel, 2002.

————. *Through the Eye of the Needle: Wealth, the Fall of Rome, and the Making of Christianity in the West, 350–550 AD.* Princeton: Princeton University Press, 2012.

Bruce, Dickson D., Jr. "W. E. B. Du Bois and the Idea of Double Consciousness." *American Literature* 64, no. 2 (June 1992): 299–309.

Bruno-Jofré, Rosa del Carmen. *Methodist Education in Peru: Social Gospel, Politics, and American Ideological and Economic Penetration, 1888–1930.* Montreal: Wilfrid Laurier University Press, 1988.

Buechler, Hans, and Judith Maria Buechler. *The Bolivian Aymara*. New York: Holt, Rinehart, and Winston, 1971.

———. *The Masked Media: Aymara Fiestas and Social Interaction in the Bolivian Highlands*. The Hague: Mouton, 1980.

Bull, Malcolm. "The Seventh Day Adventists: Heretics of American Civil Religion." *Sociology of Religion* 50, no. 2 (July 1989): 177–87.

Bull, Malcolm, and Keith Lockhart. *Seeking a Sanctuary: Seventh-day Adventism and the American Dream*. San Francisco: Harper and Row, 1989.

———. *Seeking a Sanctuary: Seventh-day Adventism and the American Dream*. 2nd ed. Bloomington: Indiana University Press, 2006.

Burga, Manuel. "Los profetas de la rebelión, 1920–1930 (imaginación y realidad en una sublevación andina)." In Deler and Saint-Geours, *Estados y naciones en los Andes: Hacia una historia comparativa; Bolivia-Colombia-Perú*, 465–517. Lima.

———. *Nacimiento de una utopía: Muerte y resurrección de los incas*. Lima: Instituto de Apoyo Agrario, 1988. http://sisbib.unmsm.edu.pe/bibvirtual/libros/2006/nacimien_utop/contenido.htm.

Burga, Manuel, and Alberto Flores Galindo. *Apogeo y crisis de la república aristocrática*. Lima: Ediciones Rikchay Perú, 1981.

Burns, Kathryn. *Into the Archive: Writing and Power in Colonia Peru*. Durham NC: Duke University Press, 2010.

Butler, Jon. "The Midwest's Spiritual Landscapes." In *Finding a New Midwestern History*, edited by Jon Lauck, Gleaves Whitney, and Joseph Hogan, 196–210. Lincoln: University of Nebraska Press, 2018.

Butler, Jonathan M. "Adventism and the American Experience." In *Rise of Adventism: Religion and Society in Mid-Nineteenth Century America*, edited by Edwin S. Gaustad, 198–206. New York: Harper and Row, 1974.

———. "From Millerism to Seventh-day Adventism: Boundlessness to Consolidation." *Church History* 55, no. 1 (March 1986): 50–64.

Bynum, Caroline. "Violent Imagery in Late Medieval Piety." *Bulletin of the German Historical Institute*, no. 30 (Spring 2002): 3–36.

Caglar, Ayse S. "Hyphenated Identities and the Limit of 'Culture.'" In *The Politics of Multiculturalism in the New Europe*, edited by Tariq Modood and Pnina Werbner, 169–85. London: Zed Books, 1997.

Canessa, Andrew. "Evangelical Protestantism in the Northern Highlands of Bolivia." *Studies in World Christianity* 4, no. 1 (1998): 21–40.

Cañizares-Esguerra, Jorge. *Puritan Conquistadors: Iberianizing the Atlantic World. 1550–1700*. Stanford: Stanford University Press, 2006.

Cataño, Gonzalo. "La Nueva Historia y sus predecesores." *Revista de economía institucional* 20, no. 39 (2018): 119–58.

Cayton, Andrew R. L., and Susan E. Gray, eds. *The American Midwest: Essays of Regional History*. Bloomington: Indiana University Press, 2001.

Celestino, Olinda. *Migración y cambio estructural: La comunidad de Lampián*. Lima: Instituto de Estudios Peruanos, 1972.

Cervantes, Fernando. *The Devil in the New World: The Impact of Diabolism in New Spain.* New Haven: Yale University Press, 1994.

Chambers, Sarah C. *From Subjects to Citizens: Honor, Gender, and Politics in Arequipa, Peru, 1780–1854.* University Park: Pennsylvania State University Press, 1999.

———. "Little Middle Ground: The Instability of a Mestizo Identity in the Andes, Eighteenth and Nineteenth Centuries." In *Race and Nation in Modern Latin America,* edited by Nancy P. Applebaum, Anne S. Macpherson, and Karin Alejandra Rosenblatt, 32–56. Chapel Hill: University of North Carolina Press, 2003.

Clayton, Lawrence A. *Peru and the United States: The Condor and the Eagle.* The United States and the Americas. Athens: University of Georgia Press, 1999.

Cobley, Evelyn. *Modernism and the Culture of Efficiency: Ideology and Fiction.* Toronto: University of Toronto Press, 2009.

Coffey, John, and Paul C. H. Lim. *The Cambridge Companion to Puritanism.* Cambridge, UK: Cambridge University Press, 2008.

Cohen, Erik. "The Missionary as Stranger: A Phenomenological Analysis of Christian Missionaries' Encounter with the Folk Religion of Thailand." *Review of Religious Research* 31, no. 4 (1990): 337–50.

Cohen, Esther. "Towards a History of European Physical Sensibility: Pain in the Later Middle Ages." *Science in Context* 8, no. 1 (1995): 47–74.

Cohen, Lizbeth A. "Embellishing a Life of Labor: An Interpretation of the Material Culture of the American Working-Class Homes, 1885–1915." *Journal of American Culture* 3, no. 4 (1980): 752–75.

Coleman, John E. "Ancient Greek Ethnocentrism." In *Greeks and Barbarians,* edited by John E. Coleman and Clark Walz, 175–220. Bethesda MD: CDL Press, 1997.

Comaroff, John L., and Jean Comaroff. "Fashioning the Colonial Subject." In *Of Revelation and Revolution,* vol. 2, *The Dialectics of Modernity on a South African Frontier,* edited by J. L. Comaroff and J. Comaroff, 218–73. Chicago: Chicago University Press, 1997.

Condori Mamani, Gregorio, Asunta Quispe Huamán, Ricardo Valderrama Fernández, and Carmen Escalante Gutiérrez. *Andean Lives: Gregorio Condori Mamani and Asunta Quispe Huamán.* Austin: University of Texas Press, 1996.

Conforti, Joseph. "David Brainerd and the Nineteenth Century Missionary Movement." *Journal of the Early Republic* 5, no. 3 (1985): 309–29.

Conkin, Paul K. *American Originals: Homemade Varieties of Christianity.* Chapel Hill: University of North Carolina Press, 1997.

Connell, R. W. *Masculinities.* Berkeley: University of California Press, 2005.

Conrad, Geoffrey W., and Arthur A. Demarest. *Religion and Empire: The Dynamics of Aztec and Inca Expansionism.* Cambridge, UK: Cambridge University Press, 1984.

Contreras, Carlos. "The Tax Man Cometh: Local Authorities and the Battle over Taxes in Peru, 1885–1906." In *Political Cultures of the Andes 1750–1950*, edited by Nils Jacobsen and Cristóbal Aljovín de Loasda, 116–37. Durham NC: Duke University Press, 2005.

Cornado, Jorge. *The Andes Imagined: Indigenismo, Society, and Modernity*. Pittsburgh: University of Pittsburgh Press, 2009.

Córtes, Hernán. *Cartas de relación*. Mexico City: Editorial Porrúa, 1960.

Corwin, Sharon. "Picturing Efficiency: Precisionism, Scientific Management, and Effacement Labor." *Representations* 84, no. 1 (November 2003): 139–65.

Cotler, Julio. *Clases, estado y nación en el Perú*. Lima: Instituto de Estudios Peruanos, 1978.

Cox, Jeffrey. *Imperial Fault Lines: Christianity and Colonial Power in India, 1818–1940*. Stanford: Stanford University Press, 2002.

Cox, LaWanda F. "The American Agricultural Wage Earner, 1865–1900: The Emergence of a Modern Labor Problem." *Agricultural History* 22, no. 2 (April 1948): 94–114.

———. "Tenancy in the United States, 1865–1900." *Agricultural History* 18, no. 3 (July 1944): 96–105.

Cross, Whitney R. *The Burned-Over District: The Social and Intellectual History of Enthusiastic Religion in Western New York, 1800–1850*. Ithaca NY: Cornell University Press, 1950.

Crowley, John E. *The Invention of Comfort: Sensibilities and Design in Early Modern Britain and Early America*. Baltimore: Johns Hopkins University Press, 2001.

———. "Sensibility of Comfort." *American Historical Review* 104, no. 3 (June 1999): 749–82.

Curtis, Heather D. *Faith in the Great Physician: Suffering and Divine Healing in American Culture, 1860–1900*. Baltimore: Johns Hopkins University Press, 2007.

Cutler, William G. *History of the State of Kansas*. Chicago: A. T. Anderson, 1883.

Dachs, Anthony J. "Missionary Imperialism: The Case of Bechuanaland." *Journal of African History* 13, no. 4 (October 1972): 647–58.

Damsteest, P. Gerard. *Foundations of the Seventh-day Adventist Message and Mission*. Grand Rapids MI: Eerdmans, 1977.

Danbom, David B. *Born in the Country: A History of Rural America*. Baltimore: Johns Hopkins University Press, 1995.

Danohof, Clarence H. *Change in Agriculture: The Northern United States, 1820–1870*. Cambridge MA: Harvard University Press, 1969.

Davies, Thomas M, Jr. *Indian Integration in Peru*. Lincoln: University of Nebraska Press, 1974.

———. "The Indigenismo of the Peruvian Aprista Party: A Reinterpretation." *Hispanic American Historical Review* 51, no. 4 (November 1971): 626–45.

Dean, Carolyn. *Inka Bodies and the Body of Christ: Corpus Christi in Colonial Cuzco, Peru*. Durham NC: Duke University Press, 1990.

Degler, Carl N. *Neither Black nor White: Slavery and Race Relations in Brazil and the United States*. Madison: University of Wisconsin Press, 1971.

de la Cadena, Marisol. *Indigenous Mestizos: The Politics of Race and Culture in Cuzco, Peru, 1919–1991*. Durham NC: Duke University Press, 2000.

de la Torre, Arturo. "La utopía viva: Asentamientos israelitas en el oriente peruano." In *Políticas divinas: Religión, diversidad y política en el Perú contemporáneo*, edited by Fernando Armas Asín, Carlos Aburto Cotrina, Juan Fonseca Ariza, and José Ragas Rojas, 97–123. Lima: Pontificia Universidad Católica del Perú, 2008.

Deler, Jean Paul, and Yves Saint-Grours. *Estados y naciones en los Andes: Hacia una historia comparativa*. Vol. 2. *Bolivia-Colombia-Ecuador-Perú*. Lima: Instituto de Estudios Peruanos, 1986.

Demera, Juan Diego. "Trayectorias del protestantismo y redefiniciones étnicas entre los indígenas guambianos en Colombia." *Revista Ciencias Sociales*, no. 20 (July 2008): 107–27.

Denenbach-Salazar Sáenz, Sabine. "Que el patrón no más, quitándose los zapatos, pastee las animales: Limitaciones y posibilidades de la historia oral para a comprensión de la resistencia indígena (Puno, Perú, comienzas del siglo XX)." In *Los mundos de abajo y los mundo de arriba: Individuo y sociedad en las tierras bajas, en los Andes y más allá*, edited by María Susana Cipolletti, 489–528. Quito: Abya Yala, 2004.

———. "Relaciones complejas: Estrategias del hacendado mestizo, del hacendado indígena, y de los campesinos indígenas en un pleito sobre amparo de posesión por despojo de tierras." In *Ensayos de historia andina*, edited by Luis Millones, 153–65. Lima: Fondo Editorial del la Facultad de Ciencias Sociales, UNMSM, 2005.

d'Epinay, Christian Lalive. *Haven of the Masses: A Study of the Pentecostal Movement in Chile*. London: Lutterworth Press, 1969.

Dercon, Stefan, and Daniel Ayalew. "Where Have All the Soldiers Gone: Demobilization and Reintegration in Ethiopia." *World Development* 26, no. 9 (September 1998): 1661–75.

Deregori, Carlos Ivan. "Harvesting Storms: Peasant *Rondas* and the Defeat of Sendero Luminoso in Ayacucho." In Stern, *Shining and Other Paths*, 128–57.

DeVault, Ileen A. *Sons and Daughters of Labor: Class and Clerical Work in Turn-of-the-Century Pittsburgh*. Ithaca NY: Cornell University Press, 1990.

Devine, Tracy L. "Indigenous Identity and Identification in Peru: Indigenismo, Education, and Contradictions of State Discourse." *Journal of Latin American Cultural Studies* 8, no. 1 (June 1999): 63–74.

Dick, Everett N. "The Millerite Movements, 1830–1845." In Land, *Adventism in America*, 1–36.

Dirks, Nicholas B. *Colonialism and Culture*. Ann Arbor: University of Michigan Press, 1992.

Domínguez, Jorge. *Essays on Mexico, Central and South America: Scholarly Debates from the 1950s to the 1990s.* New York: Garland Publishing, 1994.

Dorfman, Ariel, and Armand Mattelart. *Para leer al pato Donald: Comunicación de masa y colonialismo.* Buenos Aires: Siglo XXI, 1972.

Douglas, Mary. *Purity and Danger: An Analysis of Concepts of Pollution and Taboo* [in Hebrew]. Tel Aviv, Israel: Resling, 2010.

Drinot, Paulo. "Historiography, Historiographic Identity, and Historical Consciousness in Peru." *Estudios Interdisciplinarios de América Latina y el Caribe* 15, no. 1 (January 2004): 65–88.

Dudden, Faye E. *Serving Women: Household Service in Nineteenth-Century America.* Middletown CT: Wesleyan University Press, 1983.

Dunch, Ryan. "Beyond Cultural Imperialism: Cultural Theory, Christian Missions, and Global Modernity." *History and Theory* 41, no. 3 (October 2002): 301–25.

Duncan, Kenneth, and Ian Rutledge (with the Collaboration of Colin Harding). *Land and Labour in Latin American: Essays on the Development of Agrarian Capitalism in the Nineteenth and Twentieth Centuries.* Cambridge, UK: Cambridge University Press, 1977.

Dunkerley, James. *Bolivia: Revolution and the Power of History in the Present; Essays.* London: Institute for the Study of the Americas, 2007.

Earle, Rebecca. "'Two Pink Pairs of Satin Shoes!!' Race, Clothing, and Identity in the Americas (17th–19th Centuries)." *History Workshop Journal*, no. 52 (Autumn 2001): 175–95.

Easterlin, Richard A. "Population Change and Farm Settlement in the Northern United States." *Journal of Economic History* 36, no. 1 (March 1976): 45–75.

Elsbree, Oliver W. *The Rise of the Missionary Spirit in America, 1790–1815.* Eugene OR: Wipf and Stock, 2013.

Engerman, Stanley L., and Robert E. Gallman. *The Cambridge Economic History of the United States.* Cambridge, UK: Cambridge University Press, 2008.

Engs, Ruth C. *Clean Living Movements: American Cycle of Health Reform.* Westport CT: Greenwood Publishing Group, 2000.

Erie, Carlos M. N. *War against Idols: The Reformation of Worship from Erasmus to Calvin.* Cambridge, UK: Cambridge University Press, 1986.

Escobar, Gabriel. *Organización social y cultural del sur del Perú.* Mexico City: Instituto Indigenista Interamericano, 1967.

Favre, Henri. "The Dynamics of Indian Peasant Society and Migration to Coastal Plantations in Central Peru." In Duncan and Rutledge, *Land and Labour in Latin America*, 253–68.

———. *El indigenismo.* Mexico City: Fondo de Cultura Económica, 1998.

Findlay, James. "Moody, 'Gapmen,' and the Gospel: The Early Days of the Moody Bible Institute." *Church History* 31, no. 3 (September 1962): 322–35.

Fitts, Robert K. "The Archaeology of Middle-Class Domesticity and Gentility in Victorian Brooklyn." *Historical Archaeology* 33, no. 1 (March 1999): 39–62.

Fitzpatrick-Behrens, Suzan. *The Maryknoll Catholic Mission in Peru, 1943–1989: Transnational Faith and Transformation*. Notre Dame IN: University of Notre Dame Press, 2011.

Flores Galindo, Alberto. *In Search of an Inca: Identity and Utopia in the Andes*. Cambridge, UK: Cambridge University Press, 2010.

Florey, Francesca A., and Avery M. Guest. "Coming of Age among US Farm Boys in the late 1800s: Occupational and Residential Choices." *Journal of Family History* 13, no. 2 (April 1988): 233–49.

Fonseca Ariza, Juan. *Misioneros y civilizadores: Protestantismo y modernización en el Perú (1915–1930)*. Lima: Pontificia Universidad Católica del Perú, 2002.

Foote, Nicola. "*Monteneros* and *Macheteros*: Afro-Ecuadorian and Indigenous Experiences of Military Struggle in Liberal Ecuador, 1895–1930." In *Military Struggle and Identity Formation in Latin America: Race, Nation, and Community during the Liberal Period*, edited by Nicola Foote and René D. Harder Horst, 83–107. Gainesville: University Press of Florida, 2010.

Forman, Charles W. "II. The Americans." *International Bulletin of Missionary Research* 6, no. 2 (April 1982): 54–56.

Foster, Gaines M. *Moral Reconstruction: Christian Lobbyists and the Federal Legislation of Morality, 1865–1920*. Chapel Hill: University of North Carolina Press, 2002.

Francois, Marie Eileen. "The Products of Consumption: Housework in Latin American Political Economies and Cultures." *History Compass* 6 (January 2008): 207–42.

Freston, Paul. "Pentecostalism in Latin America: Characteristics and Controversies." *Social Compass* 45, no. 3 (September 1998): 335–58.

Fudge, Erica. *Brutal Reasoning: Animals, Rationality, and Humanity in Early Modern England*. Ithaca NY: Cornell University Press, 2006.

Fuenzalida, Fernando, Enrique Mayer, Gabriel Escobar, François Bourricaud, and José Matos Mar, eds. *El indio y el poder en Perú*. Lima: Instituto de Estudios Peruanos, Moncloa-Campodónico Editores Asociados, 1970.

Furniss, Elizabeth. "Resistance, Coercion, and Revitalization: The Shuswap Encounter with Roman Catholic Missionaries, 1860–1900." *Ethnohistory* 42, no. 2 (Spring1995): 231–63.

Gallegos, Luis. *Manuel Z. Camacho: Biografía de un aymara*. Puno, Peru, 1984.

Gallo, Ezequiel. "The Cereal Boom and Changes in the Social and Political Structure of Santa Fe, Argentina, 1870–95." In Duncan and Rutledge, *Land and Labour in Latin America*, 323–42.

García Jordán, Pilar. *Cruz y arado, fusiles y discursos: La construcción de los Orientes en el Perú y Bolivia, 1820–1940*. Lima: IEP, 2001.

———. *Fronteras, colonización y mano de obra indígena en la amazonía andina (siglos XIX–XX)*. Lima: Pontificia Universidad Católica del Perú, 1998.

————. "Iglesia y vida cotidiana en el Perú finisecular: Conflictos alrededor de la religión, el matrimonio y la muerte." *Boletín americanista*, no. 38 (September 1988): 63–75.

Garrard-Burnett, Virginia. "Indians are Drunks and Drunks are Indians: Alcohol and Indigenismo in Guatemala, 1890–1940." *Bulletin of Latin American Research* 19, no. 3 (July 2000): 341–56.

————. *Living in the New Jerusalem: Protestantism in Guatemala*. Austin: University of Texas Press, 1998.

Garrard-Burnett, Virginia, and David Stoll. *Rethinking Protestantism in Latin America*. Philadelphia: Temple University Press, 1993.

Gelles, Paul H. *Water and Power in Highland Peru: Cultural Politics of Irrigation and Development*. New Brunswick NJ: Rutgers University Press, 2000.

Geremek, Bronislaw and Agnieszka Kolakowska. *Poverty: A History*. Oxford: Blackwell Publishers, 1994.

Gilhus, Ingvild Saelid. *Animals, Gods, and Humans: Changing Attitudes to Animals in Greek, Roman, and Early Christian Ideas*. New York: Routledge, 2006.

Gill, Anthony J. *Rendering unto Caesar: The Catholic Church and the State in Latin America*. Chicago: University of Chicago Press, 1998.

————. "The Struggle to Be Soul Provider: Catholic Responses to Protestant Growth in Latin America." In *Latin American Religion in Motion*, edited by William Kenan and Joshua Prokopy, 17–43. New York: Routledge, 1999.

Gill, Lesley. "Creating Citizens, Making Men: The Military and Masculinity in Bolivia." *Cultural Anthropology* 12, no. 4 (November 1997): 527–50.

————. "'Proper Women' and City Pleasures: Gender Class and Contested Meaning in La Paz." *American Ethnologist* 20, no. 1 (February 1993): 72–88.

Gilroy, Paul. *The Black Atlantic: Modernity and Double Consciousness*. Cambridge MA: Harvard University Press, 1993.

Glick, Thomas F., Miguel Angel Puig-Samper, and Rosaura Ruiz. *The Reception of Darwinism in the Iberian World: Spain, Spanish America, and Brazil*. Boston: Springer, 2001.

Godoy, Ricardo A. "The Fiscal Role of the Andean Ayllu." *Man* 21, no. 4 (December 1986): 723–41.

Gonzales, Michael J. "Capitalist Agriculture and Labor Contracting in Northern Peru, 1880–1905." *Journal of Latin American Studies* 12 (November 1980): 291–315.

Gonzales, Ondina, and Justo Gonzales. *Christianity in Latin America: A History*. Cambridge, UK: Cambridge University Press, 2007.

Goslin, Thomas S. "Protestantism in Peru." *Journal of the Presbyterian Historical Society* 26, no. 3 (September 1948): 149–64.

Gotkowitz, Laura. *Revolution for Our Rights: Indigenous Struggles for Land and Justice in Bolivia, 1880–1952*. Durham NC: Duke University Press, 2007.

————. "Trading Insults: Honor, Violence, and the Gendered Culture of Commerce in Cochabamba, Bolivia, 1870s–1950s." *Hispanic American Historical Review* 83, no. 1 (February 2003): 83–118.

Graybill, Ronald. "Millenarians and Money: Adventist Wealth and Adventist Beliefs." *Spectrum: A Quarterly Journal of the Association of Adventist Forums* 10, no. 2 (August 1979): 31–41.

Greenleaf, Floyd. *A Land of Hope: The Growth of the Seventh-day Adventist Church in South America*. Sao Paulo: Casa Publicadora Brasileira, 2011.

Grier, Katherine. *Culture and Comfort: Parlor Making and Middle-Class Identity, 1850–1930*. Washington DC: Smithsonian Books, 1988.

Griffiths, Nicholas. *The Cross and the Serpent: Religious Repression and Resurgence in Colonial Peru*. Norman: University of Oklahoma Press, 1996.

Gruzinski, Serge. *Images at War: Mexico from Columbus to Blade Runner (1492–2019)*. Durham NC: Duke University Press, 2001.

Guevara Velasco, Agustín. *Apuntes sobre mi patria*. Vol. 3, *Departamento de Puno*. Cuzco, Peru: Editorial H. G. Rozas, 1954–55.

Guillet, David. "Land Tenure, Ecological Zone, and Agricultural Regime in the Central Andes." *American Ethnologist* 8, no. 1 (February 1981): 139–56.

Hall, Catherine. *Civilizing Subjects: Colony and Metropolis in English Imagination, 1830–1867*. Chicago: University of Chicago Press, 2002.

Hall, Edith. *Inventing the Barbarian: Greek Self Definition through Tragedy*. Oxford, UK: Clarendon Press, 1989.

Hall, Stuart. "Culture, Community, and Nation." *Cultural Studies* 7, no. 3 (October 1993): 349–63.

Halttunen, Karen. "Cotton Mather and the Meaning of Suffering in the 'Magnalia Christi Americana." *Journal of American Studies* 12, no. 3 (December 1978): 311–29.

Handy, Robert T. *A Christian America: Protestant Hopes and Historical Realities*. Oxford: Oxford University Press, 1984.

Hanke, Lewis. "Pope Paul III and the American Indians." *Harvard Theological Review* 30, no. 2 (April 1937): 65–112.

Hanson, Karen T. "The World in Dress: Anthropological Perspectives on Clothing, Fashion, and Culture." *Annual Review in Anthropology* 33 (October 2004): 369–92.

Harder Horst, René D. "Breaking Down Religious Barriers: Indigenous People and Christian Churches in Paraguay." In *Resurgent Voices in Latin America: Indigenous Peoples, Political Mobilization, and Religious Change*, edited by Edward L. Cleary and Timothy J. Steigenga, 65–93. New Brunswick NJ: Rutgers University Press, 2004.

————. "The Catholic Church, Human Rights Advocacy, and Indigenous Resistance in Paraguay, 1969–1989." *Catholic Historical Review* 88, no. 4 (October 2002): 224–25.

——— . "The Politics of Schooling in the Non-Literate Third World: The Case of Highland Peru." *History of Education Quarterly*, no.18 (Winter 1978): 419–43.

Hayter, Earl W. *The Troubled Farmer, 1850–1900*. Dekalb: Northern Illinois University Press, 1968.

Hefner, Robert W. *Conversion to Christianity: Historical and Anthropological Perspectives on a Great Transformation*. Berkeley: University of California Press, 1993.

Heilman, Jaymie. *Before the Shining Path: Politics in Rural Ayacucho, 1895–1980*. Stanford: Stanford University Press, 2010.

Henretta, James A. "Families and Farms: Mentalité in Pre-Industrial America." *William and Mary Quarterly* 35, no. 1 (January 1978): 3–32.

Herzig, Rebecca. *Suffering for Science: Reason and Sacrifice in Modern America*. New Brunswick NJ: Rutgers University Press, 2006.

Hiatt, Willie. "Flaying 'Cholo': Incas, Airplanes, and the Construction of Andean Modernity in 1920s Cuzco, Peru." *Americas* 63 no. 3 (2007): 227–358.

Hobsbawm, Eric. *Bandits*. London: Weidenfeld and Nicolson, 2010.

Holms, Urban T., III. *A History of Christian Spirituality: An Analytical Introduction*. Harrisburg, PA: Morehouse Publishing, 2002.

Horowitz, Daniel. "Frugality or Comfort: Middle-Class Styles of Life in the Early Twentieth Century." *American Quarterly* 37, no. 2 (July 1985): 239–59.

Howard-Malverde, Rosaleen. "Pachamama Is a Spanish Word: Linguistic Tension between Aymara, Quechua, and Spanish in Northern Potosí." *Anthropological Linguistics* 37, no. 2 (July 1995): 141–68.

Hron, Madelaine. *Translating Pain: Immigrant Suffering in Literature and Culture*. Toronto: University of Toronto Press, 2009.

Hunefeldt, Christine. "La guerra y la reconformación del poder local: Puno (1879–1890)." *Allpanchis* 22, nos. 35–36 (December 1990): 147–82.

Hunefeldt, Christine, and Misha Kokotovic. "Power Constellations in Peru: Military Recruitment around the War of the Pacific in Puno." In *Power, Culture, and Violence in the Andes*, edited by Christine Hunefeldt and Misha Kokotovic, 50–84. Brighton, UK: Sussex Academic Press, 2009.

Hunnicutt, Benjamin Kline. "The Jewish Sabbath Movement in the Early Twentieth Century." *American Jewish History* 69, no. 2 (December 1979): 196–225.

Hunt, William C., and Edwin M. Bliss. *Religious Bodies: 1916*. Washington DC: Government Printing Office, 1919. https://archive.org/details /religiousbodies00blisgoog?ref=ol&view=theater.

Hutchison, William R. *Errand to the World: American Protestant Thought and Foreign Missions*. Chicago: University of Chicago Press, 1993.

Ignative, Noel. *How the Irish Became White*. New York: Routledge, 1995.

Irurozqui, Marta. *La armonía de las desigualdades: Elites y conflictos de poder en Bolivia, 1880–1920*. Madrid: Consejo Superior de Investigaciones Científicas, Centro de Estudios Regionales Andinos Bartolomé de Las Casas, 1994.

Isbell, Billie Jean. *To Defend Ourselves: Ecology and Ritual in an Andean Village*. Austin: Institute of Latin American Studies, University of Texas Press, 1978.

Jackson, Robert H. *Race, Cast, and Status: Indians in Colonial Spanish America*. Albuquerque: University of New Mexico Press, 1999.

Jacobsen, Matthew. *Whiteness of a Different Color: European Immigration and the Alchemy of Race*. Cambridge MA: Harvard University Press, 1998.

Jacobsen, Nils. *Mirages of Transition: The Peruvian Altiplano, 1780–1930*. Berkeley: University of California Press, 1993.

Jenkins, Philip. *The New Faces of Christianity: Believing in the Bible in the Global South*. Oxford: Oxford University Press, 2006.

Johnson, Doug R. *Adventism on the Northwestern Frontier*. Berrien Springs MI: Andrews University Press, 1996.

Johnson, Paul E. *A Shopkeeper's Millennium: Society and Revival in Rochester, New York, 1815–1837*. New York: Hill and Wang, 2005.

Jones, Greta. *Social Hygiene in Twentieth Century Britain*. London: Croom Helm, 1986.

Joseph, Gilbert M., Catherine LeGrand, and Ricardo Donato Salvatore. *Close Encounters of Empire: Writing the Cultural History of U.S.–Latin American Relations*. Durham NC: Duke University Press, 1998.

Kagan, Richard L. "From Noah to Moses: The Genesis of Historical Scholarship on Spain in the United States." In *Spain in America: The Origins of Hispanism in the United States*, edited by Richard Kagan, 21–49. Urbana: University of Illinois Press, 2002.

Kahl, Sigrun. "The Religious Roots of Modern Poverty Policy: Catholic, Lutheran, and Reformed Protestant Traditions Compared." *European Journal of Sociology* 46, no. 1 (January 2005): 91–126.

Kalbermatter, Pedro. *20 años como misionero entre los indios del Perú (apuntas autobiografías)*. Parana: Editorial Nueva Impresora, 1950.

Kaplan, Amy. "Manifest Domesticity." *American Literature* 70, no. 3 (1998): 581–606.

Kapsoli, Wilfredo. *Ayllus del sol: Anarquismo y utopía andina*. Lima: Tarea, 1984.

――――. *El pensamiento de la Asociación Pro Indígena*. Cuzco, Peru: Centro de Estudios Regionals Andinos Barolomé de Las Casas, 1980.

――――. *Guerreros de la oración: Las nuevas iglesias en el Perú*. Lima: Servicio Ecuménico de Pastoral y Estudio de Comunicación, 1994.

――――. *Los movimientos campesinos en el Perú*. Lima: Ediciones Atusparia, 1987.

Kapsoli, Wilfredo, and Wilson Reátegui. *El campesinado peruano: 1919–1930*. Lima: Universidad Nacional Mayor de San Marcos, 1987.

Katzman, David M. *Seven Days a Week: Women and Domestic Service in Industrializing America*. Urbana: University of Illinois Press, 1981.

Kelly, Catherine E. "'Well Bred Country People': Sociability, Social Networks, and the Creation of a Provincial Middle Class, 1820–1860." *Journal of the Early Republic* 19, no. 3 (October 1999): 451–79.

Kessler, J. B. *A Study of the Older Protestant Missions and Churches in Peru and Chile*. Goes, Netherlands: Ooaterbaan and Le Cointre N. V, 1967.

Kevles, Daniel J. *In the Name of Eugenics: Genetics and the Uses of Human Heredity*. Cambridge MA: Harvard University Press, 1995.

Kimmel, Michael S. *Consuming Manhood: The Feminization of American Culture and the Recreation of the Male Body, 1832–1920*. London: Routledge, 2003.

———. *The History of Men: Essays on the History of American and British Masculinities*. Albany: State University of New York, 2005.

Kingma, Kees. "Demobilization of Combatants after Civil Wars in Africa and Their Reintegration into Civilian Life." *Policy Science* 30, no. 3 (August 1997): 151–65.

Klaiber, Jeffrey L. *The Catholic Church in Peru: A Social History*. Washington DC: Catholic University Press, 1992.

———. *Religion and Revolution in Peru, 1824–1976*. Notre Dame: University of Notre Dame Press, 1977.

Klarén, Peter Flindell. *Peru: Society and Nationhood in the Andes*. Oxford: Oxford University Press, 2000.

Klein, Herbert S. *A Concise History of Bolivia*. Cambridge, UK: Cambridge University Press, 2003.

Kloppenburg, Jack R., Jr., and Charles C. Geisler. "The Agricultural Ladder: Agrarian Ideology and the Changing Structure of U.S. Agriculture." *Journal of Rural Studies* 1, no.1 (January 1985): 59–72.

Klor de Alva, Jorge. "Spiritual Conflict and Accommodation in New Spain: Toward a Typology of Aztec Responses to Christianity." In *Inca and Aztec States, 1400–1800: Anthropology and History*, edited by George A. Collier, Renato Rosaldo, and John D. Wirth. New York: Academic Press, 1982.

Knight, George. *A Brief History of Seventh-day Adventism*. Hagerstown MD: Review and Herald Publishing Association, 2004.

———. *A Search for Identity: The Development of Seventh-day Adventist Beliefs*. Hagerstown MD: Review and Herald Publishing Association, 2000.

Komonchak, Joseph A., Mary Collins, and Dermot A. Lane. *The New Dictionary of Theology*. Dublin: Gill and MacMillan, 1987.

Koslofsky, Craig. *The Reformation of the Dead: Death and Ritual in Early Modern Germany, 1450–1700*. London: Macmillan Press, 2000.

Kristal, Efraín. *Una visión urbana de los Andes: Génesis y desarrollo del indigenismo en el Perú, 1848–1930*. Lima: Instituto de Apoyo Agrario, 1989.

Kruggeler, Thomas. "Changing Consumption Patterns and Everyday Life in Two Peruvian Regions: Food, Dress, and Housing in the Central and Southern Highlands (1820–1920)." In *The Allure of the Foreign: Imported*

Goods in Postcolonial Latin America, edited by Benjamin Orlove, 31–66. Ann Arbor: University of Michigan Press, 1997.

Kulikoff, Allan. The Agrarian Origins of American Capitalism. Charlottesville: University of Virginia Press, 1992.

Lambert, Ronald D. "Reclaiming the Ancestral Past: Narrative, Rhetoric, and the 'Convict Stain.'" Journal of Sociology 38, no. 2 (2002): 111–27.

Lamoreaux, Naomi R. "Rethinking the Transition to Capitalism in the Early American Northeast." Journal of American History 90, no. 2 (September 2003): 437–61.

Land, Gary, ed. Adventism in America: A History. Grand Rapids MI: Eerdmans, 1986.

———. Historical Dictionary of the Seventh-day Adventist Church. Lanham MD: Scarecrow Press, 2005.

Langer, Erick D. Expecting Pears from an Elm Tree: Franciscan Mission on the Chiriguano Frontier in the Heart of South America, 1830–1949. Durham NC: Duke University Press, 2009.

———. "The Franciscan Missionary Enterprise in Nineteenth-Century Latin America." Americas 68, no. 2 (October 2011): 167–78.

Langer, Erick D., and Robert H. Jackson. The New Latin American Mission History. Lincoln: University of Nebraska Press, 1995.

Larsen, Timothy, and Daniel J. Treier. The Cambridge Companion to Evangelical Theology. Cambridge, UK: Cambridge University Press, 2007.

Larson, Brooke. Trials of Nation Making: Liberalism, Race, and Ethnicity in the Andes, 1810–1910. Cambridge, UK: Cambridge University Press, 2004.

La Serna, Juan Carlos. Misiones, modernidad y civilización de los "campas": Reconstrucción histórica del proyecto misionero adventista ente los asháninkas de la selva central peruana (1920–1948). Lima: Universidad Nacional de San Marcos, 2012.

Laurie, Bruce. Artisans into Workers: Labor in Nineteenth-Century America. New York: Noonday Press, 1989.

Lears, Jackson. Rebirth of a Nation: The Making of Modern America, 1877–1920. New York: Harper Collins, 2009.

Le Goff, Jacques. Time, Work, and Culture in the Middle Ages. Chicago: University of Chicago Press, 1980.

Leibner, Gerardo. El mito del socialismo indígena: Fuentes y contextos peruanos de Mariátegui. Lima: Pontificia Universidad Católica del Perú, 1999.

———. The "New Indians": The Emergence of Mass Politics in Peru, 1895–1932 [in Hebrew]. Tel Aviv: Ramot Publishing, 2003.

———. "Radicalism and Integration: The Tahuantinsuyu Committee Experience and the Indigenismo of Leguía Reconsidered, 1919–1924." Journal of Iberian and Latin American Research 9, no. 2 (2003): 1–24.

Leinaweaver, Jessica B. The Circulation of Children: Kinship, Adoption, and Morality in Andean Peru. Durham NC: Duke University Press, 2008.

———. "On Moving Children: The Social Implications of Andean Child Circulation." *American Ethnologist* 34, no. 1 (February 2007): 163–80.

Leonard, Olen E. "La Paz, Bolivia: Its Population and Growth." *American Sociological Review* 13, no. 4 (August 1948): 448–54.

Lesser, Jeffrey. *Negotiating National Identity: Immigrants, Minorities, and the Struggle for Ethnicity in Brazil*. Durham NC: Duke University Press, 1999.

Lewellen, Ted C. "Deviant Religion and Cultural Evolution: The Aymara Case." *Journal for the Scientific Study of Religion* 18, no. 3 (1979): 243–51.

———. *Peasants in Transition: The Changing Economy of the Peruvian Aymara; A General System Approach*. Boulder CO: Westview Press, 1978.

———. *Political Anthropology: An Introduction*. Westport CT: Praeger, 2003.

Linden, Ian, and Jane Linden. *Church and Revolution in Rwanda*. New York: Holmes and Meier Publishers, 1977.

Lindert, Peter. "Long-Run Trends in America Farmland Values." *Agricultural History* 62, no. 3 (July 1988): 45–85.

Long, Guillaume, David Rosnick, Cavan Kharrazian, and Kevin Cashman. "What Happened in Bolivia's 2019 Vote Count? The Role of the OSA Electoral Observation Mission." Washington DC: Center of Economic and Policy Research, 2019. http://cepr.net/images/stories/reports/bolivia-elections -2019-11.pdf?v=3.

Love, Thomas. "Cash Cows and Fighting Bulls: Redefining Identity, Maintaining Control in Southwestern Peru." Paper presented at the Twenty-First International Congress of the Latin American Studies Association, Chicago, Illinois, September 24–26, 1998. http://biblioteca.clacso.edu.ar/ar /libros/lasa98/Love.pdf.

Lyons, Barry J. *Remembering the Hacienda: Religion, Authority, and Social Change in High Land Ecuador*. Austin: University of Texas Press, 2006.

MacCormack, Sabine. "'The Heart Has Its Reasons': Predicaments of Missionary Christianity in Early Colonial Peru." *Hispanic American Historical Review* 65, no. 3 (August 1985): 443–66.

———. "Pachacuti: Miracles, Punishment, and the Last Judgment; Visionary Past and Prophetic Future in Early Colonial Peru." *American Historical Review* 93, no. 4 (October 1988): 960–1006.

———. *Religion in the Andes: Vision and Imagination in Early Colonial Peru*. Princeton: Princeton University Press, 1991.

MacCulloch, Diarmaid. *The Reformation: A History*. New York: Penguin Books, 2004.

Mahoney, Timothy R. *Provincial Lives: Middle Class in the Antebellum Middle West*. Cambridge, UK: Cambridge University Press, 1999.

Maisch, Gonzalo P. *Racismo y mestizaje y otros ensayos*. Lima: Fondo Editorial del Congreso del Perú, 2007.

Mallet, Shelley. "Understanding Home: A Critical Review of Literature." *Sociological Review* 52, no. 1 (February 2004): 62–89.

Mallon, Florencia E. *The Defense of Community in Peru's Central Highlands: Peasant Struggle and Capitalist Transition, 1860–1940.* Princeton: Princeton University Press, 1983.

——. *Peasant and Nation: The Making of Postcolonial Mexico and Peru.* Berkeley: University of California Press, 1995.

Manrique, Nelson. "Campesinado, guerra y conciencia nacional." *Revista andina* 4, no. 1 (1986): 161–72.

——. "Historia y utopía en los Andes." *Márgenes, encuentro y debate,* no. 8 (December 1991): 201–11.

——. *Yawar Mayu: Sociedades terratenientes serranas, 1879–1910.* Lima: Instituto Francés de Estudios Andinos, 2014. http://books.openedition .org/ifea/1821.

Marriam, William R., William C. Hunt, William A. King, Le Grand Powers, and S. N. D North. "Twelfth Census of the United States, Taken in the Year 1900." In *Agriculture: Farms, Livestock, and Animal Products,* 5 no. 1. Washington DC: United States Census Office, 1902. https://www2.census .gov/library/publications/decennial/1900/volume-5/volume-5-p5.pdf.

Marsh, Margaret. "From Separation to Togetherness: The Social Construction of Domestic Space in American Suburbs, 1840–1915." *Journal of American History* 76, no. 2 (September 1989): 506–27.

Martin, David. *Tongues of Fire: The Explosion of Protestantism in Latin America.* Oxford, UK: Blackwell, 1993.

Martin, Richard T. "The Role of Coca in the History, Religion, and Medicine of South American Indians." *Economic Botany* 24, no. 4 (October 1970): 422–38.

Martínez Riaza, Ascensión. "Política regional y gobierno de la Amazonia peruana: Loreto (1883–1914)." *Histórica* 23, no. 2 (March 1999): 393–462.

Marty, Martin E. *Righteous Empire: The Protestant Experience in America.* New York: Harper and Row, 1977.

Marzal, Manuel. *El rostro indio de Dios.* Lima: Pontificia Universidad Católica del Perú, 1991.

——. *Estudios sobre religión campesina.* Lima: Pontificia Universidad Católica del Perú, Fondo Editorial, 1977.

——. *La transformación religiosa peruana.* Lima: Pontificia Universidad Católica del Perú, 1983.

Marzal, Manuel, Catalina Romero, and José Sánchez Paredes. *La religión en el Perú al filo del milenio.* Lima: Pontificia Universidad Católica del Perú, 2002.

Masterson, Daniel M. *Militarism and Politics in Latin America: Peru from Sánchez Cerro to Sendero Luminoso.* New York: Greenwood Press, 1991.

Matthews, Glenna. *"Just a Housewife": The Rise and Fall of Domesticity in America.* New York: Oxford University Press, 1987.

Matthews, James K. "Clock Towers for the Colonized: Demobilization of the Nigerian Military and the Readjustment of Its Veterans to Civilian Life."

International Journal of African Historical Studies 14, no. 2 (January 1981): 254–71.

Maxwell, David. "Writing the History of African Christianity: Reflections of an Editor." *Journal of Religion in Africa* 36, nos. 3–4 (January 2006): 379–99.

May, Henry F. *Protestant Churches and Industrial America*. New York: Harper and Row, 1967.

Mayer, David. "Midwestern Industrialization and the American Manufacturing Belt in the Nineteenth Century." *Journal of Economic History* 49, no. 4 (December 1989): 921–37.

McAnany, Emile G., and Kenton T. Wilkinson. "From Cultural Imperialism to Takeover Victims?" *Communication Research* 19, no. 6 (1992): 720–45.

McClintock, Anne. *Imperial Leather: Race, Gender, and Sexuality in the Colonial Contest*. New York: Routledge, 1995.

McCrossen, Alexis. *Holy Day, Holiday: The American Sunday*. Ithaca NY: Cornell University Press, 2000.

McEvoy, Carmen. *La utopía republicana: Ideales y realidades en la formación de la cultura política peruana, 1871–1919*. Lima: Pontificia Universidad Católica del Perú, 1997.

McIntyre, Kathleen. *Protestantism and State Formation in Postrevolutionary Oaxaca*. Albuquerque: University of New Mexico Press, 2019.

Meethan, Kevin. "Remaking Time and Space: The Internet, Digital Archives, and Genealogy." In *Geography and Genealogy: Locating Personal Pasts*, edited by Dallen J. Timothy and Jeanne Kay Guelke, 99–115. Aldershot, UK: Ashgate Publishing Limited, 2008.

Melling, David J. "Suffering and Sanctification in Christianity." In *Religion, Health, and Suffering*, edited by J. R Hinnells and R. Porter, 46–65. London: Kegan Paul International, 1999.

Méndez, Cecilia. "De indio a serrano: Nociones de raza y geografía en el Perú (siglos CVIII–XXI)." *Histórica* 35, no. 1 (August 2011): 53–102.

———. "Incas sí, indios no: Notes on Peruvian Creole Nationalism and Its Contemporary Crisis." *Journal of Latin American Studies* 28, no. 1 (February 1996): 197–225.

———. "Militares populistas: Ejército, etnicidad y ciudadanía en el Perú." In *Repensando la subalternidad: Miradas críticas desde/sobre América Latina*, edited by Pablo Sandoval, 561–98. Lima: Instituto de Estudios Peruanos, 2009.

———. *The Plebeian Republic: The Huanta Rebellion and the Making of the Peruvian State, 1820–1850*. Durham NC: Duke University Press, 2005.

Méndez Notari, Carlos. *Desierto de esperanzas. De la gloria al abandono. Los veteranos chilenos y peruanos de la guerra del 1979*. Santiago, Chile: Centro de Estudios Bicentenario, 2009.

Milanich, Nara. "The Casa de Huérfanos and Child Circulation in Late Nineteenth Century Chile." *Journal of Social History* 38, no. 2 (Winter 2004): 311–40.

Miles, Robert, and Malcolm Brown. *Racism*. London: Routledge, 2003.

Miller, Daniel R. *Coming of Age: Protestantism in Contemporary Latin America*. Lanham MD: University Press of America, 1994.

Mills, C. Wright. *White Collar: The American Middle Class*. New York: Oxford University Press, 1951.

Mizruchi, Susan L. *The Science of Sacrifice: American Literature and Modern Social Theory*. Princeton: Princeton University Press, 1998.

Morgan, Douglas. *Adventism and the American Republic: The Public Involvement of a Major Apocalyptic Movement*. Knoxville: University of Tennessee Press, 2001.

———. "Adventism, Apocalyptic, and the Cause of Liberty." *Church History* 63, no. 2 (June 1994): 235–49.

Munzar, Stephan R. "Self-Abandonment and Self Denial: Quietism, Calvinism, and the Prospect of Hell." *Journal of Religious Ethics* 33, no. 4 (December 2005): 747–81.

Nash, Mary. "Social Eugenics and Nationalist Race Hygiene in Early Twentieth Century Spain." *History of European Ideas* 15, nos. 4–6 (August 1992): 741–48.

Nelson, Edward T. *Fifty Years of History of the Ohio Wesleyan University, Delaware, Ohio, 1844–1894*. Cleveland OH: Cleveland Printing and Publishing Co., 1895.

Neth, Mary C. *Preserving the Family Farm: Women, Community, and the Foundations of Agribusiness in the Midwest, 1900–1940*. Baltimore: Johns Hopkins University Press, 1995.

Nora, Pierre. "Between Memory and History: Les Lieux de Mémoire." *Representations*, no. 26 (Spring 1989): 7–24.

Nugent, David. "Building the State, Making the Nation: The Bases and Limits of State Centralization in 'Modern' Peru." *American Anthropologist* 96, no. 2 (June 1994): 333–69.

Numbers, Ronald L. *Prophetess of Health: Ellen G. White and the Origins of Seventh-Day Adventist Health Reform*. Knoxville: University of Tennessee Press, 1992.

Numbers, Ronald L., and Jonathan M. Butler. *The Disappointed: Millerism and Millenarianism in the Nineteenth Century*. Knoxville: University of Tennessee Press, 1993.

Nunn, Frederick M. "Professional Militarism in Twentieth-Century Peru: Historical and Theoretical Background to the *Golpe de Estado* of 1968." *Hispanic American Historical Review* 59, no. 3 (August 1979): 399–405.

Olick, Jeffrey K., and Daniel Levy. "Collective Memory and Cultural Constraint: Holocaust Myth and Rationality in German Politics." *American Sociological Review* 62 (December 1997): 921–36.

Olitzky, Kerry M. "The Sunday-Sabbath Movement in American Reform Judaism: Strategy or Evolution." *American Jewish Archives* 34, no. 1 (January 1982): 75–89.

Olivar-Smith, Anthony. "The Pishtaco: Institutionalized Fear in Highland Peru." *Journal of American Folklore* 82, no. 326 (October 1969): 363–68.

O'Malley, Michael. "Work and Task Orientation: A Critique of American Historiography." *Time and Society* 1, no. 3 (September 1992): 341–58.

Orlando Melo, Jorge. "De la Nueva Historia a la historia fragmentada: La producción histórica colombiana en la última década del siglo." *Boletín cultural y bibliográfico* 36, nos. 50–51 (1999): 165–84.

Orlove, Benjamin S. "Down to Earth: Race and Substance in the Andes." *Bulletin of Latin American Research* 17, no. 2 (May 1998): 207–22.

Orlove, Benjamin, and Ricardo Godoy. "Sectorial Fallowing Systems in the Central Andes." *Journal of Ethnobiology*, no. 6 (Summer 1986): 169–204.

Orozco, Monica. "Not to Be Called Christian: Protestant Perceptions of Catholicism in Nineteenth Century Latin America." In *Religion and Society in Latin America: Interpretive Essays from Conquest to Present*, edited by Lee M. Penyak and Walter J. Petry, 174–89. New York: Orbis Books, 2009.

Orsi, Robert. "The Religious Boundaries of an In-Between People: Street Feste and the Problem of the Dark-Skinned Other in Italian Harlem, 1920–1990." *American Quarterly* 44, no. 3 (September 1992): 313–47.

Orta, Andrew. *Catechizing Culture: Missionaries, Aymara, and the New Evangelization*. New York: Columbia University Press, 2004.

Ortiz, Renato. "Revisitando la noción de imperialismo cultural." In *Comunicación, cultura y globalización*, edited by José Miguel Pereira and Mirla Villadiego Prins, 46–63. Bogota: CEJA, 2003.

Ossio, Juan. "Cultural Continuity, Structure, and Context: Some Peculiarities of the Andean Compadrazgo." In *Kinship Ideology and Practice in Latin America*, edited by Raymond Smith, 118–46. Chapel Hill: University of North Carolina Press, 1984.

Owensby, Brain P. *Intimate Ironies: Modernity and the Making of Middle-Class Lives in Brazil*. Stanford: Stanford University Press, 2001.

Padilla, María José. "Identidades creyentes en tiempos de cambio: Católicos y adventistas aimaras del distrito de Pilcuyo, Puno." *Allpanchis* 29, no. 50 (June 1997): 9–63.

Pagden, Anthony. *The Fall of the Natural Man: The American Indian and the Origins of Comparative Ethnology*. Cambridge, UK: Cambridge University Press, 1982.

Parker, David S. *The Idea of the Middle Class: White-Collar Workers and Peruvian Society, 1900–1950*. University Park: Pennsylvania State University Press, 1998.

Pascoe, Peggy. "Miscegenation Law, Court Cases, and Ideologies of Race in Twentieth Century America." *Journal of American History* 83, no. 1 (June 1996): 44–69.

Pastor, Gonzalo. "Peru: Monetary Exchange and Exchange Rate Policies, 1930–1980." IMF Working Paper, June 2012. https://www.imf.org/external/pubs/ft/wp/2012/wp12166.pdf.

Patterson, Thomas C. *Inventing Western Civilization*. New York: Monthly Review Press, 1997.

Perkins, Judith. *The Suffering Self: Pain and Narrative Representation in the Early Christian Era*. New York: Routledge, 1995.

Pesalozzi, Hansuelli. "Sectorial Fallow System and the Management of Soil Fertility: The Rationality of the Indigenous Knowledge in the High Andes of Bolivia." *Mountain Research and Development* 20, no. 1 (February 2000): 64–71.

Petkova, Kristina, and Pepka Oyadjieva. "The Image of the Scientist and Its Functions." *Public Understanding of Science*, no. 3 (April 1994): 215–24.

Piel, Jean. "The Place of the Peasantry in the National Life of Peru in the Nineteenth Century." *Past and Present*, no. 46 (February 1970): 108–33.

Pike, Fredrick B. *The United States and Latin America: Myths and Stereotypes of a Civilization and Nature*. Austin: University of Texas Press, 1992.

Pineo, Ronn F., and James A. Bear. *Cities of Hope: People, Protest, and Progress in Urbanizing Latin America, 1870–1930*. Boulder: Westview Press, 1998.

Platt, Tristan. *Estado boliviano y ayllu andino: Tierra y tributo en el norte de Potosí*. Lima: Instituto de Estudios Peruanos, 1982.

———. "Liberalism and Ethnocide in the Southern Andes." *History Workshop Journal* 17, no. 1 (March 1984): 1–18.

———. "Simón Bolívar, the Sun of Justice and the Amerindian Virgin: Andean Conceptions of the Patria in Nineteenth-Century Potosí." *Journal of Latin American Studies* 25, no. 1 (February 1993): 159–85.

Poole, Deborah A. "Landscapes of Power in a Cattle-Rustling Culture of Southern Andean Peru." *Dialectical Anthropology*, no. 12 (December 1998): 367–98.

———. *Vision, Race, and Modernity: A Visual Economy of the Andean Image World*. Princeton: Princeton University Press, 1997.

Porter, Andrew. "Cultural Imperialism and Protestant Missionary Enterprise." *Journal of Imperial and Commonwealth History* 25, no. 3 (September 1997): 367–91.

———. *Religion versus Empire? British Protestant Missionaries and Overseas Expansion, 1700–1914*. Manchester, UK: Manchester University Press, 2004.

Porter, Robert P., and Carroll D. Wright. *Report on the Statistics of Agriculture in the United States, Eleventh Census: 1890*. Washington DC: Government Printing Office, 1895. https://www.census.gov/library/publications/1895/dec/volume-5.html.

Post, Stephan. "Disinterested Benevolence: An American Debate of the Nature of Christian Love." *Journal of Religious Ethics* 14, no. 2 (1986): 356–68.

Pratt, Mary Louise. *Imperial Eyes: Travel Writing and Transculturation*. London: Routledge, 2008.

Prieto, Andrés. *Missionary Scientists: Jesuit Science in Spanish South America, 1570–1810*. Nashville TN: Vanderbilt University Press, 2011.

Pullan, Brian. "Catholics, Protestants, and the Poor in Early Modern Europe." *Journal of Interdisciplinary History* 35, no. 3 (January 2005): 441–56.

Putnam, Jackson. "The Turner Thesis and the Westward Movement: A Reappraisal." *Western Historical Quarterly* 7, no. 4 (October 1976): 377–404.

Radcliffe, Sarah A. "Marking the Boundaries between the Community, the State, and History in the Andes." *Journal of Latin American Studies* 22, no. 3 (October 1990): 575–94.

Radcliffe, Sarah A., and Sallie Westwood. *Remaking the Nation: Place, Identity, and Politics in Latin America.* London: Routledge, 1996.

Ramírez, Susan E. *The World Upside Down: Cross-Cultural Contact and Conflict in 16th Century Peru.* Stanford: Stanford University Press, 1996.

Ramos, Gabriela, and Henrique Urbano. *Catolicismo y extirpación de idolatrías: Siglos XVI–XVIII; Charcas, Chile, México, Perú.* Cuzco: Centro Bartolomé de Las Casas, 1993.

Ramos Zambrano, Augusto. *Movimientos campesinos de Azángaro (Puno), Rumi Maqui.* Puno, Peru: Universidad Nacional del Altiplano, 1985.

Randell, Robert. "Qoyllur Rit'i: An Inca Fiesta of the Pleiades; Reflections on Time and Space in an Andean World." *Bulletion de l'Institut Francais d'Estudes Andinas* 11, nos. 1–2 (1982): 37–81.

Rasell, Marc. *Exploring the Heavenly Sanctuary: Understanding Seventh-day Adventist Theology.* Bloomington IN: AuthorHouse, 2009.

Rasnake, Roger. *Domination and Cultural Resistance: Authority and Power among an Andean People.* Durham NC: Duke University Press, 1988.

Reed, Colin. *Pastors, Partners, and Paternalists: African Church Leaders and Western Missionaries in the Anglican Church in Kenya, 1850–1900.* Leiden: Brill, 1997.

Rengifo, Antonio. "Esbozo biográfico de Ezequiel Urivola y Rivero." In *La reforma agraria en la encrucijada*, edited by Amando Samper Gnecco. Teaching Materials no. 189. Bogota: IICA, Programa Nacional de Capacitación Agropecuaria, 1971.

Rénique, José Luis. "Apogee and Crisis of a 'Third Path': *Mariateguismo*, 'People's War,' and Counterinsurgency in Puno, 1987–1994." In Stern, *Shining and Other Paths*, 307–38.

———. *La batalla por Puno: Conflicto agrario y nación en los Andes peruanos.* Lima: Instituto de Estudios Peruanos, Sur, CEPES, 2004.

Roberts, Brian. *American Alchemy: The California Gold Rush and Middle-Class Culture.* Chapel Hill: University of North Carolina Press, 2000.

Roberts, Dana L. "From Missions to Mission to Beyond Missions: The Historiography of American Protestant Foreign Missions since World War II." *International Bulletin of Mission Research* 18, no. 4 (October 1994): 146–62.

Roberts, Dorothy E. "Who May Give Birth to Citizens: Reproduction, Eugenics, and Immigration." *Rutgers Race and Law Review* 1 (1998): 129–37.

Roca, Erasmo. *Por la clase indígena.* Lima: Pedro Barrantes Castro, 1935.

Román, Reinaldo L., and Pamela Voekel. "Popular Religion in Latin American Historiography." In *The Oxford Handbook of Latin American History*, edited by José C. Moya, 454–89. Oxford: Oxford University Press, 2011.

Romero, Emilio. *Monografía del departamento de Puno*. Lima: Imprenta Torres Aguirre, 1928.

Roniger, Luis, and Mario Sznajder, "The Politics of Memory and Oblivion in Redemocratized Argentina and Uruguay." *History and Memory* 10, no. 1 (Spring 1998): 133–69.

Rothstein, Morton. "America in the International Rivalry for the British Wheat Market, 1860–1914." *Mississippi Valley Historical Review* 47, no. 3 (December 1960): 401–18.

Rowe, David L. "Millerites: A Shadow Portrait." In Numbers and Butler, *Disappointed*, 1–17.

———. *Thunder and Trumpets: Millerite and Dissenting Religion in Upstate New York, 1800–1850*. Chicago: Scholars Press, 1985.

Saignes, Thierry. *Borrachera y memoria: La experiencia de lo sagrado en los Andes*. Lima: Instituto Francés de Estudios Andinos, 1993.

Salisbury, Neal. "Red Puritans: The 'Praying Indians' of Massachusetts Bay and John Eliot." *William and Mary Quarterly* 31, no. 1 (January 1974): 27–54.

Sanders, Elizabeth. *Roots of Reform: Farmers, Workers, and the American State, 1877–1917*. Chicago: University of Chicago Press, 1999.

Sapiets, Marite. "One Hundred Years of Adventism in Russia and the Soviet Union." *Religion in Communist Lands* 12, no. 3 (December 1984): 256–73.

Sater, William F. *Andean Tragedy: Fighting the War of the Pacifica, 1879–1884*. Lincoln: University of Nebraska Press, 2007.

Schmidt, Bettina E. "Fiestas Patronales in the Ecuadorian Andes: The Meaning for the Villagers and the Attitude of the Churches." *Transformation* 23, no. 1 (January 2006): 54–60.

Schwartz, Gary. *Sect Ideologies and Social Status*. Chicago: University of Chicago Press, 1970.

Schwartz, Richard W. "The Perils of Growth, 1886–1905." In Land, *Adventism in America*, 95–139.

Semple, Rhonda A. "The Conversion and Highest Welfare of Each Pupil: The Work of the China Inland Mission at Chefoo." *Journal of Imperial and Commonwealth History* 31, no. 1 (January 2003): 29–50.

Sennett, Richard. *Families against the City: Middle-Class Homes of Industrial Chicago, 1872–1890*. Cambridge MA: Harvard University Press, 1970.

Serns, Dan. "Why Not Try This . . . ? Read a Mission Story." Website of Dan Serns. Posted April 25, 2013. https://danserns.wordpress.com/2013/04/25/why-not-try-this-read-a-mission-story-3/.

Sexton, James D. "Protestantism and Modernization in Two Guatemalan Towns." *American Ethnologist* 5, no. 2 (May 1978): 280–302.

Sharkey, Heather J. *American Evangelists in Egypt: Missionary Encounters in the Age of Empire*. Princeton: Princeton University Press, 2008.

Shesko, Elizabeth. "Mobilizing Manpower for War: Towards a New History of Bolivia's Chaco Conflict, 1932–1935." *Hispanic American Historical Review* 95, no. 2 (May 2015): 299–334.

Signes, Thierry. *Borrachera y memoria: La experiencia de lo sagrado en los Andes*. Lima: Instituto Francés de Estudios Andinos, 1993.

Skeggs, Beverley. *Formations of Class and Gender: Becoming Respectable*. London: Sage Publications, 1997.

Smith, Gavin. *Livelihood and Resistance: Peasants and the Politics of Land in Peru*. Berkeley: University of California Press, 1991.

Sobrevilla Perea, Natalia. *The Caudillo of the Andes: Andrés de Santa Cruz*. Cambridge, UK: Cambridge University Press, 2011.

Solange, Alberro. *La actividad del Santo Oficio de la inquisición en Nueva España, 1571–1700*. Mexico City: Instituto Nacional de Antropología e Historia, 1981.

Solberg, Carl E. "Peopling the Prairies and the Pampas: The Impact of Immigration on Argentine and Canadian Agrarian Development, 1870–1930." *Journal of Interamerican Studies and World Affairs* 24, no. 2 (May 1982): 131–61.

Sowell, Thomas. *Ethnic America: A History*. New York: Basic Books, 1981.

Spalding, Arthur W. *Captains of the Host: A History of the Seventh Day Adventists*. Washington DC: Review and Herald, 1949.

Spalding, Karen. "Class Structure in the Southern Peruvian Highlands, 1750–1920." *Radical History Review*, no. 9–10 (1975): 5–27.

Stahl, Ferdinand A. *In the Land of the Incas*. Mountain View CA: Pacific Publishing Press, 1920.

Stain, William W. *Hualcan: Life in the Highlands of Peru*. Ithaca NY: Cornell University Press, 1961.

Starr, Paul. *The Social Transformation of American Medicine: The Rise of a Sovereign Profession and the Making of a Vast Industry*. New York: Basic Books, 1982.

Stavely, Keith W. F. *Puritan Legacies: Paradise Lost and the New England Tradition, 1630–1890*. Ithaca NY: Cornell University Press, 1987.

Stepan, Nancy Leys. *The Hour of Eugenics: Race, Gender, and Nation in Latin America*. Ithaca NY: Cornell University Press, 1991.

Stephen, Lynn. "The Creation and Re-Creation of Ethnicity: Lessons from the Zapotec and Mixtec of Oaxaca." *Latin American Perspectives* 23, no. 2 (April 1996): 17–37.

Stern, Alexandra M. *Eugenic Nation: Faults and Frontiers of Better Breeding in Modern America*. Oakland: University of California Press, 2016.

Stern, Steve J. *Resistance, Rebellion, and Consciousness in the Andean Peasant World: Eighteenth to Twentieth Centuries*. Madison: University of Wisconsin Press, 1987.

———. *Shining and Other Paths: War and Society in Peru, 1980–1995*. Durham NC: Duke University Press, 1998.

Stevens, Laura M. *The Poor Indians: British Missionaries, Native Americans, and Colonial Sensibility.* Philadelphia: University of Pennsylvania Press, 2004.

Stoler, Ann L. "Making Empire Respectable: The Politics of Race and Sexual Morality in Twentieth Century Colonial Cultures." *American Ethnologist* 16, no. 4 (November 1989): 634–60.

Stoll, David. *Is Latin America Turning Protestant?* Berkeley: University of California Press, 1990.

Stott, Richard. "Artisans and Capitalist Development." *Journal of the Early Republic* 16, no. 2 (July 1996): 257–71.

Strayer, Robert. "Mission History in Africa: New Perspectives on an Encounter." *African Studies Review* 19, no. 1 (April 1976): 1–15.

Ströbele-Gregor, Juliana. *Indios de piel blanca: Evangelistas fundamentalistas en Chuquiyawu.* La Paz: Hisbol, 1989.

Sutton, William R. *Journeymen for Jesus: Evangelical Artisans Confront Capitalism in Jacksonian Baltimore.* University Park PA: Penn State University Press, 1998.

Swedberg, Richard. "Tocqueville and the Spirit of American Capitalism." In *On Capitalism*, edited by Victor Nee and Richard Swedberg, 42–71. Stanford CA: Stanford University Press, 2007.

Szeminski, Jan. *La utopía tupamarista.* Lima: Pontificia Universidad Católica del Perú, 1993.

———. "Why Kill a Spaniard: New Perspectives on Andean Insurrectionary Ideology in the Eighteenth Century." In *Resistance, Rebellion, and Consciousness in the Andean Peasant World: Eighteenth to Twentieth Centuries*, edited by Steve Stern, 166–92. Madison: University of Wisconsin Press, 1987.

Tamayo Herrera, José. *Historia social e indigenismo en el altiplano.* Lima: Ediciónes Trentaitrés, 1982.

Tannenbaum, Frank. *Slave and Citizen.* New York: Knopf, 1946.

Tapia, Marcelino. "Protestantismo y política en Bolivia: Entre la sociedad civil y el estado." In *Protestantismo y política en América Latina y el Caribe: Entre la sociedad y el estado*, edited by Tomás Gutiérrez Sánchez, 117–44. Lima: CEHILA, 1996.

Teel, Charles. "The Radical Roots of Peruvian Adventism." *Spectrum* 21, no. 1 (December 1990): 5–18.

Theobald, Robin. "From Rural Populism to Practical Christianity: The Modernism of the Seventh Day Adventist Church." *Archives de Sciences Sociales des Religions* 60 (July 1985): 109–30.

Thome, Susan. "The Conversion of Englishmen and the Conversion of the World Inseparable: Missionary Imperialism and the Language of Class." In *Tensions of Empire: Colonial Cultures in a Bourgeois World*, edited by Fredrick Cooper and Ann Laura Stoler, 238–62. Berkeley: University of California Press, 1997.

Thompson, Carl. *Travel Writing.* London: Routledge, 2011.

Thompson, Edward P. "Time, Work-Discipline, and Industrial Capitalism." *Past and Present*, no. 38 (1967): 56–97.

Thurner, Mark W. *From Two Republics to One Divided: Contradictions of Postcolonial Nation Making in the Andes*. Durham NC: Duke University Press, 1997.

Ticona, Alejo Esteban. *Memoria, política y antropología en los Andes bolivianos: Historia oral y saberes locales*. La Paz: Plural Editores, Agroecología Universidad Cochabamba, 2002.

Tinsman, Heidi. "The Indispensable Services of Sisters: Considering Domestic Service in the United States and Latin American Studies." *Journal of Women's History* 4, no. 1 (Spring 1992): 37–59.

Todorov, Tzvetan. *The Conquest of America: The Question of the Other*. Norman: University of Oklahoma Press, 1984.

Tomlinson, John. *Cultural Imperialism: A Critical Introduction*. London: Continuum, 1991.

Toqueville, Alexis de. *Democracy in America*. Penn State Electronic Classics. University Park: Pennsylvania State University, 2002. http://seas3.elte.hu/coursematerial/LojkoMiklos/Alexis-de-Tocqueville-Democracy-in-America.pdf.

Tranburg, Hanson. "The World in Dress: Anthropological Perspectives on Clothing, Fashion, and Culture." *Annual Review in Anthropology* 33 (October 2004): 369–92.

Trawick, Paul. "The Moral Economy of Water: Equity and Antiquity in the Andean Commons." *American Anthropologist* 103, no. 2 (June 2001): 361–79.

Tschopik, Harry. *The Aymara of Chucuito*. New York: The American Museum of Natural History, 1951.

Turner, Frederick C. "Catholicism and Nationalism in Latin America." *Social Compass* 18 (December 1971): 593–607.

Turner, Terence S. "The Social Skin." *Journal of Ethnographic Theory* 2, no. 2 (August 2012): 486–504.

Twain, Mark. *The Innocents Abroad, or The New Pilgrims' Progress*. New York: Random Publishing Group, 2003.

Twinam, Ann. *Public Lives, Private Secrets: Gender, Honor, Sexuality, and Illegitimacy in Colonial Spanish America*. Stanford: Stanford University Press, 1999.

Valcárcel, Luis. *Memorias*. Lima: Instituto de Estudios Peruanos, 1981.

———. *Ruta cultural del Perú*. Mexico City: Fondo de Cultura Económica, 1945.

———. *Tempestad en los Andes*. 1927; reprint, Lima: Editorial Universo, 1975.

Van den Berg, Hans. *Diccionario religioso aymara*. Iquitos, Peru: Ceta-Idea, 1985.

Van den Berghe, Pierre, and George Primov. *Inequality in the Peruvian Andes: Class and Ethnicity in Cuzco*. Columbia: University of Missouri Press, 1977.

Van Dijkhuizen, Jan Frans. "Partakers of Pain: Religious Meaning of Pain in Early Modern England." In *The Sense of Suffering: Constructions of Phys-

ical Pain in Early Modern Culture, edited by Jan Frans van Dijkhuizen and Karl A. E. Enenkel, 189–220. Leiden: Brill, 2009.

Van Young, Eric. "Popular Religion and the Politics of Insurgency in Mexico, 1810–1821." In *The Politics of Religion in an Age of Revival: Studies in Nineteenth Century Europe and Latin America*, edited by Austen Ivereigh, 74–113. London: Institute of Latin American Studies, 2000.

Vásquez Palacios, Felipe. "Democratic Activity and Religious Practice of Evangelicals in Mexico." In *Evangelical Christianity and Democracy in Latin America*, edited by Paul Freston, 37–39. Oxford: Oxford University Press, 2008.

Velásquez Silva, David Víctor. "Indios, soldados sin patria: La conscripción militar en el Perú durante el siglo XIX." *Historia*, no.1 (November 2018): 56–72.

Von Nardoff, Ellen. "The American Frontier as a Safety Valve: The Life, Death, Reincarnation, and Justification of a Theory." *Agricultural History* 36, no. 3 (July 1962): 123–42.

Voss, Kim. *The Making of American Exceptionalism: The Knights of Labor and Class Formation in the Nineteenth Century*. Ithaca NY: Cornell University Press, 1993.

Wade, Peter, Carlos Lopez Beltrán, Eduardo Restrepo, and Richard Ventura Santos. *Mestizo Genomics: Race Mixture, Nation, and Science in Latin America*. Durham NC: Duke University Press, 2014.

Walker, Charles F. *The Tupac Amaru Rebellion*. Cambridge MA: Harvard University Press, 2016.

Webster, Steven. "Native Pastoralism in the South Andes." *Ethnology* 12, no. 2 (April 1973): 115–33.

Weismantel, Mary. *Cholas and Pishtacos: Stories of Race and Sex in the Andes*. Chicago: University of Chicago Press, 2001.

———. "Maize Beer and Andean Social Transformation: Drunken Indians, Bread Babies, and Chosen Women." *MLN* 106, no. 4 (September 1991): 861–79.

Weismantel, Mary, and Stephen F. Eisenman. "Race in the Andes: Global Movements and Popular Ontologies." *Bulletin of Latin American Research* 17, no. 2 (May 1998): 121–42.

Wilcox, Harry E. *In Perils Oft*. Nashville: Southern Publishing Association, 1961.

Willems, Emilio. *Followers of a New Faith: Cultural Change and the Rise of Protestantism in Brazil and Chile*. Nashville TN: Vanderbilt University Press, 1967.

Williams, C. P. "'Not Quite Gentlemen': An Examination of Middling Class Protestant Missionaries from Britain, 1850–1900." *Journal of Ecclesiastical History* 31, no. 3 (1980): 301–15.

Wilson, Fiona. *Citizenship and Political Violence in Peru: An Andean Town, 1870s–1970s*. New York: Palgrave Macmillan, 2013.

——— . "Indian Citizenship and the Discourse of Hygiene/Disease in Nineteenth Century Peru." *Bulletin of Latin American Research* 23, no. 2 (April 2004): 165–80.

Wilson, William A., and Marie Cornwall. "Powers of Heaven and Hell: Mormon Missionary Narratives as Instruments of Socialization and Social Control." In *Contemporary Mormonism: Social Science Perspectives*, edited by Marie Cornwall, Tim B. Heaton, and Lawrence A. Young, 207–17. Urbana: University of Illinois Press, 2001.

Wolfenzon, Carolyn. "El 'Pishtaco' y el conflicto entre la costa y la sierra en 'Lituma en los Andes' y 'Madeinusa.'" *Latin American Literary Review* 38, no. 75 (January 2010): 24–45.

Yeager, Gertrude M. "Elite Education in Nineteenth-Century Chile." *Hispanic American Historical Review* 71, no. 1 (February 1991): 73–105.

Yepes del Castillo, Ernesto. *Perú, 1820–1920: Un siglo de desarrollo capitalista*. Lima: Instituto de Estudios Peruanos, 1972.

Yoder, Frank. "Rethinking Midwestern Farm Tenure: A Cultural Perspective." *Agricultural History* 71, no. 4 (October 1997): 457–78.

Zakim, Michael. *Ready-Made Democracy: A History of Men's Dress in the American Republic, 1760–1860*. Chicago: University of Chicago Press, 2003.

Zakim, Michael, and Gary J. Kornblith. *Capitalism Takes Command: The Social Transformation of Nineteenth-Century America*. Chicago: University of Chicago Press, 2012.

Zulawski, Ann. "Hygiene and 'the Indian Problem': Ethnicity and Medicine in Bolivia, 1910–1920." *Latin American Research Review* 35, no. 2 (January 2000): 107–29.

——— . *Unequal Cures: Public Health and Political Change in Bolivia, 1900–1950*. Durham NC: Duke University Press, 2007.

Zunz, Oliver. *Making of Corporate America*. Chicago: University of Chicago Press, 1990.

Index

Italicized page numbers refer to illustrations.

Andes / Andean society (*cont.*)
123–24; and the New History school,
xix; personal relationships in, 170;
Protestantism in, 114; race and racism in, 6, 23–26, 200; religion and politics in, xvi–xvii, 7, 70, 122; religious
ceremonies and sacraments in, 22;
religious freedom in, 120; religious
minorities in, 126; social alliances in,
15–16, 19, 156; social hierarchies in,
29–30, 69–70, 200–201, 212–13; and
temporal conflicts, 121; and tenure, 20;
transactions in, 218n7; violence and
military-society relations in, 205–6
Añez, Jeanine, xv
angels of Revelation, 85–90, 109, 129
Anglican churches, 123, 202
Anglo-Chilean Antofagasta company, 4–5
Anglo-Saxons, 99
annual tribute, 66–67
antimissionary stance, 86–88
antislavery organizations, 54
Antofagasta, 4–5
apocalyptic art, 87
apocalyptic hostility, 90
apoderado movement, 184
Arequipa, Peru, 5, 7–8, 11, 13, 41, 115,
123, 163
Argentina, 11, 98, 114, 122, 228n10
aristocracy, 58, 141
Aristocratic Republic, 8–11, 41, 73, 175
Armas Asín, Fernando, 243n20
army recruitment, 9–10, 14–16, 20, 31
article four of the 1860 constitution, 42–
44, 114
Asociación Pro-Indígena, 54, 168, 176,
182–84, 186, 193, 205
assimilation, 27–30
Atacama Desert, 4
attacks on buildings, 74–76
Atun Huaylas, 38
Atusparia uprising (1885), 59
Aves sin nido (Matto de Turner), 53–54
Ayacucho, Peru, 206
Ayahunca, Don Genaro, 193–94
Ayala, José Luis, 23, 197
Aymara Indians: as Adventist converts,
xviii, 73; Adventist influence with,

36; and banditry among ex-military
men, 204; and the Catholic Church,
239n30; and decolonization, 184; and
Ferdinand Stahl, 168–72; Hispanic
acculturation of, 53; and Indian conscription, 9; and Indian tribute, 66;
and Indigenous clothing, 47, 220n41;
and Indigenous languages, 48–50; and
Nicolás de Piérola, 5. *See also* Camacho, Manuel Z.
Azángaro Province, 32–33, 52, 139, 188

banditry, 204–5
baptism, xviii, 39, 63, 118, 121, 173, 178–79
Baptists, xviii, 89, 114, 120, 126, 226n15
Barber, G. H., 11
Basadre, Jorge, 8
Bastian, Jean-Pierre, 202, 217n16
Bates, Joseph, 85
Battle Creek MI, 94, 109, 207
Battle Creek Sanitarium, 155, 176
Battle of Ayacucho, 60
Beltrán, Ramon, 117–18
Berrien Springs MI, 103
Bible, xv, xvii, 11–12, 35, 49, 55, 63, 69–
70, 185–86, 201–2
Bible societies, 124
bilingualism, 49–50
biological essentialism, 23–24, 40, 162, 200
blue law legislation, 107–8, 120, 125–26
Bolivia: and expansion of Pentecos-
tal churches, xix; first missionaries
in, 114; and the Inca Union, 117; and
Indian mission identification, 156; and
indigenismo, 54; and Peru, 4; recent
events in, xv–xvii, 215–16nn1–2; religious liberty granted in, xvii–xviii,
216n6; and republicanism, 58; and separation of church and state, 7; Seventh-
day Adventist converts, staff, and
institutions in, 37; Seventh-day Adventist membership in, 36; and taxes, 66–
67; and the War of the Pacific, 4–5
Bravo, Tomás, 124
Brazil, xix, 114
British Columbia, 168
British commodities, 235n72
British missionaries, 114, 126, 231n76

cultural codes, 33, 163, 169
cultural essentialism of material arti-
    facts, 143
cultural identity and traits, 23, 30, 40,
    136, 161, 200, 203, 236n12
cultural imperialism, xx, 213
cultural oppression, 26, 31
Cupita, Pedro, 199
Cusqueño *indigenista*, 55
Cuzco, Peru, 24, 40, 54, 57, 122, 141, 234n58

Daniells, Arthur, 155, 175
death and resurrection, 56
debt, 150
decolonization, xvi, 184–85
Degregori, Ivan, 206
de la Cadena, Marisol, 23–24, 40, 234n58
del Carpio, Pablo, 17–18, 65, 71–72, 77,
    219n21
demobilization, 12, 20, 205
democratic practices, 163, 193
departmental committees, 183
dependence, 157, 162–68, 171, 178, 194, 213
d'Epinay, Christian Lalive, 33
deviation, 29
disciplinary measures, 29, 149–50
disputes and violence, 16–20
domestic service, 144–46
Douglas, Mary, 29
draft, 8–10, 15
dress code, 24–25, 46, 135. *See also*
    clothing

earnings. *See* salaries
ecclesiastical authorities and hierarchy,
    58–59, 70, 123
Ecuador, xvii, 117, 216n6
ecumenical trends in Christianity,
    238n11
education, 36–37, 63–67, 102–4, 112,
    158–59, 161, 177, 195, 200–201, 206–10,
    213. *See also* Puno English School
elders on water rights, 17–18
elementary schools, 36
Elias, Norbert, 132
elites: in Battle Creek MI, 207; and com-
    fort, 130, 141–43; and the Comité, 187,
    190; and conversion, 54–55; in Cuzco,

141, 234n58; and domestic service,
    144; and Indian presence in provincial
    towns, 157; in Lima, 5–6, 8–10, 53–55;
    in Puno, 141–42; and the Puno English
    School, 180–82; in Soqa, 199; and
    superiority of missionaries, 144, 158–
    59; and view of Adventists, 124. *See
    also* Aristocratic Republic; kurakas;
    regional elites
Elliot, Chas, 108–9
employment. *See* labor; white-collar
    employment
Encinas, José Antonio, 60–61, 63, 168
Enlightenment, 27, 53
enlisted soldiers, 9–10, 218n16
eschatology, 87, 90, 108, 190
Escuela Militar de Aplicación de Chor-
    rillos, 8
Etchison, Tris and Bent, 81
ethnicity, 23–24, 99–100, 220n34, 220n39
Evangelicals, xvii–xix, 120, 124, 151,
    216n12
Evangelical Union of South America,
    116–17, 122, 232n86
evangélicos, xviii, 123
evangelism, 164, 175–77
evangelization, 53, 110, 136, 155–56,
    163–66
exceptionalism, 128, 136
exclusion of Protestant weddings, 41
expansion of Evangelicalism, xviii–xix
expenses, 139, 148–50, 180, 238n17
exploitation, 7, 9, 33, 36, 45, 63–65, 68,
    185–86
export economies, xix
ex-soldiers. *See* veterans
extended families, 19–21

faena, 76–77
Fair Labor Standard Act in 1938, 210
farmers, 94–98, 100–104, 105, 206–9,
    229n37
festivities and agriculture, 62
feudal characteristics of the Andean
    social structure, 70
fiestas, 21, 32, 44–46, 50, 55, 59–60, 77,
    221n71
First Amendment, 166, 191–92

195–96; and Frank Westphal, 124–25; and land disputes, 20, 65–66; photograph of, 48; and ties to the Comité, 186; and violence against Catholic Indians, 73–74

Huanca, Pablo, 74

Huancané Province, 77, 185, 196–97

Huancané rebellion, 50, 204

Huancayo, 59

Huarochirí Province, 115

huaylinos, 38

Hutu Church, 239n30

hybridity, 28–29, 31, 39

hydraulic cosmology, 61

hydrological cosmology, 17

hygiene, 30, 46–50, 55, 157–58, 186, 202

idolatry, 55, 57, 75, 119, 179, 190–91

Iglesias, Miguel, 6

Illinois, 103

immigrants, 16, 33, 42, 94, 99–100, 114–15, 144

immortality of the soul, 56, 125

imperialism, 83, 90, 181, 185, 213

imported goods, 140–42

in-betweens, 30

Inca empire, xvi, 51–53, 183, 187–91, 241n63

Inca Union Mission, 117, 127, 150, 170, 231n80

incomes. *See* salaries

Indian Day, 183

Indian-ness: and clothing, 24; and the Comité, 186; and conversion, 50, 51; hegemonic notions of, 29, 31, 34, 171, 208–9; and the Puno English School, 181; and rebranding, 203–4; and regeneration, 160–62, 211–12

Indian question, 7, 63

Indians: Catholic, xviii, 51–52, 73–75; and comfort, 133–36; and the Comité, 183–88; and communal cohesion, 15–16, 57–60; and conscription, 8–9; and consumption patterns, 141–44; and *contribución personal*, 66–67; and conversion, 50–53; and domestic service, 144–45; and education, 36–37, 63–67, 200–201; and Ferdinand Stahl,

151, 155–56, 173–79; and Harry Wilcox, 174–79; and hygiene, 46–47; and Jorge Pinazo, 16–19; and language, 47–50; and litigation, 71–78; and mestizos, 22, 25–26, 27–31, 179–82, 187–88, 212; and missionaries' superiority, 158–59; and modifications to the mission, 179–82; in provincial towns, 157–58; and race and racism, 23–26; and racial identity, 38–40; refraining from coca and alcohol and fiestas, 44–46; and tax extortion, 31–32; and upper classes, 158–59; and veterans, 10–11, 27–31; and the War of the Pacific, 5–8. *See also* Adventist Indian converts; Aymara Indians; Indian-ness; Indigenous peoples; Quechua Indians; regeneration

indigeneity and decolonization, xvi

indigenismo, 7, 53, 54, 176

indigenistas, 7, 54–56, 63–64, 73, 184, 191, 193, 201–2. *See also* Encinas, José Antonio

Indigenous Congress, 183

Indigenous peoples: and the Catholic Church, 58–60; and the Comité, 183–88, 191–92; and education, 200–201; and Ferdinand Stahl, 151, 158, 173–79; and hygienist discourse, 47; and Indigenous imagination, 237n33; languages of, 48–49; leadership of in the Adventist Church, 179; in Paraguay, 202–3; and political activism, 174, 184; and Protestant missionary efforts, 83; in provincial towns, 157–58; and rejection of coca and alcohol, 44–45; and the return of the Inca, 188; and self-sufficiency, 178; and teachers, 166–67; and upward mobility, 21–22. *See also* conversion

industrialism, 99, 103, 135, 207

industrialization, xx, 90, 100–103, 148

inheritance, 20, 101–2, 161, 219n24

integration/reintegration, 9–10, 19–23, 27–30, 33–34, 63, 171, 193–97, 202–5. *See also* enlisted soldiers; veterans

intellectuals, 6–7, 30, 41–42, 51, 54, 122–23, 184, 199

inter caetera bull, xvi

mosques, 75
mutual aid networks, 102
mutual alliance treaty, 5
mutual dependence, 157, 171, 194–95, 213. *See also* reciprocal relationships

national fiscal policies, 31–32
nationalism, 60, 69
national unity, 123
native leadership, 34, 179, 237n46. *See also* veterans
naturalization process, 67
natural resources, 11, 14–23, 32, 61
negotiations, 9, 13, 15, 20, 147, 164–65, 204, 212
new middle class. *See* middle class
New Testament, 85
New York Conference in 1903, 111
nitrate exports, 4–5
non-Catholic Christians, 37, 41, 122–26
nongovernmental organizations, 205
North American missionaries, 82–83, 114, 119, 143
Northern Baptist Convention, 89
Northern Peru, 122
Nueva Historia (New History school), xix

obligatory military service, 66
Occopampa, 75–76
occupational choices, 9, 100, 103, 105, 109, 204
Ohio Wesleyan College, 89
ojotas, 24–25
old middle class. *See* middle class
overassessment, 32
ownership, 16–21, 101–2, 134–35. *See also* controlling labor; hacienda owners

pachacuti, 188
padrinazgo, 169–70
Pallalla, Peru, 193–94
Panama, 122
papacy, 86
papal bull, 1493, 57
Paraguay, 202–3
Pardo, José, 42
parishes, 22
Partido Constitucional, 6

patriotism, 69, 167
patronage networks, 5, 10, 19, 98, 209. *See also* integration/reintegration; relationships
patronato real, xvi
patron saint festivals, 57
Pauro, Pedro, 20, 65, 186, 194
peasant communities, 6, 10, 14–15, 32–33, 61–62, 68, 121, 126, 183, 188, 193, 202, 206
Pentecostal churches, xviii, xix
Pentecostal Church of Nazarene, 88–89, 122
Penzotti, Francisco, xvii–xviii
Perry, Franklin L., 11, 115, 117, 119, 127
Peru: Adventist Mission in, 113–20; Adventist presence in, 39, 126; and the Aristocratic Republic, 8–11; Catholic Church in, 7, 60; and the Comité, 183; converts in, xix; educational system in, 36–37; and evangelization efforts, 166; Harry Wilcox's journey to, 82–84; as hierarchical caste-based society, 27; and Nicolás de Piérola, 5–8; political developments in, 73; and political instability in the nineteenth century, 4–5; popular religion in, 58–60; Protestant outreach in, 122–23; race and racism in, 23–26, 156, 220n38; and relation between church and state, 40–44; religious liberty in, xvii, 120, 192; Seventh-day Adventist converts, staff, and institutions in, 37; Seventh-day Adventist membership in, 36; and the War of the Pacific, 4–7, 30. *See also* Puno, Peru
petitions, 64–65, 71, 173–74
Philippines, 90
phobias among regional elites, 31
Picotani hacienda, 139
Piérola, Nicolás de, 3, 5–9, 14, 25, 41, 68
Pilco, Francisco, 20
Pinazo, Benigno, 45
Pinazo, Jorge, 16–19, 30, 45, 219n21
Pizarro, Francisco, 75
Platería mission and school, 43, 49, 77, 120, 134, 151, 160, 169, 173–74, 181, 194
Pohle, William, 137–38, 146, 149, 234n53
politeness, 146–47

284   Index

politico-religious hierarchy, 17–18, 21–
  22, 32–33, 44, 71, 76, 139, 166–68, 203
politics: and activism, 192–93; and activities, 196–97; and Adventists' representation, 199–200; and blue law legislation,
  107–8; and citizenship, 58, 67–69; and
  communal cohesion, 57–63; and conversion, 201–4, 209; local, 54, 59–61, 167–
  68, 171, 192, 200, 203; and missionaries'
  outreach, 166–69; and passivity, 191–92;
  and standing connected to status, 135
popular religion, 58–60, 67
population growth and density, 14, 22,
  101, 203, 218n4, 219n24
Porfirian society, 202
poverty, 160
power structures, 24, 152, 164–65, 170,
  194, 203, 210–14
Prada, Manuel González, 7, 30
Prado, Javier, 6–7
Prado, Mariano, 4–5, 73
Presbyterians, 120, 123, 126
priests, 21, 45, 52, 55–56, 59, 70, 123–24.
  See also Toalino, Father
private property, 191, 219n22
production modes, 98, 177–78
professional education, 102, 159
professional middle class. See middle class
prohibitions of public worship, xvii
property claims, 18–20
property taxes, 31–32, 66, 68
propio, 139
proselytization, xvii–xviii, 123, 131,
  180, 209
protestantes, 123
Protestantism / Protestant churches:
  and Adventism, 35–36, 88, 119–
  20, 122–26, 128–29; and the Catholic Church, 86; conversion to, 32–33,
  37–38, 117; cosmopolitan approach
  of, 180; and education, 200; and foreign missionary enterprise, xvii–xix,
  55, 82–83; and ideals of self-denial
  and sacrifice, 151; and image of Christ,
  148; and imperialism, 90; and national
  integration, 202–3; and racial or ethnic terms in mission names, 156; and
  religious freedom, 41–42, 187; and

rural schools, 166–67; and sacrifice,
  129, 137; in South America, 114–17
Protestant Reformation, 55, 75, 119
provincial towns, 157
public education, 161, 200
publishing, 109–11
Puerto Rico, 90
Pullman County WA, 96
Puma, Rita, 186
Puno, Peru: Adventist community in,
  121–22; Adventist population in,
  216n13; and article four of the 1860
  constitution, 42–43; and the Catholic Church, 123–24; and citizenship,
  66; and the Comité, 185–87; and commodities, 141–42, 209; and Ferdinand Stahl, 11, 35, 55, 155–57, 174, 195,
  236n6; and German missionaries,
  231n80; and Harry Wilcox, 81–82, 176–
  77; and Indian education, 63; material
  conditions in, 126, 129, 137; missionaries to, 96–97, 101, 103, 207; and natural
  resources, 13–14, 22; population density in, 218n4; and the Puno English
  School, 181–82; Seventh-day Adventist
  school system in, 177, 200; and the traditional system, 33. See also Camacho,
  Manuel Z.; Lake Titicaca Mission
Puno English School, 180–82
Pura Pura, Challapampa, 155–56
purgatory, 56
purification, 47, 52, 159. See also
  regeneration
purity, 190. See also hygiene

Qorimaywa, Severo, 27
Quechua Indians, xviii, 5, 9, 48–50

race and racism: in the Andes, 23–26, 137,
  156, 180–82, 208–9; Anglo and Latin
  American attitutes on, 161–62; and the
  Catholic Church, 124; and class, 142–44,
  158–59; and education, 208–9; Flores
  Galindo on, 220n38; and political outreach, 165–66; and privilege, 213–14;
  and racial identity, 23–24, 28–31, 38–
  40, 45, 47, 50, 200–201, 212; and whiteness, 158–59, 210. See also Indian-ness

radical political activism, 174
railroad, 140–41
reciprocal relationships, 10, 19, 36, 44–45,
  50, 61, 64, 66, 67–69, 139, 141, 167–68
recognition, xvi, 49, 73, 195, 213
recruitment: and conscription, 9–10,
  14–16; of labor, 36, 66–68; by Nicolás
  de Piérola, 5, 8; and phobias among
  regional elites, 31; and the Student
  Volunteer Movement for Foreign Missions (svm), 82, 89; terms of, 20, 22
redemption, 50–51, 85, 175, 188–91, 195,
  227n18, 238n11
Reform Judaism, 106
regeneration: and citizenship, 67–70;
  contrasted with the Comité, 185; conversion as, 50–53; and departure of
  missionaries, 193, 195; and division
  between the social and the religious,
  55; and education, 63–67; and Hispanic acculturation, 53; and hydraulic
  cosmology, 61; and Indian-ness, 160–
  62, 211–12; and indigenistas, 201–2;
  and power structures, 211–13; and the
  Puno English School, 181–82; and religious renewal, 54–55; and the Seventh-
  day Adventist framework, 190; and
  veterans, 168. See also conversion
regional elites, 9–10, 31, 36, 59, 68, 218n14
rehabilitation, 51
reintegration. See integration/
  reintegration
relationships, 68–69, 169–71, 218n7. See
  also reciprocal relationships
religion: and ceremonies and sacraments, 21–22, 66–67; and communal cohesion, 58; and employment, 113,
  146; and festivals, 21–22, 32, 43–44, 57–
  59; freedom of, xvii, 40–43, 90, 120, 123,
  187, 191–92, 209; and landscape, xvii,
  xix, 44, 84, 94; and minorities, 119, 126;
  and politics, xvi–xvii, 40, 57, 59–61, 192,
  209–10; and rituals, 18, 58–59, 62, 68;
  and symbols, xv–xvi, 58, 75–76. See also
  Adventist Indian converts; conversion
religious change. See conversion
religious suppression. See freedom of
  religion

Rénique, José Luis, 206
reorganization of the Adventist Church,
  155, 177
Republic of Indians, 52
respectability, 130, 133, 135, 140, 180, 211
restoration, 51–52, 188–91
Revelation, 85–86
Review and Herald, 108
Richie, John, 120
rights, Indigenous, 71–72, 182–84, 208
rights over natural resources, 17–18, 20,
  21–22
rituals, 18, 58–59, 62, 68, 205
rivalries, 22, 167
Roca, Erasmo, 34, 221n75
Romaña, Eduardo López de, 9
Rouillón, Juan Antonio, 138
Rumi Maqui rebellion, 77, 182, 188
rural clergy, 22, 123–24
rural life, 53–54, 61–62, 93, 135–36,
  206–7, 229n26
rural middle class, 94–100
rural migrants, 16, 115
rural schools, 34, 36, 64, 166–67
Russia, 191, 229n28

Sabbatarian Baptists, 226n15
Sabbath: and blue law legislation, 108–
  9; and evangelism, 164; importance
  of, 208; and Jews, 106–7; and the
  job market, 105–7; and the Millerite
  movement, 85–86; observance of on
  the seventh day of the week, 98–99,
  226n15; Saturday observance of, 113,
  115–19, 126, 137; and temporal conflicts, 111–13, 117–18, 121
sacraments, 21–22, 45, 59
sacrifices, 107, 129–31, 136–37, 140, 143–
  48, 149–51, 159–60, 209, 211–13
saints, 55, 57–60, 75–76
salaries, 103, 137–39, 150, 166, 229n37,
  234n53, 234n58, 238n17
sales of religious literature, 110
San Cristóbal, Santa Fe Province, 98
sanctuary doctrine, 85, 129
Santos Chajo, Miguel, 16–19
satisfaction, 149
Saturday. See Sabbath

schools: and adults, 216; attacks on, 187, 194; and centralization of the educational system, 36–37; and dependence between missionaries and converts, 171; establishment of for Indians, 200–201; funding of, 166–67, 178; and Jesuits, 53; and the Lake Titicaca Mission, 71; number of, 104, *110*, 222n3; and the Puno English School, 180–82; and regenerated Indians, 63–65; and reorganization of the Seventh-day Adventist school system in Puno, 177

Schwartz, Gary, 210

second coming of Christ, 86, 189–90

Second Episcopal Conference, 199

Second Great Awakening, 84

sectorial fallowing, 62

secular authorities, 192, 201

secularization, 40, 203

secular professions, 131, 137

secular time, 98, 106

self-denials, 127–37, 138, 143, 151

self-re-Indianization, 27–29

self-sufficiency, 178

selling religious literature, 109, 175–76

separation between church and state, xvi, 7, 40–44, 61, 70, 122–23, 187, 192

Seventh-day Adventism: antimissionary stance of, 86–88; and Comité activists, 185–91; and communal cohesion, 77–78; conversion to, xviii, 38; converts, staff, and institutions, 1915–28, 37; and cosmological anxieties, 61, 37; doctrines of, 124–25, 128–29, 137, 151; ethnic composition of, 99–100; global membership of, 92; and health reform, 46–47; and labor, 98–99; and Manuel Z. Camacho, 11–12; and medical evangelism, 175–76; membership in Bolivia, Peru, and the Lake Titicaca Mission to 1930, 36; and the new middle class, 210; and number of schools in the United States, *110*; as only non-Catholic Christian denomination in the rural Altiplano, 37, 122; presence of in Latin America, 115–20, *116*; presence of in the United States, 95–96; and the rural middle class, 94–100;

shut-door policy of, 84–86, 114; and student enrollment in Seventh-day Adventist educational institutions in the United States, *111*; theological and eschatological change in, 86–90; and white-collar employment, 104–13. *See also* General Conference; Sabbath

sexuality and sexual conduct, 162

Shepard, Reid, 100, 103

shepherds, 13

Shining Path (Sendero Luminoso), 206

Shuswaps, 168

shut-door policy, 84–86, 87, 99, 109, 114, 227n18

sibling relationships, 169–70

slavery, 87

sleeping arrangements, 133

Smith, Joseph, 84

social hierarchies, 27, 69–70, 77, 161, 200–201, 213

social mobility, 21–22, 27–28, 38, 113, 131, 155, 161, 185, 210

social relations, 19, 23, 29, 44–45, 156. *See also* communal life

social stigmas, 148

socioeconomic characteristics: of Indian-ness, 24–25, 31–32, 96, 121; of Millerites, 94–95; of missionaries, xx, 96, 121, 180–81, 207–8; of rural clergy, 124

socio-religious economic obligations, 32

sola fide, 88

Soqa, 199, 203, 206

soul's immortality, 56, 125

South American Union Conference, 125

sovereignty, xvi, 27, 57–58, 60, 67–70, 75, 162

Spain, 60

Spanish-American War, 90

Spanish conquest, xvi, 57

Spanish language, 25–26, 37, 46–50, 63, 200–201, 211, 221n48

Spanish material culture, 52–53

Spanish monarchy, 58

Spanish Reconquista, 75

Spanish-speaking children, 180

sponsorship of events, 21, 32, 44, 213, 221n71

Stahl, Ferdinand: and analysis of social structures, 142–43; arrival of in Puno, 11, 35; conversion of, 155–56; departure of, 173–74, 194–95; early life of, 100–102; and economic burdens, 145, 150–51; and Edgar Maxwell, 150–51; and Harry Wilcox, 174–80; and intracommunal reform, 71; and the Lake Titicaca Mission, 151, 173, 231n80; and quest for an Indian mission, 157–60; and relationships with Indian converts, 155–56, 168–71; and reliance on converts, 163–65; salary of, 137–39, 234n53; and tribulations, 189

stamp tax, 67

standardization of time, 106, 112–13, 117

standard of living, 97, 133–34, 136–37, 143–44, 152, 211

stream. *See* natural resources

Stroessner, Alfredo, 202

student enrollment of Adventist colleges, 111–12, *111*

Student Volunteer Movement for Foreign Missions (SVM), 82, 89, 127–28, 148

Sunday Blue Laws. *See* blue law legislation

Sunday observance, 86, 98–99, 106–8, 117–19

superiority, 70, 158–59, 162, 163, 166, 172

supreme court, 120

SVM (Student Volunteer Movement for Foreign Missions), 82, 89, 127–28, 148

symbolic capital, 119

symbolic essence of commodities, 142–43

symbolic reciprocity, 66–67

symbolism, 58, 191

symbols, religious, xv–xvi, 73, 75

Tahuantinsuyu. *See* Comité Central Pro-Derecho Indígena Tahuantinsuyu

Tamayo, Luis Felipe Luna, 33

Tarapacá Province, 4–6

Tarma, 157–58

taxes, 4–5, 15, 31–32, 40, 63–67, 68

teachers: and comfort associated with middle-class identity, 143–44; and Comité figures, 186; and evangelization efforts, 163, 166–67; and growth of Adventism, 35–36; and language, 47–

49; photo of at the Lake Titicaca Mission, *49*; and reciprocal relationships, 69; and reorganization of Seventh-day Adventist school system, 177–79; veterans as, 33–34, 36, 65, 204, 221n75

temperance movement, 46

temporal conflicts, 111–13, 117–18, 121

Ten Commandments, 85, 88, 99. *See also* Sabbath

theology, 46, 50–51, 55, 75–76, 86–87, 123

Thomann, Eduardo, 11, 157

Thompson, E. P., 106

Tiahuanaco, xvi

tithes, 58, 180, 238n17

Toalino, Father, 118–20, 138–39

Tocqueville, Alexis de, 130

Toledo Reforms, 52, 57

transgressing racial or ethnic categories, 28–30

treason, 67

Treaty of Ancón, 6

tribulations, 189

tribute, 57–58, 64–67

Túpac Amaru, Diego Cristóbal, 52

Túpac Amaru II Rebellion, 52–53, 188

Tutsi class, 239n30

ultimatum given to converts, 195–96, 213

Umachi, Moho Province, 74–75

uniforms of Indian veterans, 27–29

Union College NE, 89, 111–12, 231n69

United States: and the Adventist antimissionary policy, 86–87; and citizenship, 67–70; and class formation, 98, 100–104; and comfort, 134, 233n33; and commodities, 140–43; domestic service in, 144–45; and evangelization efforts, 166; foreign policies of, 83, 90; health reform movement in, 46; and imperialism, 83; and Mendelian notions of inheritance, 161–62; number of Adventist Church members in, 89; and political passivity, 191–92; and the Protestant foreign missionary enterprise, 82–83; and religious freedom, 119–20; and religious minorities, 126; rural life in, 206; and salaries, 138; Seventh-day Adventist pres-

ence in, 95–97; Seventh-day Adventist
schools in, 110; and slavery, 87; student
enrollment in Seventh-day Adventist
educational institutions in, 111
unofficial sacraments, 59
upper classes, 142, 158, 180
upward social mobility, 21–22, 27–28, 210
urbanization, xx, 101, 103, 144
Urco farm, 122
Urviola, Ezequiel, 174
U.S. Bureau of Education, 112
U.S. embassy, 165–66
Utawilaya, 35
utopia, Andean idea of, 51, 188–90

Valcárcel, Luis, 10, 55, 141, 174
Valdéz, Santos, 29
Valparaíso, Chile, 11
Van Young, Eric, 60
Varney, Curtis, 140
Varney, Frank, 130–32, 146
Vatican II, 199
veneration of Catholic saints, 58–59
veterans: and acculturation, 23–26; and
banditry, 204–5; and centralization
efforts, 9; and cooperation with missionaries, 156–57; demands of, 10–11;
and good citizenship, 65–66; and Indian
leadership in the Adventist Church, 179;
and Indian political activities, 167–68,
193–97; and indigenismo, 54; mestizo-
ness of, 27–31; in the politico-religious
hierarchy, 21–23; and racial identity,
38–40; as Seventh-day Adventist Indigenous converts, 31–34, 171, 204–6; and
social hierarchy, 70; and struggle over
natural resources, 16–21; as teachers,
33–34, 36, 65, 204, 221n75

Victorian values, 127, 132, 137
Villca, Juan de Dios, 66
violence, 16, 29, 35, 71–78, 125, 182,
205–6
Virgin of Las Mercedes, 60
visual culture, Adventist, 87

wages, 103–4, 110, 138, 146–48
Walla Walla Seventh-day Adventist Col-
lege, 96–97
Wancho Lima, 77
war booty, 6
war efforts, 19
War of the Pacific, 4, 8, 19, 30, 40, 59,
218n16
water management, 17–18
wealth, 32
Weismantel, Mary, 23–24, 29–30
Wesleyan College, 112
Western dress, 47, 135, 141
Westphal, Frank H., 114, 124–25, 169
White, Ellen, 85, 87, 94, 129, 178
White, James, 85, 94, 178, 227n22
white-collar employment, 102–13, 129,
131, 135–36, 138–40, 146, 149, 171, 207,
229n37
White Fathers, 239n30
whiteness, 158–59, 210
Wilcox, Belle, 81, 131, 145
Wilcox, Harry, 81–84, 88, 113, 151, 174–
79, 180–81, 195, 208
Willems, Emilio, 33
women, 14, 28, 131, 144, 175, 220n41
Wood, Thomas, 114
wool, 13, 16, 140
World War I, 13, 73, 129, 144, 175, 221n57

Zulen, Pedro, 9, 54, 182

CPSIA information can be obtained
at www.ICGtesting.com
Printed in the USA
LVHW101125181022
730966LV00003B/127